Jerry Baker's

VINEGAR

THE KING OF ALL CURES!

www.jerrybaker.com

Other Jerry Baker Books:

Jerry Baker's Live Rich, Spend Smart, and Enjoy Your Retirement!
Jerry Baker's Fix It Fast and Make It Last!
Jerry Baker's Solve It with Vinegar!
America's Best Practical Problem Solvers
Jerry Baker's Can the Clutter!
Jerry Baker's Speed Cleaning Secrets!
Jerry Baker's Homespun Magic
Grandma Putt's Old-Time Vinegar, Garlic, and 101 More Problem Solvers
Jerry Baker's Supermarket Super Products!
Jerry Baker's It Pays to Be Cheap!

Grandma Putt's Green Thumb Magic
Jerry Baker's The New Impatient Gardener
Jerry Baker's Supermarket Super Gardens
Jerry Baker's Dear God...Please Help It Grow!
Secrets from the Jerry Baker Test Gardens
Jerry Baker's All-American Lawns
Jerry Baker's Bug Off!
Jerry Baker's Terrific Garden Tonics!
Jerry Baker's Backyard Problem Solver
Jerry Baker's Green Grass Magic
Jerry Baker's Great Green Book of Garden Secrets
Jerry Baker's Old-Time Gardening Wisdom

Jerry Baker's Backyard Birdscaping Bonanza
Jerry Baker's Backyard Bird Feeding Bonanza
Jerry Baker's Year-Round Bloomers
Jerry Baker's Flower Garden Problem Solver
Jerry Baker's Perfect Perennials!

Jerry Baker's Grow Younger, Live Longer!
Healing Remedies Hiding in Your Kitchen
Jerry Baker's Cure Your Lethal Lifestyle!
Jerry Baker's Top 25 Homemade Healers
Healing Fixers Mixers & Elixirs
Grandma Putt's Home Health Remedies
Nature's Best Miracle Medicines
Jerry Baker's Supermarket Super Remedies
Jerry Baker's The New Healing Foods
Jerry Baker's Amazing Antidotes!
Jerry Baker's Anti-Pain Plan
Jerry Baker's Oddball Ointments and Powerful Potions
Jerry Baker's Giant Book of Kitchen Counter Cures

To order any of the above, or for more information on Jerry Baker's amazing home, health, and garden tips, tricks, and tonics, please write to:

Jerry Baker, P.O. Box 1001, Wixom, MI 48393
Or, visit Jerry Baker online at:

www.jerrybaker.com

Jerry Baker's

VINEGAR

THE KING OF ALL CURES!

www.jerrybaker.com

Published by American Master Products, Inc.

Executive Editor: Kim Adam Gasior
Managing Editor: Debby Duvall
Writer: Vicki Webster
Design and Layout: Alison McKenna
Copy Editor: Nanette Bendyna
Indexer: Nan Badgett

Publisher's Cataloging-in-Publication
(Provided by Quality Books, Inc.)

    Baker, Jerry, author.
      Vinegar--the king of all cures! / Jerry Baker.
      pages cm
      Includes index.
      ISBN 978-0-922433-24-7

      1. Vinegar--Therapeutic use. 2. Vinegar--
    Miscellanea.   I. Title.

    TP429.B35 2016   664'.55
                    QBI16-900060

Printed in the United States of America
6 8 10 11 9 7   hardcover

Table of CONTENTS

CHAPTER 4 Bon Appétit!

part two ▶ INSIDE YOUR HOME

CHAPTER 5 Kitchen & Bathroom

CHAPTER 6 Around the House

CHAPTER 7 Family & Friends

part three ▶ **OUTSIDE YOUR HOME**

CHAPTER 8 Lawn & Garden

CHAPTER 9 Outdoor Structures

CHAPTER 10 By Land or By Sea

APPENDIX

INDEX

CONTENTS

INTRODUCTION

If the title of this book sounds like an exaggeration, consider this fact: Since the dawn of recorded history, folks throughout the world have been using vinegar to cure or prevent just about every kind of health, beauty, household, and other problem under the sun. Think about it: What other single product can vanquish flu viruses, soften your skin, shine your hair, clean just about every surface in your home—and turn a ho-hum meal into a five-star fine dining experience? The answer is: NONE! Vinegar is one of a kind, the King of All Cures! In these pages, you'll find thousands of terrific tips, tricks, and tonics to put the potent power of vinegar at your beck and call. For example, you'll learn how to use this majestic marvel to:

- Relieve aches and pains from the top of your head to the tips of your toes—with none of the potential side effects of prescription or OTC painkillers (Chapter 1)

- Shave years off your appearance—at a fraction of the cost of commercial beauty products (Chapter 2)

- Avert culinary catastrophes, ranging from too-greasy French fries to messy, mushy meringue (Chapter 3)

- Whip up remarkable recipes that'll delight even the pickiest people in your household (Chapter 4)

- Demolish the most stubborn grease, grime, mold, and mildew—both indoors and out (chapters 5, 6, 9, and 10)

- Keep your pets flea-free all summer long—without resorting to toxic shampoos and sprays (Chapter 7)

- Banish pesky pests, dastardly diseases, and wicked weeds from your lawn and garden (Chapter 8)

And the royal remedies don't stop there! In every chapter, you'll find fabulous features like: **Word to the Wise**, which

contains ultra-simple secrets for curing all kinds of problems. For instance, simply adding more vinegar to your diet helps fend off osteoporosis (page 44), and a quick and easy DIY trap keeps bugs from buggin' you when you're working outdoors (page 301).

You'll also discover how Grandma Putt and her cohorts rose to the occasion in **Old-Time Vim and Vinegar**. These time-tested tricks work just as well today as they did in days of yore. Sneak preview: By spraying one common item with white vinegar, you can use it to deodorize and humidify a baby's room and make it safer at the same time (page 228). And here's another classic gem: an all-natural facial treatment that's a skin cleanser, toner, and astringent all in one (page 50).

That's Historical is heaps of fun. But many of its fascinating facts and tantalizing tidbits go one step further, giving you practical know-how you can use today. For instance, we'll

share a truly ancient curse that can lower your stress level in high-way traffic (page 308). And you'll discover General Sam Houston's secret for staying healthy and chipper well into old age (page 6).

Quick & Quirky offers up exactly what the name implies: tips for putting vinegar to work in all kinds of fast, offbeat ways. Just a couple of examples: When cotton pants come out of the dryer sporting some wrinkles, don't iron them—just spray them with a vinegar-water solution, and hang 'em up to air-dry (page 216). And before you head outside to work (or play!) on a cold winter day, wash your hands with vinegar. It'll make your fingers stay limber longer (page 288).

Fantastic Formulas are foolproof mixtures that'll solve or prevent household dilemmas of all kinds. Two cases in point: The food-safe ingredients in Wicked Wonder Salsa will kill every kind of bad bug under the sun—including black widow spiders (page 268). And DIY Do-It-All Cleaner works every bit as well as those expensive "miracle" sprays to clean floors, greasy countertops, kitchen and bathroom fixtures, and appliances—no rinsing needed (page 161).

Finally, we've included plenty of **Excellent Elixirs** (health and beauty fixers) that can't be beat. Some, like Rosy Vinegar Splash, are straight out of Grandma Putt's treasure trove. She used this mild facial astringent every day to keep her skin firm and supple (page 52). Others are up-to-the-minute concoctions from 21st-century cosmetic and natural health gurus. The Toxin-Tossin' Bath Blend (page 9) will help remove toxins from your system with none of the dangerous side effects produced by many commercial detox remedies. As a bonus, it will boost your magnesium levels, soothe irritated skin, and relax you all over. Ahhhhh...

REMARKABLE RECIPE

I See a Very Red Spread

It's hard to believe that anything this delicious—and this simple—could actually help save your eyesight, but it's true! The secret lies in the powerful antioxidants found in the peppers, garlic, and red-wine vinegar.

- **1 cup of ricotta cheese**
- **1 jar (7 oz.) of roasted red peppers, drained and chopped**
- **1 tbsp. of chopped garlic (fresh or from a jar)**
- **1 tbsp. of red-wine vinegar**
- **½ tsp. of dried oregano**
- **½ tsp. of ground red pepper**
- **½ tsp. of paprika**

Mix all of the ingredients together in a blender until smooth. Use the spread on sandwiches, or serve it with your favorite crackers or chips. Yield: About 1½ cups

part ONE
For Good Living

For centuries, folks have relied on vinegar as a first-class health and beauty aid. In this section, you'll discover some of the best ways to treat yourself and your family to the amazing feats of this simple, but oh-so-powerful, wonder worker. In addition to both classic and cutting-edge remedies, I'll share some of my favorite food recipes that feature various types of vinegar. Why here, you ask? Well, in addition to its other health benefits, vinegar can pack a load of delicious flavor with next to no calories, which makes it a valuable weight-loss aid. Plus, studies have shown that combining vinegar with complex carbohydrates reduces post-meal blood glucose levels, which can be a big help in controlling or preventing diabetes.

chapter one ▶ TO YOUR HEALTH!

Throughout history, there's not a single product you can name that has played a more superstar role in health care than vinegar has. Hippocrates, the father of medicine, prescribed it for numerous ailments. Helen of Troy bathed in it to relax her body and mind. World War I medics used it to treat soldiers' wounds. Active folks, from samurai warriors to Sam Houston, drank it as a fortifying tonic. And that's just for starters! Best of all, vinegar works its healing magic every bit as well here in the 21st century as it did in days of yore!

RELIEF FOR ACHES & PAINS

2 Truly Wacky Ways to Cure a Headache

Over the years, folks have come up with more headache remedies than you can shake an aspirin bottle at. Two of the weirdest—and most effective—involve vinegar:

- Dip a large white cotton cloth in vinegar—either white or apple cider vinegar (ACV)—and wring it out. Put it against your forehead, and tie it tightly in the back. Keep it there until the pain backs off, which should be within 30 minutes or so.

- Soak three or four thin potato slices in vinegar (again, either white or ACV will do). Then tie a bandanna around your head,

For any health or beauty remedy that calls for apple cider vinegar, always use the raw, organic, unfiltered kind (available in health-food stores and in the health-food sections of most supermarkets). You'll know it by its cloudy consistency, with strand-like sediment at the bottom of the bottle. This so-called "mother" contains the enzymes and friendly bacteria that give ACV its miraculous healing power.

and tuck the potato slices into it at your temples and forehead. Leave it on for a few hours. When you take it off, the spuds will be hot and dry—and your head should be cool, calm, and ache-free!

Tame a Toothache

Got a tooth that hurts like the dickens? No problem! Rinse your mouth with a mixture made from 2 tablespoons of apple cider vinegar, 1 tablespoon of salt, and 4 ounces of warm water. That should ease your misery until you can get to the dentist's office for a permanent fix.

Tame a Toothache, Take 2

Here's a kooky—but highly effective—way to soothe a sore chopper: Cut a piece of brown paper that's the size of your cheek. Soak the paper in vinegar (any kind will do), and then sprinkle one side of it with black pepper. Lay the peppered side of the paper against your face where the toothache is. Hold it in place with a bandage, and keep it there for at least 60 minutes.

Eradicate an Earache

Your inner ear is swarming with bacteria—some good and some bad. When the bad brigade gets the upper hand (so

FOR GOOD LIVING

to speak), the result is an ear infection. In some cases, it takes high-powered antibiotics to wipe it out. But very often, this simple routine will do the trick:

- Pour some white vinegar into a pan, and heat it until it's slightly warm (but not hot!). Then fill a medicine (a.k.a. eye) dropper with it.

- Tilt your head to the side so that your sore ear is facing the ceiling, and pull your ear up and back to open the passageway.

- Squeeze the dropperful of vinegar into your ear. Use your hand to move your ear around to help the fluid flow downward.

- Wait five minutes or so, and then tip your head the other way so the vinegar can drain out.

Repeat the process as needed until the pain subsides. **Note:** *If your pain is severe, or if it persists for more than two days, see your doctor.*

In the Swim with Vinegar

Attention, frequent (or even occasional) swimmers! The next time you're plagued by that annoying—and often painful—condition called swimmer's ear, mix equal parts of vinegar (either the white or apple cider kind) and rubbing alcohol. Dribble 2 or 3 drops of the solution into your afflicted ear. The vinegar will kill any bacteria that may be present, and the alcohol will help dry up the trapped water.

To prevent the problem, take along an eyedropper and a small bottle of the mixture anytime you take off for a dip in a lake or any other body of non-chlorinated water. As soon as you're through swimming for the day, dry your ears well, and put 2 drops of the solution into each ear. It'll stop bad bacteria dead in their tracks.

Alleviate Arthritis Aches

It seems that every arthritis sufferer either has a favorite remedy or is searching high and low for one that really works. Well, according to everyone I know who's tried it, this one's a jim-dandy: Mix equal parts of apple cider vinegar and honey, and store the mixture in a lidded glass jar at room temperature. Then once a day, stir 1 teaspoon of the combo and 1 teaspoon of Knox® orange-flavored gelatin powder (not sweetened Jell-O®) into 6 ounces of water, and drink it down. Before you know it, your joints should be jumpin' again!

HELP FOR HEARING-AID USERS

If you use a hearing aid, you know that while these devices are worth their weight in gold, they do tend to encourage ear infections. That's because they trap moisture inside your ear canal, and bad bacteria multiply like crazy in a moist environment. Your best defense is a good offense—namely, this two-part plan:

▶ Put the drying power of vinegar to work by using the earache remedy recommended in "Eradicate an Earache" (see page 3). Follow the routine every week or so, or as needed.

▶ Remove your hearing aid as often (and as long) as possible to give your inner ear a chance to dry out.

FOR GOOD LIVING

Banish Bursitis Pain

Whether it goes by the name of housemaid's knee, tennis elbow, or (my personal favorite) weaver's bottom, a case of bursitis is a royal pain in the you-know-what! There are plenty of topical remedies that can ease your discomfort. But here's a simple routine that works from the inside to help reduce the inflammation in your bursae, strengthen your joints, and boost your immune system: One hour before breakfast, drink a 12-ounce glass of water with ½ cup of apple cider vinegar, 2 tablespoons of honey, and 1 teaspoon of cayenne pepper mixed into it. Repeat each morning until your joints are back in business.

Ease Your Workout Woes

You say you got a little carried away with your new workout routine, and now your muscles are so sore that you can hardly move? Well, don't just lie on the couch moanin' and groanin'. Instead, saturate a soft cloth with apple cider vinegar, wring it out, and wrap it around

That's Historical

Before General Sam Houston became president of the Republic of Texas (and later the state's first governor), he enjoyed a long and illustrious military career. Despite serious battlefield injuries and the strains of public life, he stayed healthy and spry well into old age. He credited that feat to a potion he made from 5 parts grape juice, 3 parts apple juice, and 1 part apple cider vinegar. In case you want to give it a try, Sam's recommended dose is ½ cup of the tasty tonic each day. (Vinegar also plays a healthful supporting role in Sam Houston's Famous BBQ Sauce. You'll find the tangy recipe on page 100.)

your aching area. Leave it on for 20 minutes. If you still feel achy, repeat the procedure every three to four hours until the pain is gone for good—and it will be soon because the vinegar helps to draw out the lactic acid that causes your muscles to feel stiff and sore in the first place. **Note:** *Attention, runners! This remedy also works wonders to relieve the pain of shin splints.*

Leapin' Liniment!

No matter what has caused the pain in your muscles or joints, a gentle rubdown with this vintage vinegar recipe will ease it fast. Mix 2 egg whites with ½ cup of apple cider vinegar and ¼ cup of olive oil. Massage the lotion into the painful areas, and wipe off the excess with a soft cotton cloth. (Just be careful not to get any of the stuff on sheets, clothes, or upholstery fabric!)

VINEGAR AND HONEY are a classic health-care combo, but the duo's magic works only if you mix pure, unprocessed (preferably organic) honey with your unprocessed, unfiltered ACV. The common commercial brands of honey undergo a heating and filtering process that kills off the health-giving enzymes and nutrients. You can find the good stuff in health-food stores, farmers' markets, and natural-food sections of most supermarkets.

Soak the Soreness Away

Whether you strained a tendon on the tennis court, pulled a back muscle on the golf course, or your legs are simply aching from a marathon shopping spree, never fear—vinegar is here! Simply pour 2 cups of ACV into a tub of warm bathwater. If you have some peppermint oil on hand, stir in a few drops to intensify the relaxing action. Then step in, sit back, and feel the aches—and your cares—float away.

Nix Nighttime Muscle Miseries

Muscle cramps are bad enough any time of day, but—like other physical or mental problems—they seem a thousand times worse when they strike in the wee hours of the morning. Fortunately, this remarkable remedy can usually save the day, er, night: Mix 1 tablespoon of calcium lactate (available in pharmacies and health-food stores) with 1 teaspoon of apple cider vinegar and 1 teaspoon of honey in half a glass of warm water. Drink it down, and the pain should back off within 20 minutes or so, allowing you to get some sleep.

QUICK & QUIRKY

Stave Off Muscle Cramps—If your muscles are prone to cramping—regardless of the time of day—here's a neat trick that should put an end to that nonsense: Before each meal, drink a glass of water with 2 teaspoons each of apple cider vinegar and honey mixed into it.

Quiet Your Barkin' Dogs

Has a long, hectic day left your feet aching so much that you can't sleep? Then crawl out of bed and fill a basin halfway full of luke-warm water. Stir in 1 cup of ACV and soak your sore tootsies for at least 15 minutes—the longer, the better!

Toxin-Tossin' Bath Blend

Books and the Internet are swarming with remedies that claim to rid your body of nasty toxins. But some of these concoctions cause more harm than good. This formula produces no dangerous side effects. Plus, in addition to clearing the junk from your system, it'll boost your magnesium levels, soothe skin irritations, and relax you all over. (This recipe makes enough for one bath.)

- ¼ **cup of baking soda**
- ¼ **cup of Epsom salts**
- ¼ **cup of sea salt**
- **1 qt. of boiling water**
- ⅓ **cup of apple cider vinegar**
- **10 drops of peppermint or lavender oil (optional)**

Dissolve the first three ingredients in the boiling water, and set the mixture aside. Fill your bathtub with warm water, and pour in the vinegar. Add the other ingredients, and swish the water around with your hand to disperse them. Then step into the tub, relax, and soak for 30 minutes or so. **Note:** *You may feel a little light-headed, so be careful getting out of the tub!*

Bid Bye-Bye to Bruises

Ouch! You weren't looking where you were going and walked right into the coffee table. Not to worry—if you act fast, you can chase the pain away and stop ugly black-and-blue marks from forming. How? Just soak a piece of cotton gauze in either white or apple cider vinegar, and tape it to the injured site for 60 minutes.

Timely Tinctures

Alcohol is the liquid (a.k.a. menstruum) that's most often used in commercial herbal tinctures. But warmed (not boiled!) apple cider vinegar will work just fine, and it's definitely the way to go if you'd like to add your tincture to food, you're making it for children

FOR GOOD LIVING

or pets, or you're sensitive to alcohol. The process is as easy as 1, 2, 3, 4. Just gather up ½ cup or so of fresh or dried herbs (leaves, flowers, or both), a bottle of ACV, and a clean glass jar with a screw-on top. Then follow this four-step routine:

STEP 1. Harvest your fresh herbs, rinse, towel dry, and chop them finely. Or simply measure out the dried versions.

STEP 2. Put the herbs in the jar, and pour in the vinegar until it reaches 2 to 3 inches above the top of the herb layer.

THE BETA-CAROTENE FOUND IN ACV is a powerful antioxidant, which helps neutralize the free radicals that cause cancer, Alzheimer's, and other degenerative diseases. (Bear in mind, though, that ACV cannot cure those diseases!)

STEP 3. Cover the jar with a tight-fitting lid, and put it in a warm, dark place. Let the mixture sit for at least four to six weeks—the longer, the better. During that period, shake the bottle now and then to keep the herbs from packing down on the bottom.

STEP 4. Strain out the solids, and pour the liquid into clean, fresh bottles. Label them, and store them in a cool, dark place out of reach of children or pets. The tincture will retain its full potency for about a year. After that, although it will still taste just fine and will be perfectly safe to consume, its medicinal effect will start to decline.

Note: *To use your tincture, either put a drop or two directly under your tongue, using a medicine (a.k.a. eye) dropper. Or mix the drops into a cup of hot or warm water to make instant herbal tea. As for what herbs to use, see "Vinegar & Herbs—A Power-Packed Health-Care Pair" (at right).*

VINEGAR & HERBS—A POWER-PACKED HEALTH-CARE PAIR

When it comes to solving health problems, vinegar and herbs are a match made in heaven. In each case, the herbs you want to use depend on the job(s) at hand. Here are some of the best choices:

- **Basil** fights cold and flu infections, eases migraines, relieves stress, helps cure depression, and removes warts.

- **Bay** helps prevent tooth decay and eases headache pain.

- **Chamomile** reduces pain and inflammation in the digestive tract and relaxes both body and nerves.

- **Dill** calms upset stomachs, relieves muscle spasms, freshens breath, and stimulates the flow of breast milk in nursing mothers.

- **Garlic** kills bacteria, clears lung congestion, lowers blood sugar and cholesterol levels, and boosts circulation.

- **Marjoram and oregano** act as effective antiseptics, soothe sore throats, and relieve aching joints and muscles.

- **Parsley** aids digestion, controls blood pressure, improves immunity, bolsters bones, heals the nervous system, and eases joint pain.

- **Peppermint** energizes mind and body and relieves nausea.

- **Rosemary** stimulates memory and boosts energy and mood.

- **Sage** restores vitality and strength, fights fevers, and soothes mucous membrane tissue—thereby curing sore gums.

- **Thyme** detoxifies the body (especially the liver), boosts the immune system, fights fatigue, and kills parasites.

Note: *Herbal vinegar can also add a powerful punch to your beauty kit. You'll find some dandy tips on that score in Chapter 2.*

Caution: *If you're on medication of any kind (even aspirin), you suffer from any chronic condition, or you're pregnant or think that you might be pregnant, check with your doctor before taking these or any other herbs.*

Cut the Clogs

To help clear up congestion that's caused by a chest cold or sinus infection, simply add ¼ cup of apple cider vinegar to the water in your hot-steam vaporizer. Besides easing your discomfort, the vinegar will be good for the machine: It'll clear away any mineral deposits in the water tubes that can clog up the works. **Note:** *Check with the manufacturer before you use vinegar in a cool-mist vaporizer. The acidic fluid can damage some models.*

3 Wacky Ways to Clear Clogged Sinuses

Clogged sinuses driving you crazy? Put apple cider vinegar to work! Two or three times a day, use one of these remarkable remedies—or try all three and see which one works best for you.

- Drink a glass of warm water with 2 teaspoons of ACV mixed in it.

- Mix 2 tablespoons of ACV and 1 tablespoon of honey in 8 ounces of warm water, and sip.

- Mix 1 cup of ACV and 1 cup of water in a pan. Heat it on the stove, then inhale the steamy vapors while keeping your mouth and eyes closed. And be careful not to burn yourself!

Word to the Wise

While vinegar is generally one of the safest healers, it does interact with some medications, including digoxin (Lanoxin®), insulin, and diuretic drugs. So if you're taking any of those meds, check with your doctor before you use vinegar in medicinal quantities. Also, if you are pregnant or think you might be pregnant, ask your obstetrician how much vinegar is safe for you to consume.

Steam-Clean Your Allergies

Inhaling ACV vapors can do more than relieve sinus congestion (see "3 Wacky Ways to Clear Clogged Sinuses," at left). It's also just what the doctor ordered to clear up seasonal allergy symptoms. Use the remedy as needed to open up your nasal passages, decrease mucus production, and generally calm your allergic reactions.

IT'S A FREEZE PLAY

Thanks to a process developed at Johns Hopkins School of Medicine, vinegar is being used in developing countries as an inexpensive alternative to Pap smears. When a vinegar solution is brushed onto a woman's cervix, it turns any lesions white. They are then frozen off with the use of a metal rod chilled in a tank of very cold carbon dioxide.

5 Simple Steps to Free and Easy Airways

Since as far back as the 1600s, medical gurus have been touting the miraculous lung-clearing prowess of the vinegar-garlic-honey triad. Taking this potent syrup consistently just may keep you free of asthma symptoms. Here's your easy-breathing five-step game plan:

STEP 1. Separate and peel the cloves of three garlic bulbs.

STEP 2. Put them in a non-aluminum pan with 2 cups of water, and simmer until the garlic cloves are soft, and there is about 1 cup of water left in the pan.

STEP 3. Using a slotted spoon, transfer the garlic to a jar with a tight-fitting lid.

STEP 4. Add 1 cup of apple cider vinegar and ¼ cup of honey to the water in the pan, and boil until it's syrupy.

FOR GOOD LIVING

STEP 5. Pour the syrup over the garlic in the jar, put the lid on, and let it sit overnight, or for at least eight hours.

Every morning on an empty stomach, swallow one or two garlic cloves along with 1 teaspoon of the syrup.

Downplay Dust-Mite Allergies

For most folks, a less than pristine floor is a fairly minor annoyance. But if you're allergic to dust mites, even a few specks of dust can send your misery index into the stratosphere. One solution: Mop your hard-surface floors frequently with a mixture of ½ cup of white vinegar per gallon of water. It'll kill dust mites on contact—and shine up your floors to boot! (Coming up in parts 2 and 3, you'll find a gazillion more ways to put the cleaning power of vinegar to work, indoors and out.)

QUICK & QUIRKY

Stop Asthma Attacks in Their Tracks— Many asthma sufferers swear by this goofy-sounding trick: At the first sign of wheezing, take a breath or two from your inhaler. Then saturate two strips of white cloth in white vinegar and wrap them snugly, but not too tightly, around your wrists. If you've acted quickly enough, there's a good chance you'll avoid a full-blown attack.

Beef Up Your Chicken Soup

We all know that chicken soup is a tried-and-true weapon in the fight against cold and flu germs, including the kinds that cause bronchitis. Well, here's a way to add even more oomph to your favorite recipe (or even instant chicken broth): Heat up 1 cup of soup or broth, and stir in 1 tablespoon of apple cider vinegar, 1 crushed garlic clove, and a dash of hot-pepper sauce (to taste). Pour it into a bowl or mug, and sip yourself to good health. Repeat as necessary until you're back in the pink again.

Beat Bronchitis from the Outside

Believe it or not, vinegar can help you break up your lousy lung congestion from the outside in. Here's the easy routine:

Coat a cast-iron skillet with extra virgin olive oil, and add a handful of chopped onions, a teaspoon of apple cider vinegar, and a pinch of cornstarch.

> **VINEGAR IS A POWERFUL ACIDIC SUBSTANCE** and sniffing its fumes for too long can actually damage your mucous membranes. Using ACV steam treatments on a temporary basis to relieve a specific condition will cause no harm—but don't make it an everyday habit.

Cook the ingredients over low heat to make a paste. Let it cool to a comfortable temperature, and then spread it on a soft, clean cloth that's big enough to cover your clogged-up chest.

Lay the cloth, paste side down, on your bare chest. Cover it with plastic wrap, add another cloth, and top everything with a heating pad set on low. Relax for an hour or so. The onion will be absorbed into your body and open up your bronchial tubes pronto.

Note: *You'll know the paste has penetrated into your system because you'll have the onion breath to prove it!*

Raspberry Sore-Throat Solution

This fruity gargle is a potent potion that soothes a raw, painful sore throat in a snap!

2 cups of ripe red raspberries

2 ½ cups of white-wine vinegar

1 cup of sugar

Put the whole berries in a bowl, and add the vinegar. Cover, and refrigerate for three days. Then pour the mixture into a saucepan, stir in the sugar, and bring to a low boil. Simmer for 15 minutes, and remove from the heat. When the mixture has cooled almost to room temperature, strain it through a sieve or cheesecloth, pressing on the berries to extract as much juice as possible. Pour the potion into a glass bottle, store it in the refrigerator, and gargle with it as needed.

Clobber Coughs and Colds...

And sore throats, too, with this classic triple-threat combo: Mix equal parts of apple cider vinegar, honey, and warm water, and stir in about ¼ teaspoon of grated fresh ginger per cup of the mixture. Store it at room temperature in a covered glass jar, and take 1 teaspoon three times a day. Before you know it, your misery will be history!

3 Vivacious Vinegar Throat Soothers

Apple cider vinegar (ACV) is one of Mother Nature's most potent sore-throat relievers. Whether the pain is caused by the *Streptococcus* bacteria or a virus, you can put this valiant vanquisher to work in three ways:

Drink it. Mix 1 tablespoon each of ACV and honey in 1 cup of warm water, and sip the potion slowly. Repeat as desired once or twice a day.

Gargle it. Mix 2 teaspoons of ACV in 8 ounces of warm water, and proceed as follows: Gargle a mouthful of the solution, and spit it out. Then swallow a mouthful. Keep alternating until the glass is empty. Wait 60 minutes, and go at it again. Continue as needed until you've put your pain out to pasture.

Wear it. Just before bedtime, saturate a soft cotton cloth in a solution made from 2 tablespoons of ACV mixed with ⅔ cup of warm water. Wring out the cloth, put it on your throat, and secure it in place with a strip of dry gauze or an elastic bandage, and leave it in place overnight. By morning, your throat should feel much better. Repeat as necessary.

Word to the Wise

Never give honey in any form to a baby under one year of age. Until a youngster's gastrointestinal tract is fully operational (usually at about 12 months of age), the *Clostridium botulinum*, which honey contains, can cause infant botulism. Just to play it safe, always check with your doctor before you give honey (even as a sweetener in food) to a child under two years old.

Soothe an Overworked Throat

Is your gullet red and raw from a speaking engagement, a long round of Christmas caroling, or cheering too long and too loud for your favorite team? If so, then this trick should put you back in business fast: Gargle with a mixture of 1 tablespoon of ACV and 1 teaspoon of salt dissolved in a glass of warm water. Repeat as often as needed through the day, until you're rarin' to go again.

Quell the Inner Itch

All you ladies know that there are few more agonizing conditions than a vaginal itch caused by the *Candida albicans* yeast infection. Well, vinegar can vanquish that vexation in a hurry. Simply douche twice a day for two days with a solution made from 2 tablespoons of white vinegar in 1 quart of water. The mildly acidic shower will bid the yeast cells an unfond farewell. **Note:** *Do not use this formula any longer than two days. And never douche with vinegar—or anything else—when you don't have a yeast infection. If you do, you'll rinse out the beneficial bacteria that keep yeast and other infections at bay.*

2 Ways to Thrash Thrush

A kissin' cousin of the *Candida* fungus that causes vaginal infections (see "Quell the Inner Itch," above) can also throw off the normal balance of good versus bad bacteria in your mouth and throat. When trouble strikes there, the result is a white coating that can cause pain, bleeding, and general discomfort. Fortunately, apple cider vinegar can end that hassle fast. You can put it to work in one of two ways:

- Mix up a solution of 4 tablespoons of ACV per quart of water, and drink at least four glasses a day until your mouth is in the pink of health again.

VINEGAR IS STRONG STUFF!

To avoid upsetting your stomach, never drink it straight. Always mix it with a milder carrier, such as water, fruit juice, or honey. And if you find that the highly acidic fluid bothers your stomach, ease back on the dosage— or, if necessary, quit cold turkey.

- Rinse your mouth and gargle several times a day with a half-and-half solution of ACV and warm water.

Soak Hemorrhoids Away Overnight

Well, in a manner of speaking. Here's one of the most effective ways I know to ease the pain and itching of hemorrhoids: Soak a cotton gauze bandage in apple cider vinegar and—to put it plainly—stick it where the sun don't shine. Put on snug underwear to hold the sopping gauze in place, and toddle off to bed. You should feel blessed relief in a hurry. **Note:** *If the area is raw from scratching, you will feel some burning at first, but it should pass quickly.*

Fire Water

Don't let the name fool you! While it is true that you wouldn't want to serve this beverage at your next cocktail party, it is a lot tastier than you might think—and it packs one heck of a superstar healing punch. It can help you cure a sore throat, fend off cold and flu viruses, unstuff your sinuses, rev up your energy, and give a great big boost to your immune system. Best of all, it's a snap to make.

- **½ cup of apple cider vinegar**
- **½ cup of hot water**
- **1 tsp. of ground cayenne pepper**
- **1 tsp. of honey* (optional)**
- **1 tsp. of sea salt**
- **½ tsp. of freshly squeezed lemon juice**

Stir all of the ingredients together in a mug or heat-proof glass. Then sip the potion while it's still hot. Repeat as needed throughout the day until you're cured.

* In addition to adding a healthy kick of its own, the honey will tone down the pepper's power.

Yield: 1 serving

FOR GOOD LIVING

OLD-TIME Vim and Vinegar

Constipation got you down? Then do what Grandma Putt did whenever her (or my) inner plumbing wasn't performing up to snuff: Mix 2 tablespoons of apple cider vinegar in a glass of apple juice, grape juice, or water. Drink this mixture three times a day, and before you know it, things should once again start moving merrily along.

Stop the Flow

When your inner plumbing is working a little too smoothly, vinegar can help slow the flow, so to speak. The routine: Six times a day (before each meal and in between meals), drink a glass of water with 1 teaspoon of apple cider vinegar mixed into it. In the next 24 to 48 hours, your system should be back to normal. **Note:** *If your diarrhea continues for more than a day or two, or if you experience other symptoms, call your doctor.*

Create Health-Giving Treasure

Granted, you can buy mother-rich, unprocessed ACV in just about any supermarket (Bragg®, Fleischmann's™, and Dynamic Health™ are all good brands). But when it comes to solving health —and beauty—problems, nothin' beats your own home cookin'. The final product does take time to "brew," but the six-step process doesn't take much effort.

STEP 1. Round up 12 ripe apples (any variety, but organic if at all possible), 1 package of baker's yeast, and a quart or so of pure spring water.

STEP 2. Peel and dice the apples, and toss them (cores and all) into a stoneware crock, or a deep glass or ceramic bowl.

STEP 3. Add the yeast, and pour in enough spring water to cover the apples.

STEP 4. Cover the bowl with a piece of cheesecloth, and secure it with a rubber band. Put the container in a warm place (ideally where the temperature will stay at roughly 80°F), and let it sit for three to four months, or until the natural sugars have been converted to alcohol. (You'll know by the taste that you now have hard cider.)

STEP 5. Strain out the apples, and pour the liquid into a fresh crock or bowl. Set it back in its warm place, uncovered, and leave it for another three to four months.

STEP 6. Pour the vinegar into a glass bottle or jar. Store it at room temperature, and use it in any of the terrific health-giving tips, tricks, and tonics you'll find in this chapter.

Note: *If the apples you use have not been grown organically, be sure to wash them extra thoroughly (see "De-Pollute Your Produce" on page 45). Why? Because apples rank at the very top of the Dirty Dozen list of fruits that retain the largest amounts of pesticide residue. If any of it winds up in your ACV, it will reduce—or maybe even destroy—its medicinal value.*

Word to the Wise

If you have diabetes, confer with your doctor before you try any oral ACV remedies. Be especially careful if you have gastroparesis, a common problem in diabetics that slows down the emptying of the stomach. Some research shows that consuming ACV may make the condition worse.

In the 17th century, the bubonic plague swept across Europe, killing at least half the population, and thus becoming known as the Black Death. French folklore tells us that in Marseilles, four men repeatedly looted the homes of recently deceased victims but, miraculously, never got sick. According to one version of the story, after the thieves were arrested, they were forced to bury the dead, with the promise that if they survived, they would go free. Well, survive they did—apparently thanks to an herbal vinegar tincture concocted by one of the bad guys, who happened to be an herbalist. As the gang's resistance to the disease became well known, other folks began using the potion. Today, natural health gurus still swear by the amazing healing power of Four Thieves Vinegar (see the recipe at far right and "Good Things from Bad Guys," at right).

Good Things from Bad Guys

Ever since the 17th century, savvy folks have been tapping into the remarkable healing power of Four Thieves Vinegar (FTV), which, according to legend, was first formulated by a convicted robber. (You'll find the recipe at right and the colorful saga in the That's Historical box at left.) Here's a quartet of ways to use this wonder "drug":

Cure colds, flu, and other illnesses. Adults should take 1 tablespoon of FTV three times a day. The dosage for children is 1 teaspoon three times a day. How you take it is your call. For example, you can sip it from a spoon, add it to salad dressing, or mix it with water, fruit juice, or herbal tea.

Head off colds and flu. Use the same quantities (1 tablespoon for adults, 1 teaspoon for children) as you would to conquer a cold or flu, but for prevention purposes, taking the potion only once a day should do the trick. For additional resistance, you can also add a tablespoon or so to your bathwater, and breathe in the healing vapors while you're soaking your worries away.

Kill germs. Fend off airborne viruses as well as surface bacteria by filling a spray bottle with equal parts of FTV and water, and spritzing it into the air and onto surfaces throughout your home and office. It also makes a dandy hand sanitizer.

Repel disease-spreading insects. Or any other kind, for that matter! Pour ¼ cup of FTV into a spray bottle, and fill the balance with water. Spray the potion onto your skin and clothes whenever you venture outside into bug-infested territory.

FOR GOOD LIVING

ACV + H₂O = RELIEF

Talk about dynamic duos! Apple cider vinegar and water can solve some of the most nagging health problems under the sun. Like these, for instance:

Health Problem	The Rx
Bladder infection	2 teaspoons of ACV in a glass of water three times a day (but get your doctor's okay first)
Dizzy spell	½ teaspoon of ACV in a glass of water
Hot flashes	1 tablespoon of ACV in 8 ounces of ice water as needed
Indigestion	2 teaspoons of ACV in a glass of water once an hour until you feel relief
Morning sickness	1 teaspoon of ACV in a glass of water with approval from your obstetrician
Sinusitis or facial neuralgia	½ teaspoon of ACV in a glass of water once an hour for seven hours

Note: *If you just don't care for the taste of ACV, mix it into herbal tea or fruit or vegetable juice instead of water.*

Don't Have a Heart(burn)

Just about all of us have been here at least a few times: You eat something that doesn't agree with you, and suddenly it feels like your heart's on fire. So how do you douse the flames? Well, for starters, try to avoid the temptation to lie down. That will only increase the backflow of stomach acid into your esophagus, which is what's causing the trouble. Instead, mix 1 tablespoon of apple cider vinegar and 1 tablespoon of honey into a cup of warm water. Drink the potion standing up, and before you know it, your ticker should be as cool as a cucumber again.

Tame Tummy Turbulence

An upset stomach can strike from out of nowhere and often for no apparent reason. To stop the queasiness, drink a glass of warm water with 2 or 3 teaspoons of peppermint vinegar mixed into it. Add honey to taste if you'd like. You'll find the ultra-easy instructions for making peppermint and other herbal vinegar in "Simply Elegant..." on page 114.

TAME AN ACID...WITH AN ACID?
So how on earth, you may ask, can an acidic substance such as vinegar alleviate conditions like acid reflux and heartburn? Simple: It strengthens your stomach acid—and contrary to what the big  pharmaceutical companies would have you believe, it's weak stomach acid that causes acid reflux.

A Hasty End to Hiccups

Hiccups do not pose a real health problem, and in most cases, they end on their own within a few minutes. But when your hic, hic, hiccupping continues longer than you'd like, simply swallow a teaspoon of apple cider vinegar. No ACV on hand? Then suck on a dill pickle. The vinegar in it will accomplish the same hiccup-halting mission.

EXTERNAL WOES

Kill the Poison

Poison ivy, oak, and sumac are no match for apple cider vinegar. So the next time you have a run-in with any of these noxious weeds, split a brown paper bag open, soak it in some ACV, and lay it on the rash. It'll draw out the toxins in no time flat.

Put Prickly Heat in Its Place

This dratted condition is infamous for attacking babies, but it's actually an equal opportunity ailment. Grown-ups are every bit as likely to fall victim to the nasty welts, especially in hot, humid weather. The simple remedy: Add 1 teaspoon of apple cider vinegar to 1 cup of water, and sponge the mixture onto any itchy, rashy areas. By balancing the pH of your skin, the ACV will quickly banish the red bumps.

Save Sore, Chapped Hands

Rats! You spent too much time working bare-handed in frigid weather, and now your hands are red, raw, and burning. Not to worry! Just mix some ultra-rich hand cream with an equal amount of vinegar (any kind will do). Then every time you wash and dry your paws, follow up by smoothing a coat of cream on them. Within days, your skin will be as good as new.

VINEGAR NEVER SPOILS, and honey is the only food that never goes bad. So rest assured that whenever you mix up any vinegar-honey combo, it'll hang in there for the long haul—provided, of course, that you use the pure, natural versions.

OLD-TIME
Vim and Vinegar

You say you need to hit the garden (or maybe do a little lifeguard duty at the backyard wading pool), and you're fresh out of sunscreen lotion? No problem! Just rub your skin with a half-and-half mixture of apple cider vinegar and olive oil before heading outside. That's what folks did long before commercial sunblocks came on the scene, and in a pinch, it'll still do the job today! **Note:** *This same trick works in the winter to help protect your face from windburn or windchill.*

Get Ready for Ol' Sol

When summertime rolls around, stick a bottle of apple cider vinegar in your refrigerator to chill. Then, whenever your sizzling skin lets you know you spent too much time in the sun, pull out the bottle and pat your poor skin every 20 minutes with the cold liquid, using a washcloth or cotton pad. This trick will take the pain away fast, and as long as you don't rinse it off, it'll prevent your burned skin from blistering and peeling. **Note:** *This remedy also works well for minor burns from the stove, the barbecue grill, or a hot iron.*

Whoops—Too Late!

You say the sun has already done a number on your skin, and there's no vinegar in the fridge? No problem! Just head for the bathroom, and pour 1 cup of ACV into a tub of warm water. Then ease on in, and heave a soothing sigh of relief.

Heal Bites and Stings

When you combine the drawing power of plantain (yes, that pesky weed) and the anti-inflammatory action of ACV, what do you get? A tincture that not only relieves the symptoms of a bite or sting, but actually heals the wound! Here's how to make your own supply of this super summertime helper.

STEP 1. Gather up a bunch of plantain leaves that have not been treated with pesticides or herbicides. Wash them, tear them into pieces, and crush them to extract the volatile oils. (The bottom of a jar works well for this purpose.)

STEP 2. Pack the leaves into a large glass jar that has a tight-fitting lid, and cover them with apple cider vinegar. Store the jar in a cool, dark place for two weeks, shaking it daily.

STEP 3. When time's up, strain the liquid through cheesecloth into a clean glass jar, label it, and store it in the refrigerator. As needed, pour some of the tincture into smaller, dark-colored bottles to carry in your pocket, back-pack, or golf bag.

To use the potion, immediately dab it generously onto the site of a bite or sting. You should feel almost-instant relief.

Note: *If the culprit was a poisonous spider or snake, get medical help pronto!*

QUICK & QUIRKY

First Aid on Ice— The next time you empty a plastic egg carton, separate the top and bottom. Pour vinegar into each egg-shaped compartment in the bottom half, and pop it into the freezer. Then, whenever you need relief from a rash, bug bite, or post-sunburn itch, pull out a vinegarsicle, and rub its comfortably rounded surface over your affected skin.

Speaking of Stings...

The next time you have an encounter with the business end of an angry bee, pour undiluted vinegar (any kind you have handy will do) on the sting site. It'll eliminate the pain in no time flat and also make it easier to scrape the stinger out with a plastic credit card or flat-bladed knife. **Note:** *If you have difficulty breathing or the affected area becomes inflamed and swollen, get medical help immediately—you could be having a potentially fatal allergic reaction.*

Stingin' by the Seaside

Make that in the sea. The same vinegar splash that lends a helping hand with bee stings works just as well on the even more painful versions inflicted by jellyfish. One word of warning: Do not use vinegar if your attacker was a Portuguese man-of-war (a close cousin of the jellyfish). Scientists now tell us that, contrary to previous theories, applying the acidic fluid—or any other sustance—is likely to increase the amount of toxin released under your skin.

Word to the Wise

Anyone who spends time in the kitchen knows how easy it is to get burned by a hot stove or oven. So stop reading right now and grab a bottle of white vinegar. Pour some of it into a spray bottle, and stash it in the refrigerator. Then, the next time you need instant relief from a minor burn, spritz yourself with the chilled vinegar to cool down and soothe your sore skin.

Ring Out Ringworm

Contrary to its name, ringworm is not a worm; it's a fungus that causes circular, scaly patches on the skin. Unfortunately, it can spread like wildfire, even from one person to another. But there's a simple two-step way to douse the flames.

- Soak a gauze pad in a solution made from 1 part apple cider vinegar mixed with 4 parts distilled water, and put it on the affected area for about 30 minutes.

- The next day, repeat the process using a gauze pad soaked in a solution made from 1 teaspoon of salt dissolved in 2 cups of distilled water. Alternate these compresses—vinegar one day, salt the next. In a week or so (depending on its severity), the foul fungus should be gone.

Walk Away from Warts

Troublesome warts will vanish when you use this simple, old-time remedy. At bedtime, dab the bump with apple cider vinegar. (But don't rub it in—that could spread the virus that causes warts, and you'll wind up with more of the things than you have already.) Then soak a gauze pad in apple cider vinegar, put it over the wart, and cover it with a bandage to hold in the moisture. Leave it on overnight. In the morning, remove the bandage, but don't rinse off the vinegar. Repeat the treatment each night until the wart is gone.

DISINFECT A WOUND and head off infection with this simple trick: Cover the "owie" with baking soda, and pour vinegar over it (any kind will do). Wait until the bubbles subside, and then rinse the area thoroughly with nice warm water.

Make Hives Take a Hike

These itchy, wretched red bumps generally spring up out of nowhere in response to an allergy (most often to a food or medication) or oversensitivity to sun exposure or insect bites. Hives usually vanish almost as fast as they appear, but if yours seem determined to hang around, vinegar can give them an encouraging shove out the door. Just mix 1 tablespoon of vinegar (any kind will do) with 3 tablespoons of cornstarch to make a paste. Spread it on the red areas. By the time it dries and flakes off, your skin should be back to normal. If it's not, repeat the process—the second time should be a charm.

EXCELLENT ELIXIR

Fungus-Fighter Tonic for Nails

Powerful prescription drugs can quickly cure finger- and toenail fungi from the inside. There's just one problem: These meds can deliver side effects, including kidney damage, that are a lot worse than the pain and itch of your infected digit. So why take chances? Instead of popping pills, use this ultra-safe DIY formula.

1 part antiseptic mouthwash

1 part vinegar (white or ACV)

1 part warm water

1 tbsp. of ground cinnamon

Mix all of the ingredients in a bowl or basin. Then soak your affected hand or foot for 15 to 20 minutes every day. Granted, it will take longer to work than a doctor's prescription, but it will kill the foul fungi with no damage to your innards—and for less money.

FOR GOOD LIVING

The Fast Track to an Itch-Free Scalp—When you don't have time for a full-scale shower (see "Head for Psoriasis Relief," at right), gently massage your scalp with a half-and-half mixture of apple cider vinegar and water. It'll not only stop the itching, but it will also help reduce the inflammation and heal any associated infections.

Head for Psoriasis Relief

One of the simplest and most effective ways to ease the pain and itch of psoriasis is to relax for 20 minutes in a tub full of water with 2 cups of apple cider vinegar added to it. But if the agonizing lesions have flared up on your scalp, chances are you'd rather not soak your head in a bathtub for 20 minutes. Nor do you want to risk messing up your hair with a topical healer—at least not unless you're headed off to bed rather than out the door. Enter this shower-time treatment that's as easy as pie and neat as a pin:

- Pour 1 cup of olive oil into a bowl, and mix in 1 drop of oregano oil and 2 drops of calendula oil.

- Step into the shower, massage the mixture into your scalp, and shampoo as usual. (Be careful because the oil will make the shower floor slippery.)

- Rinse with a half-and-half solution of apple cider vinegar and water. Repeat daily or as needed until you've doused the flare-up.

Beat Boils from the Inside

There's no getting around it: Boils hurt like the dickens. But (believe it or not) vinegar tea can help make the pain vanish and the bumps vamoose. The easy R_X:

- At least twice a day, mix 1 tablespoon of apple cider vinegar and 1 tablespoon of honey in a cup of hot water, and drink up.

- Throughout the day, guzzle plenty of water.

- When the boil comes to a head, add hot packs to the routine (but continue tippling the tea and water). Three times a day, soak a soft, clean cloth in hot (but not burning hot!) water and apply it to the boil for 15 to 20 minutes.

Before you know it, the agonizing lump should be history!
Note: *Whatever you do, never squeeze a boil! And if the pain gets progressively worse, or if you see a red streak in it, get medical help immediately. The pus-filled bump may need to be drained surgically.*

VARICOSE VEINS VAMOOSE

If you're plagued by varicose veins, you know that their unsightly appearance is the least of the problem. They're also painful—and potentially dangerous because they can trigger blood clots. But before you resort to drugs or surgery, try this simple trick. Soak a couple of cloths in apple cider vinegar, and wrap them around your legs. Then lie down with your feet propped up about a foot, and hold that pose for half an hour or so. Do this twice a day until those ugly blue road maps hit the trail.

Pull the Poison Out

Here's an old-time potion that'll pull the toxins out of boils and blisters: Put about 2 tablespoons of coarsely ground slippery elm bark (available online and in health-food stores) in a 1-quart glass jar. Fill the balance of the container with boiling apple cider vinegar, and let it sit in a dark place at room temperature for a week. Then strain out the bark. To use the potion, soak a soft cloth in the fluid, and lay it on the sore for 15 minutes. Repeat several times a day. **Note:** *If the sore shows signs of infection, forget DIY treatments and see a doctor.*

If your eyes are tired and sore, and you're of a certain age, the reason may be simply that your body is behaving naturally—that is, it is less effective at producing the vital elements that are essential to keep your orbs functioning at their peak. To help restore your peepers' vitality, sip 2 teaspoons each of ACV and honey in a glass of water three times a day. **Note:** *If your eyes are still just fine, thank you, this bracing beverage will help delay the onset of trouble.*

3 Ways to Nail Athlete's Foot

We all know that you don't have to be an athlete to get athlete's foot. Fortunately, vinegar is a surefire way to kill the foul fungi that cause the problem—and keep them from coming back. Here's the routine:

- Rinse your afflicted feet several times a day with either white or apple cider vinegar.

- To avoid reinfecting yourself, soak your socks and/or panty hose in white vinegar for 20 minutes before washing them. Also, moisten a cotton ball or pad with white vinegar, and use it to wipe out any shoes or boots you've worn since contracting the condition.

- If you swim or work out at a gym or health club, keep a spray bottle of vinegar in your tote bag or locker. Then, each time you get out of the shower, spray your toes thoroughly, rinse them with clear water, and dry them well.

Lose Head Lice

Once these teeny, wingless insects get into your hair, they feast on your blood and lay their eggs (a.k.a. nits) on your hair shafts just above scalp level. And the little vampires spread like crazy through contact with contaminated hair, brushes, combs, clothing, and bedding. They can be the very dickens to get rid of, but one of the most effective eviction methods involves (you guessed it) vinegar. Here's the procedure:

STEP 1. Wash your hair with a commercial delousing shampoo that contains permethrin. Leave it in for 10 minutes, and then rinse it out with clear water.

STEP 2. Rinse again using a half-and-half solution of white vinegar and water. (The vinegar will help dissolve the bodies of the dead nits.) Massage the mixture into your hair and scalp as vigorously as you can. Then rinse your hair thoroughly with clear water to remove the vinegar odor.

STEP 3. Repeat the routine 10 days later. If you still have some lingering lice, proceed to Step 4.

STEP 4. Mix ½ cup of white vinegar with ½ cup of olive oil (any kind will do). Apply the mixture to your hair, working it in well to thoroughly coat the base of your hair shafts. Cover your hair with a shower cap, and go about your business for 60 minutes.

STEP 5. Remove the cap, step into the shower, and wash your hair with your usual shampoo. That should deep-six the lousy hordes!

DURING ANY HEAD-LICE INVASION— regardless of what products you use to treat the problem—comb your (or your child's) hair at least once a day using a fine-toothed nit comb to remove the dead larvae and any live ones that have survived the dousing. Then soak the comb in white vinegar for 30 minutes to destroy any eggs.

FOR GOOD LIVING

Ditch Jock Itch

Jock itch is caused by a fungus, and it *does* tend to afflict its namesake athletic victims (both male and female). It can spread rampantly in gyms and health clubs where the towels are washed with water that's not quite hot enough to kill the fungi. One tried-and-true trick: Once or twice a day, soak a cotton ball in vinegar (any kind will do), and dab it onto your affected skin. Continue the routine until the itching, burning, and redness are gone. **Note:** *This treatment works because the fungi cannot thrive and multiply in the acidic environment created by the vinegar.*

QUICK & QUIRKY

Give Shingles a Shove—Few conditions are more agonizing than shingles—fluid-filled blisters caused by the herpes zoster virus, which also causes chicken pox. Fortunately, one of the most effective ways to ease the pain is also one of the simplest: Lightly dab or coat the spots with apple cider vinegar. Repeat the process throughout the day until your flare-up fades.

The Eyes Have It

If your eyes are sore, tired, or puffy, the cause could be allergies, stress, a big night on the town, or simply too much time in front of a computer screen. The good news is that the dynamic duo of apple cider vinegar and blackstrap molasses can put the pep back in your peepers. It works because ACV improves your blood circulation, and blackstrap molasses is a potent source of vitamin B_1, which is essential for good eye health. Best of all, you can take your medicine either internally or externally in one—or both—of two ways:

Internally. Take 2 tablespoons of apple cider vinegar mixed with

1 tablespoon of blackstrap molasses. You can slurp it straight from a spoon, or spread it on toast, bagels, or English muffins at breakfast time.

Externally. Mix 2 teaspoons of ACV with 1 teaspoon of blackstrap molasses, and spread it onto your puffy eyelids. Leave it on for five minutes, and gently wipe it off with a moist cotton ball.

Whichever delivery method you choose, use it twice a day, and before long, your eyes should be back to normal. **Note:** *If your puffy eyes are accompanied by blurry vision, pain, or intense discomfort, call your doctor or see an optometrist ASAP.*

Marinate Your Calluses

Calluses do not pose a serious health hazard, but they can be as painful as the dickens. Here's a simple—and quick—solution: Cut a slice of onion that's big enough to cover the affected area, put it in a bowl, and pour in some wine vinegar (either red or white) to cover it. Let the onion soak for four hours or so, then lay it over the calluses, and secure it in place with plastic wrap. Put on a sock to contain the wrapper, and leave it on overnight. Come morning, you should be able to scrape away the thick, hard skin. Once you do, wash and rinse your feet thoroughly so you don't go around town smelling like a salad!

AXE ECZEMA

Or at least ease your misery. The two-part plan:

▶ Drink a teaspoon each of ACV and honey in a glass of water before each meal.

▶ Several times throughout the day, dab your sore skin with a solution of 1 teaspoon of ACV per half a cup of water.

Give Corns the Boot

This old-time corn-removing formula sounds too good to be true, but a lot of folks I know swear by it. Just before your usual bedtime, put a slice of white bread, a slice of raw onion, and 1 cup of vinegar (any kind will do) in a bowl, and let it sit for 24 hours. The next night, put the bread on top of the corn, lay the onion on top of the bread, cover it with a bandage, and go to bed. There's a good chance the corn will fall off overnight. If it doesn't, repeat the procedure until the painful bump is history.

Clear Up Cold Sores

Cold sores (a.k.a. fever blisters) are caused by the herpes simplex virus and have no direct relation to either colds or fevers. But they do hurt like crazy. Never fear—ACV can help relieve the pain. Just mix 1 tablespoon of unfiltered apple cider vinegar with 3 tablespoons of honey, and store the mixture in a lidded jar. Then dab it onto your sore(s) in the morning, late afternoon, and just before bedtime. Before you know it, your fever blisters will be bygones!

OLD-TIME
Vim
and
Vinegar

As a boy, I sure picked up my share of bloody noses (what kid doesn't?). But Grandma Putt's old-time cure worked every time. And it still does today. Just soak a cotton ball in apple cider vinegar, and gently insert it into the dripping nostril. Then, holding both nostrils closed with your fingers, breathe through your mouth for about five minutes. Slowly remove the cotton. If the bleeding hasn't stopped, repeat the procedure. **Note:** *If you have recurring nosebleeds, it could signify an underlying health condition, so see your doctor. And if blood is flowing from both nostrils, hightail it to the ER!*

Swish Away Gum Disease

Swishing your mouth with ACV on a regular basis will help prevent gum disease. It'll also give your teeth a deep-down cleaning and sweeten your breath to boot. Just be aware that over time, the acid in vinegar can damage your tooth enamel, so rinse your mouth thoroughly with clear water immediately afterward. **Note:** *For that same reason, also swirl plenty of H_2O around in your mouth whenever you use a vinegar-based gargle.*

Whittle Your Waistline

Being overweight or—even worse—obese makes you a sitting duck for every health problem under the sun. The good news is that vinegar just may help you drop your excess baggage and avoid disaster. The simple process: Before each meal, mix 1 teaspoon of apple cider vinegar in a glass of warm water (make sure it's warm!). Add a teaspoon of honey if you'd like.

ONE OF THE KEY WAYS VINEGAR HELPS maintain good health is by making your inner ecosystem more alkaline. It works because disease organisms of all kinds favor an acid environment—which is exactly what most folks have these days, thanks to an overabundance of processed food, among other things.

Then drink up. If you're like most folks, this elixir will decrease your appetite, so you'll just naturally eat less, and that—combined with getting more exercise—is the healthiest way to shed unwanted pounds! **Note:** *Proponents of this tonic claim that in addition to curbing your appetite, it'll also improve your memory.*

FOR GOOD LIVING

Great Grapes Alive!

Thanks to the Trebbiano and Lambrusco grapes it's made from, balsamic vinegar is loaded with compounds that fight cancer, strengthen your immune system, and destroy the free radicals that cause premature aging and hardening of the arteries. And here's a hot tip for all you pasta fans: The next time you order a big dinner at your favorite Italian restaurant, make sure you ask for balsamic vinegar dressing on your salad. It'll keep your blood sugar from spiking, thereby preventing the sudden fatigue (a.k.a. "sugar crash") that can set in a few hours later. **Note:** *This trick is a real winner for runners who load up on carbs before a big race.*

Calm Down!

Even if you're as thin as a rail, stress ups the odds that you'll succumb to anything from a common cold to catastrophic cancer. The good news: Whether your nerves are frayed from a busy day at the office followed by a bumper-to-bumper commute, or the state of world affairs has your anxiety level soaring off the charts, this de-stressing cocktail can help you relax: Put 1 tablespoon of apple cider vinegar and a chamomile tea bag into 1 cup of boiling water. Reduce the heat, and let it simmer for three or four minutes. Then remove the pan from the stove, pull out the tea

QUICK & QUIRKY

Fight Fatique—If you feel constantly fatigued, the reason may be that lactic acid has built up in your system, which tends to happen during periods of stress or strenuous exercise. If that's the case, this simple trick may help: At bedtime, take 3 teaspoons of apple cider vinegar mixed in 1/8 cup of honey. Continue the routine until you feel like your old self again.

bag, and pour the tea into a mug. When the brew has cooled to a comfortable drinking temperature, sit back in a cozy chair, put your feet up, and sip your cares away.

Soak Stress Away

Sipping a soothing tea isn't the only way to fight off health-damaging stress. Relaxing in a vinegar bath will also do wonders to soothe your spirits and calm your mind. There are plenty of excellent tub-time formulas, but this is one of the simplest: Just pour 1 quart of either apple cider or white-wine vinegar into your bathwater. Stir in a handful of mint leaves, rose petals, or chamomile (either fresh or dried). Then step into the tub, settle back, and think lovely thoughts. (In Chapter 2, you'll find more tub-time vinegar combos that'll soften your skin and make your stress level plummet.)

BEAT THE DRUMS FOR BALSAMIC
Repeated scientific tests have shown that balsamic vinegar—the tastiest type of all—reduces triglyceride and total cholesterol levels. What's more, it's been proven to help eliminate one of the most dangerous kinds of fat: the "spare tire" around the belly that can lead to such conditions as heart disease, sleep apnea, and type 2 diabetes. It works by activating genes that cause your body to distribute fat more evenly, rather than storing it at your waist. The jury is still out on exact dosages, but a good amount to aim for is 5 teaspoons a day, which is the amount that researchers have found to increase insulin sensitivity in diabetics.

How you take the Big B is your call: You can sip it straight from a spoon; stir it into juice, tea, or water; or use it in one of the recipes in Chapter 4, starting on page 119.

EXCELLENT ELIXIR

Fire Cider*

This combo of vinegar and tangy herbs and spices acts as a powerful decongestant, stimulates digestion, and boosts all of your body's natural health processes. Use it topically to ease muscle aches. The ingredients in this folk remedy may vary, but here's the basic recipe:

½ cup of chopped onion

½ cup of freshly grated ginger

½ cup of grated horseradish

10 garlic cloves, chopped

1 tsp. of ground cayenne pepper

1 qt. of apple cider vinegar

Honey to taste (optional)

Put the first five ingredients in a glass jar with a tight-fitting lid, and fill the balance of the jar with ACV. (If the lid is metallic, cover the jar opening with plastic wrap before you close it.) Shake it well, then store the jar in a cool, dark place, shaking it daily. After 30 days, strain the potion into a clean jar, pressing hard to squeeze as much liquid as possible out of the pulp. Set the pulp aside (see "5 Fine Ways to Put Fire Cider to Work," at right). If desired, add some honey to the vinegar, and stir well.
Not to be confused with Fire Water on page 19.

5 Fine Ways to Put Fire Cider to Work

Natural health gurus generally recommend taking 1 tablespoon of Fire Cider every day to keep your system revved up and performing at its peak. If you feel sniffles or a cough coming on—or if your stress level is elevated for whatever reason—up the dosage to 3 tablespoons a day. How you take your daily ration is your call. Of course, you can take it straight from a spoon or a shot glass, but here's a handful of tastier suggestions:

- Stir it into tomato or vegetable juice (it gives a dandy kick to a Bloody Mary!).

- Splash it on fried rice.

- Mix it into pasta sauce.

- Combine it with extra virgin olive oil to make a healthy and delicious salad dressing.

- Use the strained-out pulp to spice up stir-fries, omelets, and casseroles.

Note: *With or without honey added, Fire Cider is, well, fiery. So make sure you experiment until you find the right quantity that suits your family's heat tolerance.*

A Triumphant Triad

Worldwide studies show that a mixture made of apple cider vinegar, garlic, and honey can help prevent or cure almost every ailment under the sun, including Alzheimer's disease, arthritis, asthma, high blood pressure, obesity, ulcers, and cancer, as well as muscle aches and colds. The simple formula: Mix 1 cup of apple cider vinegar, 1 cup of honey, and 8 peeled garlic cloves in a blender on high speed for 60 seconds. Pour the blend into a glass jar that has a tight-fitting lid, and refrigerate it for five days. Then every day (ideally before breakfast) take 2 teaspoons of the mixture stirred into a glass of water or fruit juice. Researchers recommend freshly squeezed orange or 100 percent grape juice.

VARIATIONS ON A THEME OF FIRE

When you're dealing with a time-honored folk remedy like Fire Cider, the basic recipe at left is just the beginning. So feel free to improvise, according to your family's flavor preferences and the fruits, herbs, and spices you have on hand. Any of the ingredients below will ramp up the flavor and deliver an extra jolt of healing power:

▶ Juice and zest of one citrus fruit

▶ 2 jalapeño peppers, chopped

▶ 1 tablespoon of oregano, parsley, rosemary, thyme, or any combination thereof (either fresh or dried)

▶ 1 tablespoon of rose hips, chopped

▶ 1 tablespoon of turmeric

Sleep Tight

Sleepless nights are no fun—and they're not good for your health either. In fact, study after study has shown that consistently poor sleep can reduce your life span by (are you ready for this?) as much as 8 to 10 years. So if you find yourself tossing and turning when you should be cuttin' z's, try this remedy my Grandma Putt swore by: Mix about a teaspoon of apple cider vinegar into 1 cup of honey. When you go to bed, take a spoonful of the mixture, and put the container by your bedside. Then take another spoonful every hour or so during the night until you drift off to dreamland.

Secret of the Samurais

Japan's famous samurai warriors claimed they owed their strength and power to a tonic called *Tamago-su*, or egg vinegar. Folks throughout Japan still take it to maintain good health and slow down the aging process. Of course, the samurais didn't know why it worked, but we do: It prevents both the formation of damaging free radicals and the buildup of LDL (bad) cholesterol in your body. Here's how to make your own supply in two simple steps:

STEP 1. Immerse a whole, raw egg in 1 cup of rice vinegar, and let it sit, covered, for seven days.

STEP 2. When the week's up, you'll find that everything has dissolved into the vinegar except the transparent membrane that was just inside the

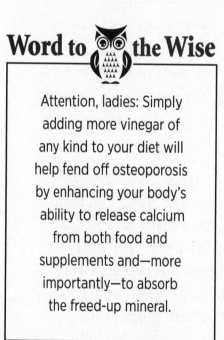

Word to the Wise

Attention, ladies: Simply adding more vinegar of any kind to your diet will help fend off osteoporosis by enhancing your body's ability to release calcium from both food and supplements and—more importantly—to absorb the freed-up mineral.

EXCELLENT ELIXIR

Cholesterol-Clobbering Punch

This remarkable—and delicious—folk remedy has helped legions of folks lower their cholesterol levels significantly.

> **2 cups of 100 percent apple juice**
>
> **2 cups of 100 percent cranberry juice**
>
> **2 cups of 100 percent white grape juice**
>
> **⅓ cup of apple cider vinegar**

Mix all of the ingredients together in a jug or pitcher, and keep it in the refrigerator. Drink one 8-ounce glass each morning and evening—and watch your Big C numbers plummet!

shell. Discard the membrane, and stir the egg-infused vinegar thoroughly. Store the tonic in a glass jar with a tight-fitting lid.

Three times a day, stir 1 or 2 teaspoons of the vinegar into a glass of hot water, and drink to a long, healthy life.

De-Pollute Your Produce

The best way to stay healthy is to eat good food. To ensure that all of your fruits and vegetables are free of pesticides, chemical fertilizers, and other toxic substances, call out the big guns (or a small spray bottle). Fill it with 2 tablespoons of vinegar (any kind), 1 tablespoon of lemon juice, and 1 cup of water. Keep the bottle by the sink, and spray all your fruits and veggies thoroughly. Then rinse 'em with clear water, and you're good to go! **Note:** *Do yourself a favor and use this potion on all of your fresh produce. After all, even organically grown crops generally contain stuff that you'd rather not eat, like the residue from manure tea, garlic- or citrus-based pesticides—or plain old garden-variety dirt.*

Test Time

Are you one of the millions of women who take calcium supplements to treat or help prevent osteoporosis? If so, you should be aware that if the pills don't break down completely and quickly after you swallow them, your body will not absorb the calcium. (And, believe it or not, some of the most highly touted pills don't pass the test.) What test, you ask? This one: Drop one of your supplements into a glass of white vinegar. Wait 20 minutes, and then take a look. If the pill is still intact, it's likely that you've been wasting your money. The reason: White vinegar has a pH level similar to that of your stomach. As scientific studies have confirmed, if a calcium supplement doesn't dissolve well in white vinegar, then it probably won't dissolve well in your tummy.

Liberate Your Minerals

We all know that minerals like calcium, potassium, and iron are essential for good health. But here's something you may not know: If you're over age 50, you could be eating heaping helpings of mineral-rich foods and still not be reaping all of their benefits. How come? Because, according to scientific studies, many folks who have passed the half-century mark don't produce enough stomach acid to draw essential minerals from their food. The simple solution: Boost your drawing power by adding more vinegar to your diet. Any kind of vinegar will do the trick, and it'll work its magic whether you use it as a dressing on dark, leafy greens, as a marinade for meat, or in any of the yummy recipes coming up in Chapter 4, starting on page 119.

Word to the Wise

Never, ever take your dose of hot-pepper vinegar from a spoon—or even taste it straight from the bottle. It can give your mouth and tongue a nasty burn. Instead, to find your comfort level, shake a drop or two of the fiery fluid onto a fork- or spoonful of food.

Tap into the Pepper Potential

Hot-pepper vinegar has been a culinary staple in American kitchens for generations (for my favorite version of the recipe, see page 117). But in recent years, medical research has shown that vinegar and capsaicin (the chemical that gives hot peppers their heat) team up to pack one heck of a health-giving wallop. Here's just a sampling of ways this zesty condiment can help you:

Lose or maintain weight. Hot-pepper vinegar increases your metabolic rate (the speed at which you burn calories). Plus, just $\frac{1}{5}$ ounce of the stuff can burn at least 76 more calories than it delivers.

Fend off major health trouble. It encourages your adrenal glands to produce cortisone, which is a key driver in preventing heart disease, diabetes, and other chronic (and potentially fatal) conditions.

Prevent heatstroke. Hot-pepper vinegar brings blood to your body's surface, thereby stimulating your sweat glands, which enable your body to keep its cool in hot weather.

FOR GOOD LIVING

EXCELLENT ELIXIR

Timely Tick Repellent

Ticks are not simply summertime nuisances. We now know that they can also spread life-threatening diseases. So make up a batch of this powerful, but gentle, repellent, and keep it on hand throughout the bad-bug season.

> **2 cups of white vinegar**
>
> **1 cup of water**
>
> **20 drops of eucalyptus oil**
>
> **20 drops of lavender oil**
>
> **20 drops of peppermint oil**

Mix all of the ingredients together, and pour the mixture into pocket-size spray bottles. Then, whenever you're in tick territory, spritz your clothes and exposed skin (but not your face!) thoroughly. The tiny terrors will keep their distance—guaranteed!

Yield: 24 ounces

Ease shingles pain. According to an old folk remedy, eating food that is laced with hot-pepper vinegar will moderate the intense pain of the lesions.

Reduce inflammation. Hot-pepper vinegar encourages your body to produce natural anti-inflammatory chemicals that can help prevent infectious diseases and generally keep your body functioning on all its "cylinders."

Note: *There are no precise dosages for hot-pepper vinegar. Simply adding it to your menu in any way you desire will give zip to your system.*

Scram, Skeeters!

As we've all learned, a mosquito bite can give you far more than an irritating itch. The diseases the little vampires spread can lay you flat on your back in a flash. So don't take any chances: Make yourself a suit of liquid "armor" by mixing 1 tablespoon of dried parsley per ¼ cup of apple cider vinegar in a large jar with a tight-fitting lid. Shake the jar thoroughly, and keep it where you can get at it easily (don't strain out the parsley). Then, before you venture outdoors, rub the lotion generously onto your exposed skin with a cotton pad. For extra protection, dip a bandanna or cotton scarf in the mixture, and tie it around your neck or hat.

chapter two

YOUR GOOD LOOKS

The earliest uses of vinegar as a beauty aid are lost in the annals of time. But we know that the same properties that make this tangy fluid one heck of a healer also give it an uncanny ability to improve your looks from the top of your head to the tips of your toes. In this chapter, you'll discover tons of traditional, not-so-traditional, and cutting-edge ways to make vinegar a key part of your beauty routine.

SKIN CARE

A Beautiful Balancing Act

You could pay an arm and a leg for a fancy facial toner that will moisturize, refresh, and purify your skin. Or you could mix 2 parts water with 1 part apple cider vinegar (ACV), and dab it onto your face with a cotton ball. Both potions will lock in moisture and reduce any inflammation. But vinegar also helps restore your skin's natural pH balance, so it's better able to shed dead skin cells and fend off blemish-causing bacteria. To add zip—and a lovely aroma—to your toner, replace the H_2O with an infusion made with your favorite herbs (see "10 Terrific Teammates" on page 50). **Note:** *If your skin is very sensitive, skip the herbs and use more water (start with 3 parts water to 1 part vinegar, and experiment until you find the right ratio). Or substitute rice vinegar, which is less acidic.*

FOR GOOD LIVING

For an ultra-simple and ultra-versatile beauty treatment, do what Grandma Putt did: Mash up some dried herbs of your choice (see "10 Terrific Teammates," below), and mix ½ cup of the herbs with 2 cups of ACV or wine vinegar (either red or white). Let the mixture sit in a cool, dark place for one to three weeks. Then use it as a skin cleanser, toner, and astringent.

Grandma Knew Best

Back in our grandmothers' day, rose water was a staple in every woman's beauty-care kit, and for good reason: It can purify and tone any type of skin, heal blemishes, hydrate dry skin, reduce redness and swelling, and much more. You can buy rose water, but it's a snap to make your own. Just put 1 cup of rose petals into a heatproof bowl, and pour in just enough boiling distilled water to cover them (about 2 cups). Cover the bowl, let the petals steep for 30 to 60 minutes, and strain the liquid into a bottle or jar. Store your rose water in the refrigerator, where it will keep for a week to 10 days. See page 52 for a skin-softening splash recipe that features rose water in a starring role. **Note:** *Rinse the petals well before you use them, and avoid any roses that have been sprayed with pesticides.*

10 Terrific Teammates

Plenty of herbs can team up with vinegar to perform fabulous feats for your health and good looks. But this double handful can produce exceptional results for your skin—whether you use them in facial formulas, or in one of the body lotions or bath blends coming up. Your best choice depends on what you want to accomplish. You can find the following champs at many farmers' markets and natural-food stores, and (in dried form) at herbal-supply stores, both online and brick-and-mortar versions.

Chamomile (flowers). Reduces inflammation, soothes, cleanses, and supplies antifungal agents.

Elder (flowers). Cleanses, tones, and acts as a gentle astringent.

Lavender (flowers). Soothes, cleanses, and reduces inflammation.

Linden (flowers). Supplies the same benefits as chamomile (above), but in a milder form that's especially good for aging skin.

Mallow. Soothes irritated skin.

Mint. Cools and refreshes.

Pot marigold, a.k.a. calendula (flowers). Cleanses, soothes, reduces inflammation; often used in a half-and-half mix with chamomile or lavender.

Rosemary. Tones, revitalizes, improves blood circulation to the capillaries.

Thyme. Fights bacteria; is especially effective on acne and eczema.

Yarrow. Tones, cleanses, heals; particularly good for aging or damaged skin.

> **TO STERILIZE GLASS JARS OR BOTTLES** for beauty formulas, fill the jar with boiling water, and let it sit for 10 minutes. Then empty the water, and let the container cool down to room temperature (or close to it) before pouring in the potion. Likewise, soak lids or caps for 10 minutes in boiling water.

Note: *To make an herbal infusion, put 2 heaping tablespoons of fresh or dried herbs in a heat-proof glass container, and pour 8 ounces of just-boiled spring water over them. Cover, and let the mixture steep for 10 to 15 minutes.*

Strain out the solids, and pour the liquid into a clean container. Use the infusion as soon as it's cooled to a skin-pleasing temperature, or store it in the fridge, where it will keep well for about five days.

EXCELLENT ELIXIR

Rosy Vinegar Splash

The key to maintaining healthy, young-looking skin is water and plenty of it. In addition to drinking a steady supply of H_2O throughout the day, using mildly astringent splashes like this one will help hydrate your skin, keeping it firm and supple.

1 cup of rose petals

4 cups of white-wine vinegar, heated to near boiling

1 cup of rose water

Put the flowers in a sterilized glass jar, pour in the vinegar, cover the jar, and set it in a dark place at room temperature for 10 days, shaking it occasionally. Then strain the liquid into a fresh jar, and add the rose water. To use the potion, pour 1 tablespoon of it into a bowl, add 1 cup of warm water, splash it onto your face, and pat dry.

Trouble-Prevention Toner

If you're stuck in a place that has little, if any, fresh air circulating—like an airplane cabin or an office building with sealed windows—the germ-infested atmosphere can take a major toll on your skin. But here's a DIY suit of liquid armor that will fight off blemish-causing fungi and bacteria and stimulate the production of vital collagen. The easy formula is made by pouring 2 cups of boiling water over a handful of chopped parsley, and letting it steep, covered, for 10 minutes or so. Then strain out the solids, and mix the liquid with ½ teaspoon of unfiltered apple cider vinegar and 20 drops of tea tree oil. Pour the mixture into a jar that has a tight-fitting lid or (if you're taking to the air) into small, FAA-approved bottles. When you're earthbound, the toner will stay fresh in the fridge for up to three weeks.

CAN'T-MISS COMBOS

Combining several kinds of herbs or flowers will ramp up the beautifying power of cosmetic vinegars in a major way. You can make your beauty potion as strong as you like, but a good proportion to start with is 1 cup of fresh petals or leaves per 2 cups of wine or apple cider vinegar. Steep for three weeks or so, and then strain and bottle it. (For the whole lowdown on making herbal and floral vinegars for culinary use, see Chapter 3.) In the meantime, here are some particularly effective combinations for hair rinses, facial toners, and bath blends:

Beauty Helpers	Ingredient Combinations
Hair rinses	Chamomile and linden flowers; fennel, horsetail, nettle, rosemary, sage, and yarrow leaves
	Lavender flowers and lemon verbena leaves
	Orange and lemon peels; mint and rosemary leaves
	Mint and rosemary leaves
	Rosemary, sage, and southernwood leaves
Facial toners	Calendula petals and witch hazel
	Lady's mantle leaves, lavender flowers, and rose petals
	Lavender flowers and mint leaves
	Lavender flowers; mint, rosemary, and thyme leaves
	Calendula petals, orange peel, and orange mint leaves
Bath blends	Bay, comfrey, lemongrass, and either peppermint or spearmint leaves
	Lavender flowers and rosemary leaves
	Orange peel, flowers, and leaves
	Chamomile flowers, orange peel, and rose petals; comfrey and peppermint leaves
	Chamomile flowers and rose petals
	Bay leaves, rose water, and whole crushed cloves
	Sage, savory, and thyme leaves; lavender flowers
	Almond oil, spearmint leaves, and witch hazel

Hot and Humid with a Chance of Oil

It's no secret that extra-oily complexions go into overdrive during the steamy summer months. That's the time to make this de-oiling toner part of your daily skin-care routine. It'll lift the dirt and debris from your pores, giving your skin a smoother appearance—and getting your day off to a refreshing start. Here's the routine:

- In a container that has a tight-fitting lid, mix 1 tablespoon each of fresh lemon and fresh lime juice, 1 teaspoon of apple cider vinegar, 1 teaspoon of pineapple juice, and ¼ cup of water.

- After cleansing, apply the formula to your face with a cotton ball, concentrating on the area extending across your forehead, down your nose, and down to your chin (a.k.a. the t-zone). This is the part of your face that is most susceptible to oil buildup.

Use the toner every day if your skin is extremely oily. For moderately oily skin, every other day should be fine. Keep the covered container in the refrigerator, and use the contents within five days. **Note:** *Use either fresh pineapple juice or juice*

That's Historical

By now, most of us know that people have been using vinegar for health and beauty purposes since before the dawn of recorded history. But that's not even half the story. Scientists tell us that vinegar actually played a key role in the creation of life on earth. How? By combining naturally with ammonia to form the simplest biologically significant building block of life as we know it. And here's another stunner of a factoid: Astronomers at the University of Illinois found vinegar floating in Sagittarius B2 North, a renowned cloud of dust and gas located 390 light-years from the center of the Milky Way.

from a can of chunk pineapple that's packed in natural juice, with no sugar added.

Tone, Don't Dry

Toners are invaluable for removing excess cold cream or cleansers from your face. But commercial versions are generally alcohol based and they can be extremely drying to your skin. Enter this gentle, all-natural alternative. To make it, mix 1 tablespoon of honey into ¼ cup of hot water, and stir in ¼ cup of apple cider vinegar. Add ½ cup of peppermint infusion to the container (see the note below), and mix thoroughly. Pour the blend into a bottle with a tight stopper. Store it at room temperature, and use it as you would any other toner, shaking occasionally between uses. **Note:** *To make peppermint infusion, cover 2 heaping tablespoons of peppermint leaves (fresh or dried) with 1 cup of freshly boiled water, and steep for 15 minutes. Strain the liquid, and use ½ cup of it for the toner.*

OLD-TIME Vim and Vinegar

Although this skin pleaser dates back to the 1600s, it's more popular today than ever before. And that's no wonder because it's cheap, easy to make, and works like a dream to smooth and firm any type of skin. The simple procedure: Mix 3 tablespoons of alcohol-free witch hazel and 1 teaspoon of apple cider vinegar in a bowl, then lightly beat in one egg white. Whip the mixture until it's foamy, and pop it into the refrigerator for five minutes or so. Apply the frothy stuff to your warm, moist skin using a cotton pad. Leave it on for at least 30 minutes (the longer the better). For best results, repeat the procedure at least once a week.

BEAUTY BONUS

For centuries, savvy women have used facial masks to solve cosmetic conundrums of all kinds—or simply to soften and beautify their skin. Here are five fine examples, all featuring the star power of vinegar.

Summertime Clarifying Mask

When Mother Nature turns up the heat, sweat, dirt, and melting makeup all add up to one thing: clogged pores. But this terrific trio will clear out the nasty crud, fend off blemish breakouts, and leave your skin soft and radiant. One major secret to this mask's success lies in pumpkin's whopping load of alpha hydroxy acids (AHAs), the cosmetic superstars that can cost you a bundle in commercial skin-care products.

Mix 4 tablespoons of canned pumpkin puree (not pumpkin pie filling!), 3 tablespoons of apple cider vinegar, and 1½ tablespoons of rose water in a bowl.

Spread the mixture onto your face, and leave it on for 15 minutes.

Rinse with warm water, and follow up with your usual cleansing and moisturizing routine.

5-Star Facial Mask

Talk about a versatile cast of characters! The oats and bran in this formula slough off dead skin cells, the cucumber and mint freshen your skin, the dairy products cleanse and soften it, and the vinegar tones it to perfection.

Gather up 1 cup of uncooked rolled oats, 1 tablespoon of wheat bran, 2 tablespoons of buttermilk, 2 tablespoons of whipping cream, 1½ table-spoons of ACV, 1 tablespoon of plain yogurt, 1 teaspoon of fresh mint leaves, and ½ medium cucumber, unpeeled and chopped.

Grind the oatmeal and bran to a powder in a blender or food processor.

Add the remaining ingredients and mix to a smooth consistency.

Spread the mixture onto your just-washed face, and leave it on for 10 to 15 minutes. Then rinse with warm water, and pat dry.

Honey, Vinegar, and Almond Mask

The trio of ingredients in this simple blend make it ideal for very dry complexions. The honey and oil soften and moisturize, while the vinegar tones and helps balance your skin.

Measure out 2 tablespoons of honey, ¼ teaspoon of vinegar (either white-wine or ACV), and ½ teaspoon of sweet almond oil.

Nuke the honey in a microwave-safe container until it's soft and pliable but not hot (20 to 30 seconds).

Stir in the vinegar and oil and immediately spread the blend onto your face. Leave it on for 15 minutes, then rinse with warm water.

Easy Does It Avocado Mask

This quick-fix formula features five of Mother Nature's most powerful skin beautifiers.

In a small bowl, mix ½ mashed avocado, ¼ cup of uncooked rolled oats, 2 tablespoons of honey, 1 tablespoon of apple cider vinegar, and 1 teaspoon of lemon juice.

Smooth the concoction onto your face, being careful not to get it in your eyes.

Wait 20 minutes or so, then rinse with warm water.

Amazing Anti-Aging Mask

Turn back the hands of time (or at least make them seem to slow down) with this earthy concoction.

Grind ¼ cup of dried lentils in a food processor or coffee grinder.

Mix the powder with ¼ cup of tomato puree, ½ teaspoon of white-wine vinegar, and about ½ inch of turmeric paste (available in tubes at Indian markets and many supermarkets).

Spread the mixture onto your freshly washed face, leave it on for about 15 minutes, and rinse with warm water.

Repeat the process two or three times a week for best results.

Shrink Your Pores

Well, in a manner of speaking. Unfortunately, nothing you can do will permanently shrink large pores. But you can make them a lot less noticeable by keeping your skin spankin' clean—and this DIY astringent does a dandy job on that score. It's a snap to make. Here's all you need to do:

- Put a chamomile tea bag in a heat-proof bowl or measuring cup, and pour 1 cup of boiling water over the bag. Cover the container, and let it sit until the tea reaches room temperature.

- Remove the tea bag, and mix 2 tablespoons of apple cider vinegar into the liquid, and pour it into a sterilized bottle. Store it in the refrigerator, where it will keep for a week.

Twice a day, smooth the astringent onto your freshly washed face with a cotton ball. The chamomile will soothe your skin, while the vinegar will kill bacteria and remove pore-clogging makeup and other debris.

Scrub Wrinkles Away

Or at least make it look like you have. In addition to removing surface debris from your skin (which any good cleanser will do), a good scrub removes dead cells, encourages the growth of new ones, and decreases the depth of wrinkles. The result: fresh, glowing, younger-looking skin. This all-natural scrub delivers the

Vinegar-Flaxseed Skin Lotion

This ultra-softening formula is an excellent everyday moisturizer for dry skin.

- **4 tbsp. of cracked flaxseed***
- **2 cups of warm water**
- **2 cups of apple cider vinegar**
- **6 tbsp. of glycerin**
- **3-4 drops of your favorite essential oil (optional)**

Put the flaxseed and water in a pan, and let it sit, covered, for 24 hours. Then bring the water to a boil, reduce the heat, and simmer for 15 minutes. Strain off the flaxseed, add the vinegar and glycerin, and bring the mixture just to the boiling point. Remove the pan from the heat, add the oil if desired, and beat thoroughly. Pour the potion into bottles with tight stoppers, store them at room temperature, and use the lotion as you would any other moisturizer. * *Pulse the whole seed in a food processor or coffee grinder for just a second or two to crack them slightly.*

"goods" better than just about any formula you could ever hope to find. To make it, simply mix ¼ cup of uncooked oatmeal (not instant), 2 ½ teaspoons of honey, 1 teaspoon of apple cider vinegar, and ½ teaspoon of warm water in a bowl. Smooth the mixture onto your face, and let it sit for 10 minutes. Then, using a soft washcloth dipped in warm water, gently scrub your skin using circular motions. Rinse with warm water, and follow up with your favorite moisturizer.

Note: *Don't use any scrub more than two or three times a week—exfoliating too often will leave your skin raw and irritated. And if you have sensitive skin or conditions like eczema or hives, consult with a dermatologist before applying any exfoliating product—either a DIY or commercial version.*

FOR GOOD LIVING

Post-Sun Softener

Even if you don't burn, a day (or even a few hours) in the sun can leave your skin dry and parched. Well, this powerful but oh-so-gentle spray will solve that problem in a hurry. To make it, follow this ultra-easy three-step process:

STEP 1. Gather the goods. You'll need a 4-ounce spray bottle plus the following ingredients: 3 tablespoons of rose water, 2 tablespoons of aloe vera gel (preferably organic), ½ tablespoon of apple cider vinegar, ¼ tablespoon of glycerin, 5 drops of peppermint essential oil, and a bottle of distilled water. (Feel free to double the recipe—in which case, of course, you'll need two 4-ounce bottles or a single 8-ounce version.)

STEP 2. Mix the first five ingredients in the bottle(s), and shake hard until the aloe is thoroughly blended in (this may take several minutes).

STEP 3. Fill the balance of the bottle(s) with distilled water, and store the potion in the refrigerator. This is essential because the all-natural formula contains no preservatives. Plus, the chilled fluid will feel cool and refreshing on your hot, scratchy skin.

CLEAN YOUR MAKEUP BRUSHES

To remove built-up powder, blusher, and other grime from your makeup brushes, mix equal parts of white vinegar and warm water in a basin, and add a couple drops of baby shampoo to soften the bristles. Swirl the brushes around in this mixture until all the yucky residue comes off, and then rinse them under warm, running water. Reshape the bristles with your fingers, and stand the brushes upright in a mug or jar to dry. They'll be as clean and fresh as the day you bought them!

Immediately following your time in the sun, spray the mixture on all exposed areas, and let it dry before covering your skin. **Note:** *You can substitute distilled water for the rose water, but try not to because rose water is more effective at soothing irritated skin.*

A Duo of Dandy Ways to Fade Dark Spots

Many middle-aged people, especially those with fair skin, develop large, flat brown marks (a.k.a. age or liver spots) on their faces and hands. They may be caused by the sun or by a nutritional deficiency, and in most cases, they're perfectly harmless. But who needs the unsightly things? Here are two ways to make 'em vamoose:

- Mix 1 tablespoon of fresh onion juice with 2 teaspoons of apple cider vinegar. Massage the mixture into the discolored areas twice a day until you no longer see spots before your eyes.

OLD-TIME
Vim and Vinegar

For centuries, herbalists have touted the relaxing, skin-toning effect of aromatic floral bath vinegars. This is one of the best: Mix 1 cup of distilled water, 1 cup of white vinegar, and ³/₄ cup of fresh lavender flowers in a glass jar with a tight-fitting lid. Shake the jar, and store it in a cool, dark place for 30 days, shaking it every week or so. When the time's up, give the jar a final shake, strain out the flowers, and then pour the floral vinegar into a decorative glass bottle. Use ¹/₂ cup or so in a tub of water (the temperature is your call). Store the blend, tightly closed, at room temperature; it will keep for two to six months.

EXCELLENT ELIXIR

Beautifying Body Cleanser

Ever since the days of Cleopatra, milk has played a key role in skin care. This vinegar-powered dairy delight will leave your skin feeling luxuriously soft and clean.

> ¼ cup of baking soda
>
> 2 tbsp. of skim milk
>
> ½ cucumber, scrubbed but not peeled
>
> ½ lemon, peeled and seeded
>
> ¼ russet potato, scrubbed but not peeled
>
> 2 tbsp. of chopped strawberries
>
> 2 tsp. of apple cider vinegar

Mix all of the ingredients together in a blender on medium-high speed for 45 to 60 seconds or until smooth. Moisten your skin with warm water, and massage the mixture all over your body—but not your face. Rinse with warm water, then with cool water. Cover any leftovers, and pop them into the refrigerator, where they'll keep for two days.

- Finely grate a 4-inch piece of fresh horseradish, and mix the pieces with ¼ cup of apple cider vinegar in a clean lidded jar. Let the mixture sit for two weeks, but shake the jar daily. Strain the liquid into a second jar, and store it in the refrigerator. Then three times a day, rub the potion into your problem areas with a cotton ball or swab.

Note: *In either case, it may be a few months before you start to see results, but be patient: It took years for the pigment to build up, so you can't expect it to vanish overnight.*

Rose Petal Vinegar Bath

A nice, long soak in this fragrant bath blend is delightful and skin pleasing anytime—but it's a special treat in the winter, when the dry air has left your skin feeling parched and itchy. Here's how to make it in four simple steps:

STEP 1. Gather up 2 cups of rose petals, from either your garden or a florist's bouquet (the fresher the better). Spread them on paper towels and let them dry overnight. Then put them in a wide-mouth mason jar.

STEP 2. Pour 1 quart of apple cider vinegar into a saucepan. Bring it to a boil over medium heat, and pour it over the rose petals.

STEP 3. Cap the jar tightly, and set it in a sunny window for two weeks.

STEP 4. Strain the rose-infused vinegar into a sterilized jar, and store it at room temperature.

To use your rosy treasure, pour 2 cups of it into a tub of water (the temperature is your call), and soak for 10 to 20 minutes.

2 Itch-Eradicating Tub Soaks

Is your skin so dry that you feel parched and itchy all over? If so—whether the cause is an arid climate or moisture-robbing furnace heat in a northern winter—then either of these tub-time additives should put an end to your discomfort. Whichever blend

FOR GOOD LIVING

you choose, mix it into your bathwater, and settle in for 20 minutes or so. Then follow up with your favorite moisturizer.

- 1 cup each of apple cider vinegar and barley flour
- ½ cup each of apple cider vinegar, wheat germ, and either olive or sesame oil

Rice and Soft

When your heels are dry and cracked, reach for some rice vinegar. Mix 1 tablespoon of it with 1 tablespoon each of honey and coarse sea salt to make a watery paste, and scrub the dead skin away. Then slather on a rich hand or foot cream, put on a pair of cotton socks to help the cream sink in, and leave them on overnight. The next morning, your heels will be noticeably softer. Repeat the procedure every night until all the thickened, dead skin is gone with the wind.

QUICK & QUIRKY

Let Your Polish Linger Longer—You carefully paint your nails and patiently wait for them to dry. Then, before you know it, the polish starts chipping off. Well, don't just grin and bear it. Instead, adopt this simple prep routine: Soak your nails in vinegar (any kind will do) for about 60 seconds. Once they've dried thoroughly, paint the surfaces as usual. The vinegar will remove the natural oils from the surface of your nails, so your polish will hang on tight!

Soak Your Way to Softness

If you prefer a less hands-on approach to foot treatments, mix equal parts of rice vinegar and water in a basin, and soak your feet for 20 to 30 minutes. Repeat the routine nightly until your skin is smooth and silky again. **Note:** *This vinegar and water remedy will also help prevent or eliminate nail fungus.*

Whiten Your Nails

You can make your fingernails whiter and stronger simply by soaking them in lemon juice for 10 minutes, once a week. Then follow up by brushing them with a half-and-half solution of white vinegar and warm water, and rinsing with clear H_2O. After a couple of treatments, you should start to see a remarkable difference.

PEP UP YOUR "PAWS"

It's annoying, all right: You've been working (or playing) hard all day, and now your hands or feet—or both—are tired and swollen. But you're headed out for the evening, and there's no time to soak your afflicted appendages. No problem! Just massage a splash of apple cider vinegar into your skin for an instant pick-me-up.

Penny-Pinching Pedicure

Why dump double-digit dollars on a beauty salon pedicure when you can treat yourself to a refreshing, pre-exfoliating foot soak for a fraction of the price? Here's the routine: Fill a pan or foot basin with 10 cups of hot water, and mix in 1 cup of apple cider vinegar, ½ cup of sea salt, and the juice of two freshly squeezed lemons. Soak your tired tootsies for about 15 minutes, pat dry, and use a pumice stone to slough off any dead or flaky skin. Then hop into the shower to rinse off.

Softer Does It

Pliable cuticles make for beautiful—and healthy—nails. And you couldn't ask for a more effective softening treatment than this one. To make it, put ¼ cup of pineapple flesh, 2 teaspoons of honey, 2 teaspoons of olive oil, ¼ teaspoon of apple cider vinegar, and 1 egg yolk in a blender. Mix on medium speed for

15 seconds. Then quickly rub the mixture onto your hands, concentrating on your cuticles and the skin around your nails. Put on plastic gloves and leave them on for 10 to 15 minutes. Remove the gloves, and rinse your hands with warm water. You'll be amazed at the difference in your skin! Apply the treatment at least once a week—or as often as every day, depending on the dryness of the weather and your skin. Cover and refrigerate any leftover mixture, and use it within three days, shaking thoroughly before each application to re-blend the oil. **Note:** *When applying, it's crucial to act fast because the olive oil has a tendency to separate from the other ingredients.*

Give Body Odor the Boot

Few things are more embarrassing than body

odor, a.k.a. BO. Here's what to do about it: Shortly before bedtime, saturate a cloth with either malt or white vinegar, and wipe your whole body down with it. Then let your skin air-dry before you hit the sack. The acid will change your skin's pH, thereby deactivating the odor-causing bacteria. Come morning, hop in the shower, and you should come out smelling like a rose—more or less. **Note:** *If the aroma persists, see your doctor. The problem may be a sign of ill health or a poor diet.*

This Aftershave Gets an A+

Commercial aftershave lotions are designed to do four things: act as an antiseptic to clean any nicks or cuts, moisturize your skin, close your pores, and soothe razor burn. Well, guess what? The acetic acid in apple cider vinegar can perform those same feats at a fraction of the cost—on gents' faces or ladies' legs. All you need to do is fill a clean bottle or jar with equal parts ACV and water, and shake well to blend them. Then splash it onto your skin as you would any other aftershave.

> **VINEGAR IS TOPS FOR WIPING OUT FOUL AROMAS OF ALL KINDS,** but it comes with a strong scent of its own. So are you simply swapping one bad smell for another? Nope! ACV's aroma vanishes as the vinegar dries.

Fire Your Antiperspirant

Most commercial deodorants are actually antiperspirants, which (as the name says loud and clear) prevent you from sweating. So what's wrong with that, you may ask? Just this: Perspiration is one of your body's most effective means of eliminating toxins.

When you close off that exit ramp, you may be asking for health problems down the road. Fortunately, there's an easy way to minimize unpleasant odor and keep the detox channels open: Instead of using regular deodorant, simply rub a little vinegar (either white or ACV) on your underarm skin. **Note:** *In a pinch, this same simple trick will keep sweaty hands and feet odor-free.*

Toss the Dirt

When working in the garden or puttering in your workshop leaves your hands as grubby as all get-out, it's time for drastic (but gentle) action. March into your kitchen, and pour a teaspoon or two of cornmeal into your palm, add a few drops of apple cider vinegar, and scrub-a-dub-dub, then rinse with cool water. Your hands will be clean and soft.

TOSS THE AROMA, TOO!

This tip is just what the doctor ordered for the gardeners in our audience. You know that there is nothing better for your plants than frequent servings of compost tea or manure tea. And you also know that when you get the stuff on your hands, it smells to high heaven. So the R$_X$ is simple: Get rid of the odor by washing your hands with dishwashing liquid, then rinsing them with vinegar. And from now on, wear plastic or rubber gloves to deep your paws clean at garden "tea" time!

Fight Cellulite!

Trying to get rid of unsightly "cottage cheese" patches on your skin? Then call on apple cider vinegar, which can help you say "see you later" to cellulite in two ways:

From the inside. Once a day, drink an 8-ounce glass of water with 2 tablespoons of apple cider vinegar and 1 tablespoon of honey mixed into it. The dynamic duo will help your body burn fat more efficiently, thereby streamlining the lumpy areas.

From the outside. Mix 3 parts apple cider vinegar with 1 part olive oil or your favorite massage oil, and gently knead the solution into the problem spots for 10 minutes twice a day. This will increase circulation and help reduce the fatty deposits—fast.

HAIR CARE

Customize Your Hair Conditioner

For centuries, women have been using vinegar to shine and condition their hair. But with a few herbal additives, you can tailor the treatment to do more than that. Add 1 cup of dried herbs to 1 quart of high-quality vinegar. Let it steep for a few weeks, strain out the solids, and pour the liquid into a clean bottle. As for the type of herbs, that depends on the effect you're looking for. Here's the rundown:

Calendula is a good all-purpose conditioner.

Chamomile puts highlights in blonde or light brown hair.

Lavender and lemon verbena add enticing fragrance.

Nettles control dandruff.

Parsley and rosemary make dark hair come alive.

Sage darkens graying hair.

Whichever combo suits your fancy, use the potion as a final rinse after shampooing, at a ratio of roughly 1 tablespoon of the "spiked" vinegar per gallon of water.

Word to the Wise

You can either rinse the herb-vinegar combo out or leave it in to prevent tangles. But beware that vinegar rinses can dry out your hair if you use them every day, so limit them to once or twice a week.

Triple-Threat Rosemary Conditioner

Here's a formula that will de-tangle, nourish, and shine up your hair to beat the band. And it couldn't be simpler to make. Just stand six to eight fresh rosemary sprigs upright in a heat-proof glass jar that's tall enough to hold them with an inch or so to spare on top. Pour in boiling water until it covers the sprigs, and let them sit overnight. Come morning, pull out the herbs, and pour the liquid into a plastic squeeze bottle. Add about 2 teaspoons of apple cider vinegar, and give the bottle a good shake. After shampooing, squirt the potion onto your head, and comb it through your hair. Then rinse with clear water, and dry and style your hair as usual. **Note:** *If your bathroom is on the warm side, refrigerate the conditioner between uses.*

QUICK & QUIRKY

Don't Go Green!
Attention, blondes and light-toned brunettes: If swimming in a chlorinated pool is giving your hair a greenish tinge, don't give up your lap time. Instead, after shampooing, rinse your hair with a solution of ¼ cup of vinegar per 2 cups of water. How often you need to repeat this procedure depends on how often you take a dip!

Fight the Frizzies

Is frizzy, flyaway hair driving you nuts? If so, then serve your tresses this beer and vinegar cocktail. It'll leave your hair clean, shiny, and more manageable than you probably thought possible. To make the potion, mix 1 cup of beer (the full-strength kind—not the "lite" stuff), ¼ cup of vinegar, and 20 drops each of lemon, rosemary, and sage essential oils in a bottle or measuring cup. After shampooing as usual, pour the rinse over your wet hair. Massage it into your scalp, and let it sit for three to four minutes.

Then rinse with clear water, and style your newly tamed mane! **Note:** *Strictly speaking, the essential oils are optional. You could accomplish the same results using just vinegar and beer, but the aroma won't be pleasant.*

Conquer the Oil Crisis

If you have oily hair, beware of commercial products that are targeted for your type of tresses. Many of them contain harsh ingredients that strip out too much oil—thereby encouraging your glands to produce even more of the stuff. On the other hand, this well-balanced blend will leave your hair shiny and manageable— without a greasy backlash. Here's the drill:

Thoroughly mix half a mashed avocado, 2 tablespoons of apple cider vinegar, 2 tablespoons of freshly squeezed lemon juice, and 1 tablespoon of full-fat mayonnaise in a bowl.

EXCELLENT ELIXIR

All-Natural Shampoo

Scads of commercial shampoos proudly sport the word *natural* in big letters on the label, but when you read the fine print on the back, you usually see a bunch of ingredients that you can't even pronounce—much less buy at the grocery store. This shampoo, on the other hand, comes straight from Mother Nature herself.

- **2 tbsp. of extra virgin olive oil**
- **1 tbsp. of lemon juice**
- **1 tsp. of vinegar**
- **1 egg**

Mix the ingredients together thoroughly in a blender. Pour the mixture into a plastic bottle, take it to the sink, tub, or shower, and use it as you would any other shampoo. The result will be hair that's clean, fresh, and natural!

FOR GOOD LIVING

Apply the combo to your hair shafts, avoiding your scalp. Wait 20 minutes, then massage the mixture onto your scalp and leave it on for five more minutes.

Rinse thoroughly with very warm water for at least two minutes.

Shampoo twice with a high-quality, deep-cleansing shampoo.

Refrigerate any leftovers in a lidded glass jar and use them within seven days.

Heroic Herbal Conditioning Rinse

No matter what type of hair you have, here's an all-around formula that'll restore its natural vitality and shine—and help it grow thicker:

- Gather up 1½ cups of water, 1 cup of fresh or dried rosemary leaves, ½ cup of apple cider vinegar, and 10 drops each of rosemary and peppermint essential oils.

- Bring the water to a boil and add the rosemary. Reduce the heat to low and steep, covered, for 45 minutes.

- Strain, let the tea cool to room temperature, and stir in the

That's Historical

We've all heard about some wild wagers, but for my money, this stunt of Cleopatra's tops 'em all: She bet Mark Antony that she could consume a meal worth one million sesterces (the equivalent of many years' wages for the average Egyptian worker). She did it, too. How? Before dinner one night, she dropped a gigantic pearl—valued at one million sesterces—into a glass of vinegar. By the end of the meal, the pearl had dissolved, and Cleo quaffed the solution for dessert. History does not record what she won, but it must have been a dilly of a payoff!

vinegar and oils. Pour the solution into spray bottles (the size is your call).

- After shampooing and rinsing, spray the potion onto your hair and massage it into your scalp, being careful to avoid your eyes. Towel dry and style your hair as usual.

Store the rinse at room temperature (in the shower if you'd like). **Note:** *Do not use this formula on color-treated or processed hair.*

> **VINEGAR OWES ITS HAIR-CARE POWER** to two biological feats: It improves circulation in your capillaries, which increases the flow of health-giving blood, nutrients, and oxygen to your scalp. Also, rinsing with vinegar closes your hair's cuticles, which open up during shampooing. And you want closed cuticles because when they're closed, more light reflects off the hair shafts.

De-Gunk Your Hair

Over time, hair sprays, gels, and other styling products can build up in your hair, making it downright dull, drab, and tangle-prone. Fortunately, there's a fast, simple way to rout out that residue. Mix equal parts of vinegar and water in a spray bottle. After shampooing, spritz the mixture onto your hair, and massage it into your scalp. Let it sit for about three minutes or so, and rinse with clear water. You'll soon have soft, shiny, silky-smooth hair that's easy to manage. **Note:** *How often you need to use this treatment depends (of course) on how often you use styling products and in what quantities. Your mirror will tell you when it's time for another round.*

FOR GOOD LIVING

A Scentsational De-Gunking Treatment

Here's another way to get rid of product buildup—and it smells great to boot. To whip it up, pour ¼ cup of vodka, 2 tablespoons of apple cider vinegar, 2 tablespoons of apple juice, and 1 teaspoon each of lemon and orange extracts in a blender. Mix on high for 20 seconds, or just enough to disperse the extracts (be aware that the potion will not be completely homogenized). Pour the mixture into a spray bottle, shake vigorously, and spray your hair thoroughly *before* shampooing and conditioning. The elixir will penetrate deep into your hair, clarifying the shafts and letting their natural highlights shine through.

Refrigerate the final product immediately and use it (and any leftovers) within five days.

Word to the Wise

Depending on the quantity you use, apple cider vinegar may darken blonde hair, and there's a slim chance that distilled or white-wine vinegar could lighten dark hair. So play it safe—experiment on an out-of-the-way strand before you try any vinegar-based shampoo or conditioner.

A 5-Step High-Intensity Cleaning

Whether the crud that's making your hair dull and lifeless is styling-product residue or plain old dirt from city streets or a long, shampoo-less camping trip, this five-step process gets the stuff out pronto:

STEP 1. Pour 4 tablespoons of aloe vera gel, 2 tablespoons of rice vinegar, and 5 ounces of water into a spray bottle. Put the cap on tightly, and shake vigorously until the ingredients are thoroughly blended.

STEP 2. Separate your hair into six to eight sections, and working with one section at a time, spray the mixture generously onto your scalp and along the length of the hair shafts.

STEP 3. Work the formula into your hair using your fingertips. Then squeeze out the cleanser—and the dirt with it.

STEP 4. Repeat the process, only this time, leave the cleanser on your hair for five minutes, and then rinse with warm water. Repeat this step if necessary.

STEP 5. Follow up with your usual shampoo and conditioner.

Get Out of the Snow

Ever feel as though you live inside one of those little snow globes, with white flakes falling on your shoulders all the time? Well, there

---

PREVENT HAIR LOSS

Or at least slow it down. Even on the most well-"clothed" heads, hair falls out and regrows constantly. But if you seem to be shedding more and growing less as the years go by, try this remedy: Combine equal parts of olive oil and rosemary essential oil in a bottle, and shake to mix thoroughly. At bedtime, massage the mixture into your scalp, and cover it with a shower cap. In the morning, wash your hair with a gentle shampoo, and rinse with 1 tablespoon of vinegar in 1 quart of warm water. Repeat the procedure each night for a few weeks. By that time, your hair income should exceed the outgo. **Note:** *Some folks claim this routine will even work to stop* *male-pattern baldness but I wouldn't lay any bets on that if I were you.*

Herbal Dandruff Treatment

In this fragrant formula, two common herbs give added oomph to the dandruff-fighting power of ACV. Rosemary calms scalp irritation, and thyme clobbers any loitering bacteria.

2 tsp. of dried rosemary

2 tsp. of dried thyme

2/3 cup of boiling water

2/3 cup of vinegar

Put the herbs in a teapot or a heat-proof glass or ceramic bowl. Pour in the water. Cover the container and steep for 15 to 20 minutes. Strain the solution into a clean 10-ounce bottle with a tight-fitting lid. Add the vinegar and shake thoroughly. Between uses, store the potion in a cool, dark place (a kitchen cabinet far away from the stove is fine).

To use the flake stopper, shampoo your hair as usual and rinse thoroughly. Then massage a dime-to nickel-size amount of the treatment into your scalp. For added healing power, massage an equal amount into your scalp just before you go to bed.

are a lot of expensive dandruff treatments that can help stop the flurries, but for my money, this simple formula works as well as any of 'em: Just mash five aspirin tablets and put them in a plastic bottle with 1/3 cup of vinegar and 1/3 cup of witch hazel. Cap the bottle and shake it thoroughly to mix the ingredients. After you shampoo as usual, comb the solution through your hair. Wait 10 minutes, rinse it out with warm water, and say farewell to the flakes.

Scrub Dandruff Away

Millions of folks suffer from dandruff. According to the Mayo Clinic, the most common cause is simply dry skin. As you might expect, the problem tends to occur more often in dry climates or in the winter months, when outdoor weather is cold and dry and heated indoor air is even drier. But, as odd as it may sound, using hair-care products with a high oil content can make the problem even worse. Second on the list of culprits is a buildup of styling products in your hair. Whichever gremlin is making the flakes fly from your head, this gentle, but powerful, scrub will help strike the right balance:

- Put ½ cup of olive oil, 2 tablespoons of cornmeal, and 1 tablespoon of apple cider vinegar in a small bowl, and stir to make a thick paste.

- Wet your hair with warm water, scoop up a handful of the mixture, and warm it up by rubbing your hands together. Massage the scrub into your scalp.

- Put on a shower cap, or cover your hair with plastic, and go about your business for 30 minutes or so.

- Remove the topper, and shampoo as usual.

Note: *This formula does not keep well, so discard any leftovers.*

OLD-TIME
Vim
and *Vinegar*

The same half-and-half mixture of vinegar and water that removes residue from hair-care products (see "De-Gunk Your Hair" on page 73) can also help you bid good-bye to your white-flake woes. The vinegar will destroy the fungus that caused the dandruff in the first place and restore the proper pH balance of your scalp to make it itch-free. Just spray the potion onto your head, work it into your scalp, and leave it on for one to two hours before rinsing with clear water. After that, to keep your dandruff from coming back, use this conditioner at least once a week, keeping it on for three minutes before rinsing.

Do the Daily Dandruff Two-Step

This intensive formula will help chase the flakes away and keep them there. Depending on the severity of your affliction, you may not need to use it every day—but the potion is gentle enough that daily treatment won't cause problems.

To make the shampoo, put 1 tablespoon of apple cider vinegar, 1 tablespoon of lemon extract, 3 egg yolks, and ½ cup of warm water in a blender. Mix on low for 20 seconds.

Make the rinse by whisking 1 tablespoon of apple cider vinegar in 1 cup of warm water.

Massage the shampoo into your scalp, and leave it on for 10 minutes. Then pour the rinse over your hair. Wash your head with clear, warm water, and follow up with your favorite conditioner.

QUICK & QUIRKY

Get Your Hair Glowing—Want to make your hair so shiny that it gleams (maybe for an extra-special occasion)? Just mix 2 tablespoons of malt vinegar in a quart of water, and use it as a final rinse. Your luxuriant locks will sparkle like the stars!

Baby Your Brushes

Getting built-up residue out of your hair is one thing (see "De-Gunk Your Hair" on page 73). To make sure your tresses stay crud-free, you also have to keep your brushes clean and fresh. Here's how:

- Remove as much hair as possible from the brush, using a comb or your fingers.

- Soak the brush for 15 minutes in a basin of warm water with ¼ cup of white vinegar and 2 teaspoons of shampoo mixed into it.

- Pull off any remaining hair, and use a toothbrush or nail brush to scrub stubborn residue from the bristles.

- Rinse the brush under warm running water. Then, to keep the bristles from breaking as they dry, lay flat brushes on their backs, and stand round ones, heads up, on their handles in a glass or similar container.

To keep your brushes sanitary—and extend their lives—perform this routine two or three times a week. Or if you don't use commercial styling products at all, clean your natural-bristle brushes once a month and synthetic brushes three or four times a month to get rid of airborne dirt that your hair picks up.

RAMP UP THE COLOR

Calling all brunettes! Want to rev up your locks' rich radiance without dropping big bucks at the beauty shop? If so, then give this terrific trick a whirl: Mix ½ cup of cocoa powder, ½ cup of plain yogurt, 1 teaspoon of apple cider vinegar, and 1 teaspoon of honey to form a smooth paste. Apply the mixture to your freshly shampooed  hair, and leave it on for two to three minutes. Then rinse and style as usual.

Brighten Dull Hair

When your locks have lost their luster, bring them back to life with this routine:

- Mix 2 tablespoons of sunflower oil with 2 egg yolks, and massage the mixture into your hair. Cover it with a shower cap, and leave it on overnight with an old towel over your pillowcase.

- Come morning, wash the mix out with your usual shampoo, and rinse with a solution of 2 tablespoons of vinegar in 1 quart of warm water.

4 Steps to Thicker, Softer Hair

The secret to this remarkable rinse lies in its all-star ingredient team: Vinegar strips out residue from styling products, lavender regenerates hair follicles, rosemary strengthens your hair shafts and helps them grow, and borax packs amazing softening power. Here's the DIY routine that'll give your hair a new lease on life:

STEP 1. Gather the goods. You'll need ½ cup of dried lavender flowers, ½ cup of dried rosemary, 3 tablespoons of vinegar, 1 teaspoon of borax, 4 cups of water, a large pot, and a 1-quart glass jar with a tight-fitting lid.

STEP 2. Bring the water to a rolling boil, remove the pot from the stove, and stir in the vinegar and borax.

STEP 3. Add the lavender and rosemary, and mix until they're thoroughly wet. Cover the pot, and let it sit for at least two to four hours (longer if possible; the longer the potion steeps, the stronger it will be).

STEP 4. When the mixture has reached a caramel-brown color, strain out the herbs, pour the liquid into the jar, and tuck it into the fridge, where it will keep for up to two weeks.

To use your hair-improvement potion, shampoo as usual, then pour the rinse over your hair so that it's completely saturated. Rinse with clear water, and follow up with your normal drying and styling procedure.

Word to the Wise

When using the vinegar-herb rinse (at right), it's okay to skip the clear-water rinse if you want to. But be aware that the herbal rinse is brownish in color, so it may stain a light-colored towel if you *don't* rinse it out.

Make Your Hair the Apple of Your Eye

When your hair starts to lose its shine, strip away the haze and bring back the glow with this ultra-simple rinse. Here's the easy-as-pie formula:

- Peel and chop 1 large apple (any kind you have in your fruit bowl will do).

- Put it in a blender with 2 tablespoons of apple cider vinegar and 2 cups of water, and mix on high speed. Strain the mixture into a bowl, discarding the solids.

- After shampooing, pour the liquid over your hair, and massage it into the strands, paying special attention to the ends. Let it sit for a couple of minutes, then rinse thoroughly with cool water.

Your hair will shine like the sun! **Note:** *Use only 1 tablespoon of vinegar if your scalp is very dry or sensitive.*

EXCELLENT ELIXIR

Nettle Growth Formula

This easy-to-make rinse helps maintain a healthy scalp and encourage hair growth.

1 tbsp. of fresh nettles, chopped*

1 cup of vinegar

2 cups of warm water

Simmer the nettles in the vinegar for 15 minutes. Strain the vinegar into a jar that has a tight-fitting lid, and store it in a cool, dark place. At shampoo time, mix ¼ of the infused vinegar in the warm water, and use it as a final rinse. Store the leftover formula in a cool, dark place. * *Be sure to wear gloves when preparing this potion—nettle hairs sting like the dickens!*

PLEASE PASS THE MAYONNAISE

Good old-fashioned mayonnaise is a valuable part of any DIY beauty arsenal. The commercial kind works fine, but with just a tiny bit of effort, you can whip up a homemade version that's even better. Simply gather up 1 egg, 1 teaspoon of salt, 1 ¼ cups of extra virgin olive oil, and ½ cup of apple cider vinegar. Then proceed as follows:

▶ In a blender or food processor, mix the egg, salt, and ¼ cup of the oil.

▶ With the machine still running, slowly pour in another ¼ cup of oil in a very thin stream, followed by ¼ cup of the vinegar.

▶ Follow up with another ¼ cup of the oil and the rest of the vinegar.

▶ Continue blending as you slowly add the remaining oil until you have thick, white, creamy mayonnaise.

Note: *The key to success is to add the ingredients slowly and steadily. You may need to practice a few times before you perfect your technique, but once you do, the store-bought stuff will never seem the same again!*

Pour the creation into a clean container with a tight-fitting lid, store it in the refrigerator, and use it in any beauty treatment that calls for mayonnaise, like these winners, for example:

Mayo for Your Mane

Mayonnaise (either store-bought or homemade) is one of the best friends a head of hair ever had. Here's a trio of ways it can make your tresses look like a million bucks:

Plain and simple. Just shampoo your hair as you normally do, towel it dry, and massage a tablespoon or so of mayo into your hair. Let it sit for 15 minutes or so, shampoo again, and rinse thoroughly before styling. Then get ready to dazzle your friends and family!

Stronger measures. For very dry or damaged hair, use mayonnaise as you would a hot-oil treatment. Just heat the mayo until it's warm (don't boil it!), and rub it into your hair. Wrap your head in a warm towel, wait 15 to 30 minutes, and shampoo with warm (not hot) water.

Intensive care. Here's an extra-strength treatment that's tailor-made for dry or damaged hair: Puree a banana in a blender until it's smooth and free of lumps. Add about 1 tablespoon each of mayonnaise and olive oil to it, and blend until creamy. Massage the mixture into your hair, wait 15 to 30 minutes, rinse with warm water, and shampoo as usual.

Put Your Best Face Forward

The marvels of mayo don't stop at the top of your head. Its creamy goodness can also work wonders for your complexion. Try one of these, for example:

Remove eye makeup. Just smooth the mayo onto your eyelids with your fingertip, and gently wipe it away with a cotton ball that's been moistened with cool water.

Clean and soften your skin. To make cold cream that's as good as any you can buy, mix ½ cup of mayonnaise, 1 tablespoon of melted butter, and the juice of 1 lemon or lime. Store the cream in the refrigerator in a tightly closed glass jar. Use it as you would any facial cleanser, and rinse with cold water.

Provide deep-down moisture. Mix 2 tablespoons of mayonnaise and 1 teaspoon of baby oil in a container. Smooth the mixture onto your face, neck, and any other part(s) of your body that could use some softening. Leave it on for 20 minutes or so, and then rinse thoroughly with lukewarm water. Presto, change-o— sleek, soft, supple skin!

Hippocrates, the Father of Medicine, routinely advised his patients to "Let food be thy medicine and medicine be thy food." Of course, he wasn't referring only to vinegar, although it does add health-giving oomph—as well as scrumptious flavor—to any dish you use it in. But that's not all! As you'll soon see, vinegar can also perform plenty of practical chores around the kitchen, from making your bread rise higher and faster to keeping food fresh longer.

COOKING WITH VINEGAR

Coming to Terms with Vinegar

Technically speaking, vinegar can be made from any substance that's sweet enough to ferment, whereupon the sugar content changes to alcohol (see "Where in the World . . . ?" on page 112). Then a second fermentation turns the alcohol to acetic acid (a.k.a. vinegar). Here's a brief rundown of the most popular types sold in the United States:

Apple cider vinegar is mild with just a slight flavor of (surprise!) apple. As we saw in chapters 1 and 2, it's the vinegar of choice for most health and beauty purposes. But it's also highly versatile in the kitchen and makes a fine recipe stand-in for just about any other kind of vinegar. You can make your own ACV by following the simple instructions in "Create Health-Giving Treasure" (see page 20). For a fast and flavorful variation on the theme, see "Festive Fruit-Scrap Vinegar" on page 113.

Distilled white vinegar (a.k.a. white vinegar) is made from grain alcohol. It's the vinegar of choice for pickles and relishes and, in small amounts, for many of the food-related tricks and tips in this chapter. However, beware of using white vinegar in large quantities because its sour, harsh taste can overpower more delicate flavors.

Wine vinegars come in red, white, sherry, and champagne varieties. They're the most versatile vinegars of all for culinary purposes. Unlike most other types, though, the homemade versions are far superior to even the most expensive store-bought brands. Fortunately, the process is simple—and fun (see "DIY Wine Vinegar" on page 109 for the ultra-easy directions).

Balsamic vinegar, generally considered the queen of all vinegars, is made from the unfermented juice of Trebbiano and Lambrusco grapes, which are unique to the Modena and Reggio areas of Italy. In the

Word to the Wise

To add a big dose of antioxidants to your diet, use red-wine vinegar in marinades and salad dressings—or simply splash it on fruits or vegetables. It packs just as many of these powerful disease fighters as red wine and grape juice do. Just be aware that if you use red-wine vinegar in any recipe that contains pale, light-colored ingredients, it may discolor the finished product.

traditional production method, the juice is boiled down to a sweet, fruity syrup and then aged in wooden barrels for anywhere from 12 to (yes, you're reading this right) 75 years or longer. Fortunately, modern producers have found ways to speed up the process, which makes this elegant treat available in American food stores at affordable prices.

Malt vinegar, which is made from barley and other grains, is mild and sweet. While it's best known as a condiment for fish-and-chips, it also makes delicious marinades and salad dressings. You can substitute it for other types of vinegar in almost any dish, too—but because it's so mild, you may want to add a little more than the recipe calls for. Like wine vinegar, the "home-cooked" variety is generally much more flavorful than commercial types (see "Make Your Own Malt Vinegar" on page 111).

{ **SOME COMMERCIAL CULINARY VINEGARS**— particularly red-wine and inexpensive balsamic varieties—contain sulfites. So if you're sensitive to those chemicals, read the labels carefully to make sure the brands you choose are all clear. }

Rice vinegar is made from rice wine. The Japanese varieties have a delicate, subtle flavor, while the Chinese versions tend to be sweet and sour and often contain sugar. Rice vinegar is (of course) an essential ingredient in Asian cuisine, but it can also add zip to standard American fare. (For one example, see the Cucumber Salad with Rice Vinegar Dressing at right.)

Infused vinegars are made by immersing herbs, fruits, veggies— or combinations thereof—in various types of vinegar and letting them steep for anywhere from a week to several months (depending on the ingredients and your taste). Gourmet-food stores and some supermarkets sell many types of infused vinegars, but it's a snap to make your own—for a lot less money.

Liven Up Limp Vegetables

Are the veggies in your produce drawer looking a little droopy? No worries! Depending on the type of vegetables, use one of these two methods to restore the crispness:

Salad greens. Add 1 teaspoon of white or apple cider vinegar to a pan of water, and let the greens soak in it for 15 minutes.

Other vegetables. Dunk them briefly in hot tap water, then immediately drop them into a bowl of ice water that's got a tablespoon of either white or apple cider vinegar mixed into it. Within a few minutes, they should perk right up!

REMARKABLE RECIPE

Cucumber Salad with Rice Vinegar Dressing

If you only think of rice vinegar as an ingredient in Asian cooking, you're in for a treat: It also makes a tasty addition to standard American fare like this super salad.

- **3 cups of peeled, thinly sliced seedless cucumbers**
- **3 tbsp. of rice vinegar***
- **2 tsp. of dark sesame oil**
- **1 tsp. of sugar**
- **½ tsp. of salt**
- **2 tbsp. of chopped dry-roasted, unsalted peanuts**
- **2 tbsp. of chopped green onions**

Combine the first five ingredients in a bowl and toss until the cucumber is thoroughly coated. Transfer it to salad plates, and sprinkle with the peanuts and green onions before serving. * *Japanese rice vinegar has a light, delicate taste. For a more robust flavor, go with a Chinese variety.*

Yield: 6 servings
For more super salad recipes, see *page 122 in Chapter 4.*

FOR GOOD LIVING

Prep Produce Early

It's an unpleasant fact of kitchen life that when you peel and slice certain fruits and vegetables, they start to turn brown almost immediately. Potatoes, apples, and pears are especially prone to changing color quickly. The simple solution: Put the pieces in a bowl, cover them with cold water, and add 1 to 2 tablespoons of vinegar (either white or ACV will do). There's just one minor catch: Although the produce will stay fresh in your refrigerator for several days, it will start to lose water-soluble vitamins after a couple of hours—so the sooner you use it, the more healthy benefits you'll enjoy!

Love 'Em Tender

Vegetables that are high in cellulose can be fibrous and stringy. That unpleasant texture doesn't alter the flavor or the nutritional content—but who needs it? Not you! So use vinegar to soften up those tough customers in a flash. You can accomplish this in one of two ways:

- When you're cooking beets, cabbage, celery, okra, spinach, or string beans, add 2 teaspoons of vinegar to the cooking water.

- Sprinkle a few drops of vinegar on raw vegetables such as broccoli, carrots, cucumbers, kale, and lettuce.

OLD-TIME *Vim and Vinegar*

Whenever you steam vegetables, take a tip from Grandma Putt: Add 2 tablespoons of vinegar to the water. The veggies will retain more of their natural color and—more importantly—a bigger supply of their health-giving vitamins. As a bonus, the vinegar will also eliminate any unpleasant odors.

Get Redder Reds and Whiter Whites

Beets, red cabbage, and red-skinned (and red-fleshed) potatoes all tend to lose much of their rosy color when they're cooked. The simple solution: Just add a spoonful of white vinegar to the cooking water. Those leaves and roots will hang on to every bit of their vibrant tones!

This same jolt of vinegar will also keep cauliflower as white as new-fallen snow. To brighten mashed potatoes, use this slightly different technique:

- Add milk to the boiled taters, as usual, and mix them to the consistency of your choice.

- Add 1 teaspoon of vinegar for each pound of spuds and beat them for one more minute.

Don't Cry over Grated Horseradish

Instead, whenever you need to grate the pungent root, chop off a chunk or two, put the pieces in a blender or food processor, and add a spoonful or so of vinegar. Then put the cover on and let 'er rip. If you use a hand grater, sprinkle the cut end of the root with vinegar, then pull a plastic bag over the whole she-bang, and grate inside that fume-containing cover. Either way, your eyes will stay dry, with none of the burning sensation fresh horseradish can produce.

Word to the Wise

Dark, leafy greens are renowned for packing potent loads of iron and calcium. Unfortunately, the leaves also contain compounds that restrict the absorption of those essential minerals. The secret to freeing up the flow: Douse the greens with vinegar (any kind is fine). It'll liberate those health-giving minerals so that none of their power goes to waste.

Don't Cry over Chopped Onions, Either

There are scads of ways to stop the flow of tears when you're chopping onions. But this is one of the easiest: Simply sprinkle vinegar generously over the surface of the cutting board before you start whacking at the bulb. Besides reducing the flow of the onion's tear-generating chemicals, the vinegar will minimize the odor that lingers on your cutting board. (For getting rid of any aroma that does remain on the board and your hands, see "Freshen Up Surfaces, Too!" on page 108.)

QUICK & QUIRKY

Cut the Grease—

If you love fried food, but you don't like the grease that usually goes with it, this tip is just for you: Add a tablespoon of vinegar to the pan or deep fryer before you pour in the oil. Whether you're making classic French fries or onion rings, Southern fried chicken, deep-fried shrimp, or homemade doughnuts, your favorite treats will come out more flavorful—and a lot less greasy.

A Hot Tip for Hot-Pepper Fans

As you know if you're a chili pepper lover, the oil inside these ultra-hot devils can deliver a painful burn. Fortunately, if that happens when you're in the kitchen, you're in luck: Immediately wash your affected skin with white vinegar, and the pain will vanish.

Better yet, whenever possible, head off trouble from the get-go by soaking your hot peppers in vinegar for three to four hours before you cut into them. It'll neutralize the trouble-causing chemicals in the oil.

Ta-Ta, Togetherness

Rice and pasta are just like a band of buddies in an old-time movie: They're bound and determined to stick together through thick and thin no matter what. In the case of the grains and noodles, there's a one-word reason for that buddy system: starch. There's also a one-word antidote: vinegar. So drop a teaspoon of it into the boiling water just before you add the rice or pasta. It'll reduce the starch—making your rice fluffy, and keeping your spaghetti, rigatoni, or lasagna from clumping so it's ready for your favorite sauce.

> **FOIL FLATULENCE**
>
> Beans are infamous for producing embarrassing, and uncomfortable, gas emissions. But they're far from the only culprits. Lots of folks have similar problems with broccoli, cabbage, cauliflower, onions, peas, and other vegetables. The secret to calming your inner exhaust system: Pinpoint your personal demons, and anytime you cook one of them, add a teaspoon of white vinegar to the water.

Beat the Canned-Food Blahs

Let's face it: Nothing can make canned foods taste like their fresh-picked or made-from-scratch counterparts. But a spoonful of vinegar will give a fresher, more robust flavor to anything that came from a can, including fruits and vegetables, as well as soups, sauces, stews, and gravy. What kind of vinegar, you ask? Well, in a pinch, even a little of the distilled white kind will do the trick. But for the best results, use whatever kind you have on hand that complements the particular vittles. For example,

Fabulous French-Style Potato Salad

This classic side dish is so tasty you may never mix mayo with your taters again!

2 lbs. of Yukon gold potatoes, scrubbed but not peeled

2 tsp. of white vinegar

½ cup of white-wine vinegar

Salt and pepper to taste

½ cup of extra virgin olive oil

⅔ cup of chopped scallions*

1 tbsp. of minced shallots

Boil the potatoes, with the white vinegar added to the water, until they're fork-tender. When the potatoes are just cool enough to handle, cut them into ½-inch slices, and put them in a large bowl. Sprinkle the vinegar, salt, and pepper over the still-warm potatoes and toss gently. Add the olive oil, tossing again. Mix in the scallions and shallots. Serve at room temperature.

Or substitute your choice of variations. Good choices include chopped olives, minced garlic, and cubed chicken; chopped tomato, diced bacon, and hard-boiled egg.

Yield: 4 servings

For another sensational spud recipe, see page 127 in Chapter 4.

balsamic is a perfect perker-upper for fruit. Red-wine vinegar does wonders for soups, stews, and sauces. And vegetables get a whole new lease on life when you douse them with herb- or fruit-infused vinegars. (Coming up in the next section, you'll find the easy-as-pie directions for making your own infused and wine vinegars.)

Keep Potatoes Firm

When you take the time and trouble to make potato salad, you want the taters to stay nice and firm. And they will if you use this simple trick: Add a spoonful or two of vinegar to the cooking water. Those spuds will hold their shape right along with the other ingredients. (Since the proof of the pudding—or in this case, potato salad—is in the tasting, make a batch of the Fabulous French-Style Potato Salad, at left, and see for yourself.)

Say Cheese!

And enjoy it longer. To keep mold from ruining hard cheese, wrap the block in a clean cloth or paper towel that you've moistened with vinegar. Then tuck it into a plastic bag or storage container, and put it in the fridge.

Keep cottage cheese fresher longer by stirring a teaspoon of vinegar into the container. In both cases, the acetic acid in the vinegar will prolong the life of the cheese without altering the flavor.

Perk Up Pimientos and Olives

Here's a slick trick for extending the refrigerator shelf life of pimientos and all kinds of olives: Whenever you remove any from the jar, pour in enough white vinegar to completely cover the contents, and screw the lid back on tightly. Those tasty tidbits should stay good to eat for several months beyond their normal expiration date. **Note:** *Let your eyes be your guide. If the liquid turns murky, milky, or shows other obvious signs of spoilage, toss the stuff out immediately.*

OLD-TIME Vim and Vinegar

If you're of a certain age, it's a sure bet that you grew up hearing this World War II–era mantra every day: "Use it up, wear it out. Make it do, or do without." Well, around our house, that philosophy applied across the board—right down to the condiments in the icebox. Whenever the mayonnaise, mustard, or ketchup dwindled to just a thin coating on the bottom of the jar, my Grandma Putt would reach for the vinegar. She'd dribble a few drops into the container, shake it hard, and presto—there'd be enough to perk up a few more sandwiches.

FOR GOOD LIVING

Keep Garlic at the Ready

In theory, fresh, dried garlic will keep for up to several months in a cool, dark environment. But real-life conditions being what they are, those bulbs can go belly-up before their time. The simple solution: Preserve your garlic, whether homegrown or store-bought, in vinegar. If you do, it'll keep for up to a year in the refrigerator. And unlike the stuff you buy in jars at the supermarket, it will retain its full fresh flavor. Here's the ultra-easy preservation procedure:

Break the garlic heads apart, peel the cloves, and put them in a large mixing bowl filled with cool water.

Clean the cloves with your fingertips to remove any dirt, and cut off any brown spots using a small paring knife.

Transfer the cleaned garlic to a colander or large strainer. Rinse thoroughly, and put the cloves into small, sterilized glass jars. (Half-pint canning jars, with either plastic or clamp-style glass lids, are perfect.)

> **NEVER USE A HAND-PAINTED PLATE** to serve a salad with a vinegar-based dressing. The vinegar will corrode the paint. Not only will that ruin your treasure, but it could also release harmful toxins into the food.

Bring white vinegar to a boil in a large, nonreactive pot. Immediately pour the vinegar over the garlic and close the jar lids tightly. (Roughly 1 cup of vinegar for each half-pint jar should be plenty, but it's always smart to err on the side of caution and boil a little more than you think you'll need.)

Let the jars sit until they reach room temperature and then stash them in the fridge. Or, if you prefer, process them in a hot-water bath or pressure canner, and store them at room temperature.

Keep Berries Fresh Longer

It just doesn't seem fair: You buy some beautiful, fresh berries at the market or maybe at a pick-your-own berry farm—but it seems that no sooner do you get them home than they're covered with fuzzy mold. Well, I'll let you in on a little secret: The key to keeping berries fresh is to kill any mold spores that may be present, and then to store the delicate fruit in just the right way. Here's how to accomplish that heroic feat in five easy steps:

STEP 1. As soon as you get the berries home, put them in a large bowl with a mixture of 1 part vinegar (either white or ACV) and 10 parts cool water.

STEP 2. Let the berries soak for three or

REMARKABLE RECIPE

Raspberry Dressing

Granted, for most folks, it's all but impossible to resist eating fresh raspberries right from the box! But do yourself a favor and save some of them for this berry fine dressing.

⅓ cup of plain yogurt

¼ cup of fresh raspberries

3 tbsp. of raspberry vinegar

2 tbsp. of mayonnaise

1 tbsp. of Dijon mustard

1 tsp. of sugar

Ground black pepper to taste

Whisk all of the ingredients together in a nonreactive bowl. Cover tightly and chill for several hours so the flavors can blend. Serve as a topping for other fresh fruit, or on a salad made with baby spinach or Bibb lettuce sprinkled with fresh raspberries and toasted walnuts. **Note:** *To toast walnuts, spread the shelled nuts in a single layer on a baking sheet, and bake at 350°F, stirring once or twice, until lightly browned and fragrant (10 to 12 minutes).*

Yield: ⅔ cup

For more delicious dressing recipes, see page 119 in Chapter 4.

FOR GOOD LIVING

four minutes. Gently move them around with your hands to help dislodge any dirt while the vinegar bath kills bacteria and mold spores.

STEP 3. Drain the clean berries in a colander, and then rinse the fruit thoroughly to remove any vinegar flavor.

STEP 4. Transfer the berries to a clean cloth towel, and very gently pat them dry with paper towels or a second cloth towel.

STEP 5. Store the fragile fruits in a lidded container that you've lined with paper towels. A clean, dry supermarket-style berry container that has holes in the sides and lid is perfect. If you use a regular, airtight storage container, leave the lid slightly ajar to prevent moisture buildup.

That's all there is to it! Raspberries and blackberries should stay in fine fettle for a week or more. Strawberries and blueberries could last for close to two weeks.

QUICK & QUIRKY

Perfectly Pleasing Pepper Storage—Vinegar is just the ticket for storing bell peppers. Just rinse 'em off, and chop or slice them into the sizes and shapes you desire. Then pop the pieces into jars, and cover them with just-boiled vinegar. Use a separate jar for each pepper color or make festive, multi-colored blends.

Preserve Fresh Herbs: A Third Option

If you grow your own herbs, or buy them in quantity, you know that both drying and freezing are excellent ways to preserve your bounty. But did you know that you can also do the job with vinegar? Here's all there is to it:

- Loosely pack sterilized jars with the fresh herbs (use only one type per jar).

- Add enough warmed vinegar to cover the tops by 1 inch, making sure that all of the leaves are immersed.

- Store the jars at room temperature, away from light and sources of heat, and use them in the same quantities as dried herbs. They should stay in fine fettle for several years.

Note: *Basil and tarragon are especially good candidates for vinegar storage.*

Eggzactly Right!

White vinegar is one of the best friends an egg lover ever had. Here's a trio of ways it can help you when you're cooking hen fruit:

- When you're boiling eggs, add 2 tablespoons of vinegar per quart of water before you turn on the heat. It will prevent the shells from cracking and also make the boiled eggs easier to peel.

- For tidier poached eggs, bring your water to a boil and then add a drop or two of vinegar to it. It'll keep the egg whites from spreading.

- Make creamier scrambled eggs with this terrific trick: Add a tablespoon of vinegar for every two eggs as they begin to thicken, and stir until they're done.

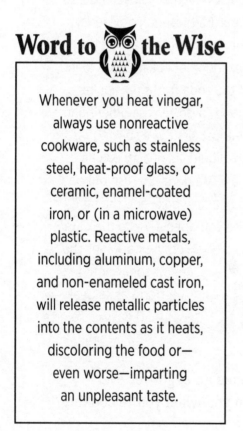

Word to the Wise

Whenever you heat vinegar, always use nonreactive cookware, such as stainless steel, heat-proof glass, or ceramic, enamel-coated iron, or (in a microwave) plastic. Reactive metals, including aluminum, copper, and non-enameled cast iron, will release metallic particles into the contents as it heats, discoloring the food or—even worse—imparting an unpleasant taste.

Oops—I Overdid It!

It happens to even the most experienced chefs: You get distracted for a moment and accidentally add too much salt or too much sugar to a recipe. Well, don't beat yourself up over it—and don't toss your dish in the garbage can. Instead, depending on the flavor mishap at hand, let apple cider vinegar save the day in one of these two ways:

Too sweet. Add a teaspoon of ACV to the pot.

Too salty. Mix in 1 teaspoon of ACV and 1 teaspoon of sugar.

Then, in either case, take a taste, and if necessary, add more of the appropriate flavor adjuster until it tastes just right.

OLD-TIME
Vim and Vinegar

If you make your own soup stock from scratch, as my Grandma Putt did, this hot tip is right up your alley: When you're cookin' up your chicken or beef bones, add a table-spoon or two of vinegar to the water. It'll draw out the calcium from the bone. Not only will that make your soup more nutritious, but it'll also give it a richer taste.

What's that? You say you make your soup with store-bought broth, or maybe bouil-lon concentrate from a jar? Not to worry: Vinegar will add zing to that, too—giving your meat, vegetable, or bean soups more of an old-fashioned, full-bodied flavor.

Practice Safe Poultry

As soon as you get an un-cooked chicken or turkey home from the store, pour ¼ cup of white vinegar into the cavity, and swish it around. It'll slow down the growth of harmful bacteria. Remember, though: The operative words here are *slow down*. Nothing can halt bacterial growth indefinitely, so make sure you cook that bird within about 48 hours.

Meaty Matters

Attention, meat lovers! The acetic acid in vinegar can solve a trio of common carni-vore conundrums:

Tough meat. Lean meat can be easier on your budget and your waistline, but (as we all know) it can also be on the tough, stringy side. The simple solution: Soak your steaks, chops, or other cuts in vinegar overnight before you cook them. You can rinse off the vinegar before cook-ing if you'd like, but it's not necessary. Either way, that meat will melt in your mouth!

Gamey game. Even folks who love venison, rabbit, and other wild game admit that the flavor can take some getting used to. If you're not fond of that, um, distinctive bite, take the edge off by soaking the meat in a half-and-half mixture of vinegar and water for at least an hour before you cook it.

Overly salty ham. Add 2 tablespoons of white or apple cider vinegar to the water that you boil the ham in. It'll draw out some of the salty taste and perk up the flavor to boot!

Note: *Speaking of ham, when you bring home an uncooked one, rub white vinegar on the cut end to prevent mold from forming before you get a chance to cook it.*

REMARKABLE RECIPE

Sam Houston's Famous BBQ Sauce

This really was the world-famous Texan's own recipe!

- **3 tbsp. of vegetable oil**
- **¼ medium yellow onion, grated**
- **2 garlic cloves, minced**
- **1 cup of ketchup**
- **¼ cup of lemon juice**
- **¼ cup of Worcestershire sauce**
- **2 tbsp. of apple cider vinegar**
- **2 tbsp. of brown sugar**
- **1 tbsp. of chili powder**
- **2 tsp. of paprika**
- **1 tsp. of hot-pepper sauce**
- **1 tbsp. of dry mustard**
- **2 tsp. of water**

Heat the vegetable oil in a pot on medium-low heat. Add the onion, stirring for five minutes. Add the garlic and stir for another minute. Add the next eight ingredients. Combine the mustard and water to form a smooth paste, and add it to the pot. Bring to a boil, then turn the heat to low, cover the pot, and simmer for 20 minutes, stirring occasionally. Brush the sauce onto the meat of your choice. *For more delicious marinade recipes, see page 119 in Chapter 4.*

Corned Beef Shrinkage

You've purchased just the right amount of corned beef to feed all of your guests on St Patrick's Day. But what you didn't count on was the shrinkage! Once this cut of meat is cooked, its size is drastically less than it was when you started. Stop the shrinkage by boiling the meat in water to which you've added a couple tablespoons of apple cider vinegar. And next year, remember to buy a larger cut of meat than you think you'll need.

Be a Bread Winner

Attention, bread bakers! Here's a trio of ways white vinegar can help you when you're fixin' to make a loaf or two (of course these tricks work just as well with home-baked rolls):

Make it rise faster. And give it a yummy texture. Just add 1 tablespoon of vinegar for every 2½ cups of flour you use. (But remember to reduce the other liquid ingredients by the amount of vinegar you use!)

Keep the crust soft. Simply brush vinegar on the top of the loaf just before you pop it into the oven.

2 QUICK CANNING TRICKS

When you're canning food, vinegar is a vital asset—regardless of whether it's part of your recipe or not. Here's how to use it:

▶ To prevent hard-water deposits from forming on the jars' sealers, add a tablespoon or two of white vinegar to the canning bath.

▶ Before you store your jars, wipe the outsides thoroughly with white vinegar. This will remove any food residue that may be on the glass, thereby eliminating the chance of mold forming.

Give it a shine. To add luster to the crust without making it soft, put your bread in the oven as usual. Then two minutes before the baking time is up, remove the loaf, brush the top with vinegar, and put it back in the oven to finish baking.

Something's Fishy

Are you a fish aficionado? If so, then make sure you keep plenty of vinegar on hand, and put it to work in one of these ways:

- To make scaling easier, rub white vinegar on the fish and let it sit for five minutes. The scales will practically fly off!

- When salmon, lobster, oysters, or clams are on the menu, soak them in vinegar for at least several hours, or even overnight. The acidic bath will tenderize the tough muscle fiber.

- For firmer, whiter fish fillets, soak them for 20 minutes in a solution of 2 tablespoons of white vinegar per quart of water.

- Bring out the flavor of any kind of fish or seafood by dousing it with a tablespoon or so of white-wine or sherry vinegar as it's poaching or frying.

- Give canned fish or seafood a fresher taste by soaking it for 15 minutes in 2 tablespoons of white vinegar and 1 teaspoon of sherry, or 2 tablespoons of sherry vinegar—whichever you have on hand.

QUICK & QUIRKY

Super-Simple Fish Topper—This wonderful white sauce takes just seconds to whip up, but its elegant appearance and fabulous flavor are worthy of the fanciest dinner party in town. To make it, just mix 2 teaspoons of white-wine vinegar per ½ cup of heavy cream. Drizzle it over baked, grilled, poached, or smoked fish—and get ready for all the "oohs" and "ahs!"

Vinegar for *Dessert*?!

Yes indeed! In addition to being a key ingredient in some mighty tasty desserts (for one example, see the Crazy Cake recipe on page 105), a jolt of white vinegar can perk up your favorite sweet treats. Here are some winning ways to put it to work in your kitchen:

Fluff up meringue. If you beat in 1 teaspoon of vinegar for every three egg whites, then that tasty topping will be fluffier and more stable to boot!

Make flakier piecrust. Simply add 1 tablespoon of vinegar to the recipe. You'll have the most mouthwatering pies in town!

Bake moister cakes. One teaspoon of vinegar mixed into the other ingredients will improve the moistness and flavor of any cake— whether it's made from scratch or a boxed mix.

Make finer frosting. Add several drops of vinegar as you beat the icing. It'll turn out smooth and creamy—with no sugaring.

Make finer frosting, take 2. To keep boiled icing from hardening, stir in ⅓ teaspoon of vinegar as the frosting is cooking.

Firm up Jell-O®. Mix in 1 teaspoon of vinegar per box of gelatin. It'll hold its shape in molds and salads, even in hot weather. What's more, it'll be easier to cut after it sets.

Word to the Wise

Ever whipped up a special dessert only to have it turn out so sweet that it almost tasted like pure sugar? Well, next time, add a teaspoon of vinegar to the recipe. It'll reduce the sweetness just enough to let you savor the true flavor of the other ingredients.

Accept Substitutions

It happens to all of us every now and then: You start whipping up a particular recipe, only to discover that you're missing a key ingredient. You can't stop what you're doing and rush to the store. But fortunately, if you've got a jug of white vinegar on hand, chances are you can avoid culinary disaster. Here's how:

Buttermilk or sour milk. Mix 1 tablespoon of vinegar with enough milk to measure 1 cup. Stir, let it sit for five minutes, use as much as your recipe calls for, and save the rest in the fridge for later.

Cream of tartar. For every teaspoon the recipe calls for, use 2 teaspoons of vinegar.

Egg. When you run short in a baking recipe (no other kind!), substitute 1 tablespoon of vinegar for each missing egg. Just one caveat: This exchange will work only if there is another leavening agent, such as baking powder, baking soda, self-rising flour, or yeast, in the recipe.

Hot-pepper sauce. Combine 1 teaspoon of vinegar with ¾ teaspoon of ground cayenne pepper for each teaspoon of sauce you need.

Ketchup. To make 1 cup of ketchup, mix 1 cup of tomato sauce with 1 tablespoon of sugar and 1 teaspoon of vinegar.

Lemon juice. Replace the amount stipulated in the recipe with half as much vinegar. Just be aware that this switcheroo works best in dishes that re-

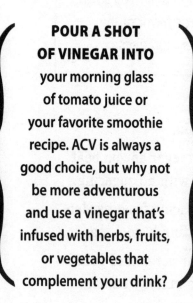

POUR A SHOT OF VINEGAR INTO your morning glass of tomato juice or your favorite smoothie recipe. ACV is always a good choice, but why not be more adventurous and use a vinegar that's infused with herbs, fruits, or vegetables that complement your drink?

quire small amounts of lemon juice. Do not use vinegar as a stand-in for lemon in drinks or canning recipes—and certainly not in lemon meringue pie!

Mustard (prepared). For each tablespoon needed, mix 1 tablespoon of dry mustard with 1 teaspoon each of vinegar, sugar, and water.

Sour cream. In a blender or food processor, mix 1 cup of cottage cheese, ¼ cup of skim milk, and 1 teaspoon of vinegar to get a creamy consistency. You might like the homemade version so much that you'll never go back to store-bought sour cream!

Wine. Mix 2 teaspoons of vinegar per cup of either grape or apple juice. Or use a mixture of 1 part wine vinegar to 3 parts water.

REMARKABLE RECIPE

Crazy Cake

This dessert rose to fame in the 1940s, when wartime rationing often left bakers bereft of standard ingredients such as eggs and butter.

3 cups of all-purpose flour
2 cups of sugar
⅓ cup of cocoa powder
2 tsp. of baking powder
1 tsp. of salt
1 tsp. of vanilla extract
2 tbsp. of white vinegar
¾ cup of vegetable oil
2 cups of cold water

Combine the first five ingredients in an ungreased 9- by 13-inch baking pan. Make three 1-inch holes in the mixture. Pour the vanilla extract into the first hole, the vinegar into the second, and the vegetable oil into the third. Then pour the water evenly over the whole surface. Mix with a fork or wire whisk until the ingredients are well blended. Bake at 350°F for 35 to 40 minutes, or until a wooden toothpick inserted in the center comes out clean. Cool completely in the pan or on a wire rack.

Yield: 15 servings

For more dessert recipes, see page 144 in Chapter 4.

FOR GOOD LIVING

TIMELY TRADE-OFFS

What happens when you want to make a recipe that calls for a specific type of vinegar, and you don't have it on hand? Just reach for this handy chart! (You might want to make a copy of it and tuck it into one of your cookbooks.)

AWOL Vinegar	Pinch Hitter (per 1 tablespoon)
Apple cider	1 tablespoon of either lemon or lime juice *or* 2 tablespoons of white wine
Balsamic	1 tablespoon of either brown rice or Chinese black vinegar *or* ½ teaspoon of sugar per tablespoon of apple cider or (preferably) red-wine vinegar
Champagne	1 tablespoon of either white-wine or rice vinegar*
Distilled white vinegar	1 tablespoon of either lemon or lime juice
Herb vinegar	1 tablespoon of either wine, rice, or apple cider vinegar plus 1 or 2 teaspoons of chopped fresh herbs
Malt vinegar	1 tablespoon of either lemon juice or apple cider vinegar
Raspberry vinegar	1 tablespoon of sherry vinegar
Red-wine vinegar	Equal parts of distilled white vinegar and red wine
Sherry vinegar	1 tablespoon of white-wine vinegar *or*, if you don't need the acidic property of vinegar, 1 tablespoon of red or white wine
White-wine vinegar	1 tablespoon of rice vinegar

* Champagne vinegar is very mild, so don't substitute any stronger type for it.

I Don't Need Your Help!

As the old adage goes, the kitchen is the heart of the home—and that's true not only for people. A couple of harmless, but highly annoying, pests are attracted to all that good food, too. Fortunately, vinegar can help you lay out a big unwelcome mat. Your strategy depends on which tiny terrors are coming to call:

Fruit flies. Pour apple cider vinegar into a jar or small bowl. Add a couple drops of dishwashing liquid, mix well, and set it on the kitchen counter. The little buggers will make a beeline for the vinegar, fall into the drink, and drown!

Ants. Simply wash your counters, backsplashes, and floor with equal parts of white vinegar and water. Ants will stay away.

Freshen the Air

Whether the unpleasant aroma in your kitchen was caused by burnt food or naturally odoriferous food like garlic, onions, or fish, vinegar can help. Just add half a cup of white vinegar to a quart of water, and let it simmer (not boil!) on the stove. Before you know it, the bad odors will be bygones. **Note:** *In a pinch, any kind of vinegar will perform this aroma-erasing feat. But don't waste the good stuff—use the cheapest distilled white vinegar you can find.*

OLD-TIME *Vim and Vinegar*

Whenever Grandma Putt got a new wooden spoon, she soaked it in apple cider vinegar overnight, and dried it off with paper towels the next morning. This kept the wood from absorbing food odors, so Grandma knew for sure that her cookies wouldn't come out of the oven bearing a telltale aroma of spaghetti sauce!

Freshen Up Surfaces, Too!

The same vinegar that removes unpleasant smells from the air can also eliminate food aromas from other odor collectors in your kitchen—namely these:

Cutting boards. Simply wipe the surface with a sponge dampened with white vinegar. L'eau de onion, garlic, or fish will be a goner!

Plastic bowls or food-storage containers. Soak a slice of bread in vinegar, tuck it into the "victim," and cover the top tightly. Let it sit overnight, then toss out the bread, and wash the item in soapy water. If any slight odor lingers, repeat the process. This trick also removes built-up food odors from lunch boxes and garbage cans.

Your hands. Sprinkle a little salt on your skin, and add a few drops of vinegar. Rub your "paws" together, then rinse with clear water. This is also a guaranteed way to erase stains left by berries or other color-sharing produce.

That's Historical

Throughout history, folks around the world have incorporated vinegar into their menus in a variety of ways. Here's a sampling of taste-tempting and not-so-enticing examples:

• In ancient Rome, one luxurious dessert was apricots cooked in a thickened syrup made from honey, wine, and vinegar and sprinkled with pepper and mint.

• Another Roman treat was turnips pickled in a creamy mustard seed and vinegar sauce.

• In the 1500s and 1600s, Europeans cooked thin slices of veal on skewers, then served them with a topping made from vinegar, butter, and sugar. The tangy sauce was flavorful—and, more importantly, robust enough to disguise the taste of meat that might be slightly (or a little more than slightly) spoiled.

• During the Middle Ages, folks throughout the Mediterranean region feasted on mutton tongue stewed in a mixture of vinegar and orange juice.

DIY Wine Vinegar

Nowadays, you can buy wine vinegar in just about every super-market. So why would you want to bother making your own? I'll tell you why: Even the expensive store-bought brands are gener-ally rushed through the fermentation process, which makes them highly acidic and lacking in flavor. On the other hand, homemade vinegar has a milder, fuller-bodied taste that gives a flavorful boost to everything from soups and sauces to (of course) vinai-grette dressings. Plus, your own "vintage" vinegar makes one of the most clever—and appre-ciated—Christmas, birthday, or hostess gifts you could ever deliver. Here's all there is to it:

STEP 1. Round up a container. A half-gal-lon glass jar with a wide mouth will do for starters. But the best, and most user-friendly, vessel for this purpose is a crock or a glass beverage container with a spigot at the bottom (like the ones sold for dispensing iced tea).
Just make sure the spigot is made of stainless steel—not aluminum, which will react with the vinegar.

Word to the Wise

For a vinaigrette dressing worthy of the fanciest five-star restaurant in town, marinate finely chopped shallots in your homemade wine vinegar for 15 minutes. Then whisk the mixture with good-quality extra virgin olive oil, add salt and pepper to taste—and modestly accept the applause from around the dinner table!

FOR GOOD LIVING

STEP 2. Buy an 8-ounce bottle of commercial mother from a wine- and beer-making supply shop. (The mother is the *Acetobacter* bacteria that convert alcohol into vinegar.)

STEP 3. Pour 2 cups of good red or white wine and 1 cup of filtered water into the crock, then add the mother. Cover the container with a double layer of cheesecloth and secure it with a rubber band.

STEP 4. Set the container in a warm (70° to 90°F), dark spot and let it stand for 1 ½ weeks. Don't disturb it, as it's important to let the mother be still while she's doing her job.

STEP 5. Add more wine to the container in three 2 ½-cup installments over the next 1 ½ weeks until it's about two-thirds full. Once a thin veil has formed on the surface, add the wine through a funnel or the tube of a bulb baster tucked under the edge of the veil. Let the

REMARKABLE RECIPE

Chicken Thighs with Red-Wine Vinegar

This simple, family-pleasing dish is a great venue for your homemade vinegar!

4 tbsp. of extra virgin olive oil

4 garlic cloves, chopped

8 boneless, skinless chicken thighs

1 tbsp. of fresh rosemary

1 ½ cups of red-wine vinegar

Pour the oil into a large skillet, add the garlic, and sauté it for about two minutes. Add the chicken and sprinkle the rosemary over it. Brown the chicken on both sides, then pour the vinegar over it. Cover and cook for about 20 minutes, turning the chicken at about the halfway mark. Then serve it up. (It's great over wild rice with a side of broccoli!) Yield: 8 servings

For another perfectly pleasing poultry recipe, see page 128 in Chapter 4.

container sit for 10 weeks, checking it and sniffing the contents periodically. If your vinegar-in-the-making ever gives off a scent like that of furniture polish, throw it out—mother and all. Then wash the crock thoroughly and start over.

STEP 6. When the vinegar smells sharp and crisp, strain it into sterile bottles through a plastic or stainless steel funnel lined with a paper coffee filter. (If you plan to start the process over, leave 2 cups of vinegar in the container and just add wine and water.)

STEP 7. If you want to keep your vinegar for more than four months, pasteurize it. To do that, simply heat the vinegar to 155°F in a stainless steel saucepan and keep it at that temperature for 30 minutes.

Whether your vinegar is pasteurized or not, store it in sterilized, well-sealed bottles in a cool, dry place.

OVER TIME, VINEGAR CAN CAUSE THE LEAD in top-quality crystal to leach out. While it's perfectly safe to serve vinegar for salads in a lead crystal cruet, don't store it in one for any length of time.

Note: *The better the wine you use, the better the end product will be. That's because good wines have a variety of complex flavors, which will create interesting, full-flavored vinegars. Typically, fruitier, younger wines result in tastier vinegars.*

Make Your Own Malt Vinegar

Wine vinegar isn't the only kind that's far superior to commercial brands. Once you've sampled the richer, heartier flavor of homemade malt vinegar, the store-bought stuff will never cut the mustard at your house again! And you don't have to start from scratch by fermenting barley, as the major manufacturers do. All you need to do is visit your local beer distributor and pick up a six-pack of your favorite brew (see note on page 113). Then lay in the same supplies you need for wine vinegar: a crock or jar and a piece of vinegar mother (see "DIY Wine Vinegar" on page 109). Once you're equipped, proceed as follows:

- In your container, mix 3 parts of your chosen brewski with 1 part filtered or distilled water.

- Cover the container with cheesecloth, and set it in a dark area at room temperature (such as a kitchen cabinet) for 24 hours.

- Remove the cover, and add a a piece of vinegar mother. Replace the cloth topper, put the container back in its resting place, and leave it to ferment for at least a week.

- Taste it to test the strength and acidity. If it suits you, strain, bottle, and pasteurize the vinegar in the same way that you would wine vinegar. On the other hand, if it isn't your cup of tea, er, vinegar, let it age until it meets your approval, tasting it every week or so. (It can be left to age as long as you like—once all the alcohol has been converted to acetic acid, the bacteria will stop working.)

WHERE IN THE WORLD . . . ?

Around the globe, folks make vinegar from whatever "fermentable" foods are most plentiful. Here in the good ol' US of A, apples fill that bill. Back in ancient Babylonia, dates were the fruit of choice. And here's what's fermenting in vinegar barrels in various parts of the planet:

China and Japan: Rice

Philippines: Sugarcane

Germany: Potatoes

Indonesia: Coconut

Nicaragua: Bananas

England: Barley

Now you have your very own malt vinegar to dress your fish-and-chips—or to use in scads of recipes, like the ones coming up in Chapter 4, beginning on page 119. **Note:** *Your beer or ale must be free of preservatives, and have an alcohol content that's between 5 and 7 percent. If it's higher than that, dilute it with another part or two of water after you pour it into the crock.*

Festive Fruit-Scrap Vinegar

Here's a fun way to make use of peelings and cores that you'd otherwise toss in the garbage can or the compost bin:

Put your fruit peelings and cores in a wide-mouth jar, crock, or glass bowl, and cover them with cold water. Apples, pears, peaches (minus pits), and grapes are good choices.

Set the container in a warm place and cover it with cheese-cloth (so air can get in but bugs will stay out).

That's Historical

Vinegar was discovered at least 10,000 years ago, when a wine vat was accidentally opened early. Instead of maturing into a delicious beverage, the fruit "morphed" into a not-so-tasty, but much more versatile, liquid. By 2000 BC, vinegar making had become a lucrative undertaking. In the late 1300s, master vinegar makers in France developed the Orleans method, by which they could make continuous batches by adding fresh wine or cider to oak barrels that contained remnants of the previous batch (the "mother"). Infused vinegars soon followed, and by the late 1700s, Parisian street markets were selling more than 50 varieties of flavored cooking vinegar. Fast forward to 1869, when the H.J. Heinz Company of Pittsburgh, Pennsylvania, became the first company to mass produce and distribute vinegar.

Add a couple of fresh cores and peelings every few days until a scum forms on top of the water. Then stop adding fruit and let the mixture thicken.

After a month, start tasting it every few days. When the vinegar is strong enough to suit your taste, strain it through a double layer of cheesecloth and pour it into sterilized bottles.

PASTEURIZED VINEGAR OF ANY KIND will keep almost indefinitely in an unopened bottle. But once the bottle has been opened (even when it's tightly capped afterward), the vinegar will only retain its full flavor for about three months. After that, although it won't actually spoil, it will gradually begin to lose its zip.

Then discard or compost the solids, and enjoy your fruity creation! **Note:** *If at all possible, use organically grown produce for this vinegar, as well as all of your infused vinegars, including herbal versions. When organic is not an option, or if you don't know how the stuff was grown, wash it thoroughly before preparation using the simple procedure described in "De-Pollute Your Produce" (see page 45).*

Simply Elegant...

Or maybe elegantly simple. Homemade herbal vinegars pack a flavor punch you'll never find in store-bought versions, and they're as easy to make as a pot of tea. Why, in just a few hours, you can whip up a year's worth of Christmas, birthday, and hostess gifts. What's more, the final product looks as grand as anything you'd buy at a fancy-food boutique—for just a fraction of the price. For each bottle, you'll need six to eight fresh herb sprigs and 1 quart of good-quality vinegar. Here's the easy-as-pie procedure:

STEP 1. Wash and dry the herbs, then pack them into clean, quart-sized glass canning jars.

STEP 2. Heat the vinegar until it's warm (don't let it boil!), pour it over the herbs, and close the lid. If you're using jars with metal lids, cover the jar openings with plastic wrap or wax paper before you screw the lids on. The inner wrap will keep the metal from reacting with the vinegar.

STEP 3. Put your filled jars in a dark place at room temperature, and let them sit for a couple of weeks.

STEP 4. When the time's up, open one of the lids and sniff. If you detect a rich, herbal aroma, your "crop" is ready. Otherwise, close the jar, and check again every week.

STEP 5. When the scent is just right, strain out the solids, pour the flavored vinegar into pretty bottles, and tuck a fresh herb sprig into each one.

That's all there is to it!

OLD-TIME *Vim* and *Vinegar*

There's almost no limit to the herbal combinations (in some cases, with a jolt of citrus zest) that work beautifully for infused vinegars. These very versatile blends were some of Grandma Putt's favorites—and they're mine, too:

Basil-Orange: White-wine vinegar, basil sprigs, and the peel from one orange.

Dill-Peppercorn: Apple cider vinegar, dill sprigs, and black peppercorns.

Garlic-Chive: Rice vinegar, two peeled, chopped garlic cloves, and chives.

Lemon-Thyme: White-wine vinegar, the peel from one lemon, and thyme sprigs.

Sage-Rosemary: Red-wine vinegar, sage, and rosemary sprigs.

FOR GOOD LIVING

REMARKABLE RECIPE

Creamy Zucchini

If you're looking for new ways to serve up summer's never-ending supply of zucchini (whether you grow it yourself or "adopt" it from gardening neighbors) try this favorite recipe of mine—made even better with DIY thyme vinegar.

3 tbsp. of extra virgin olive oil

1 lb. of zucchini, shredded

2 tbsp. of thyme vinegar

½ cup of sour cream

2 tsp. of minced fresh thyme

Salt and freshly ground black pepper to taste

Warm the oil over medium heat in a heavy, nonreactive skillet. Add the zucchini and sauté for four minutes, or until golden in color. Transfer it to a bowl, and set it aside. Add the vinegar to the pan, scraping up any zuke bits on the bottom. Cook until the liquid is reduced to a teaspoon or so. Add the sour cream and thyme, mixing well. Return the squash to the skillet and stir until it's well coated. Heat through and season to taste with salt and pepper.

Yield: 4 servings

For more very vivacious vegetable recipes, see page 131 in Chapter 4.

Simple Secrets to Very Fine Vinegar

When you make an herbal vinegar, keep these tips in mind:

Let taste be your guide. Choose the vinegar and herbs that appeal to you (see the Old-Time Vim and Vinegar box on page 115 for a handful of Grandma Putt's favorites).

Don't scrimp on the herbs. With an insufficient amount, the flavor will be weak. As a general rule, use about 2 cups of fresh herbs per quart of vinegar.

Select high-quality vinegar. Don't try to economize by using the bargain-basement stuff. If the vinegar you start with doesn't taste good, the finished product won't either—no matter how much herbal flavoring you pack into it.

Make sure the herbs are in tip-top shape. Anything that's limp, or yellowing, or (heaven forbid!) turning brown is too far gone to make high-quality vinegar.

Don't put 'em on display. Decorative bottles filled with herbal vinegar look beautiful on a windowsill with the light streaming through them. But that light will make the flavor fade fast. So make a few just-for-show batches if you want to, but keep your cooking and gift-giving supply in a cool, dark place. A pantry works well; so does a kitchen cabinet that's far away from the stove, refrigerator, or other heat source.

Ultra-Easy Hot-Pepper Vinegar

If you like spicy food—whether your taste runs to Tex-Mex, Creole, Szechuan, or simply anything that's hot, hot, hot—pepper vinegar will give it a beautiful bite. There are more complex, time-consuming ways to make the fiery stuff, but this ultra-easy method never fails to produce mighty fine results:

- Wash 12 to 15 hot peppers (whatever kind you fancy) and pierce them with a needle.

- Pack them, along with two sprigs of fresh parsley, into a sterilized 8- to 10-ounce bottle or jar.

- Fill the container with white-wine vinegar to cover the peppers and parsley completely, and cover it with a tight-fitting lid.

- Let the mixture steep for a week at room temperature. Tuck it into the fridge, and use it to your heart's (and tummy's) content.

Word to the Wise

For an extra-special visual treat, make your hot-pepper vinegar using peppers in several different shapes and colors. Pack 'em into fancy bottles or jars, add a handwritten label, and you'll have some of the most appreciated Christmas, birthday, or hostess gifts in town!

Whenever you use some of your spicy condiment, replace it with enough fresh vinegar to completely cover the peppers and parsley. It should keep for at least three to four months.

Vivacious Vegetable Vinegar

Hot peppers aren't the only vegetables that can add a flavor punch to vinegar. Lots of veggies can spark up your favorite recipes. Prepare your choice as specified in the list below and put it in a sterilized glass jar with 1 quart of red- or white-wine vinegar (either home-made or store-bought). Close the lid tightly, and let the vinegar age for at least 30 days. Strain it through cheesecloth until the fluid runs clear, and pour it into one or more sterilized bottles. As for what kind of vegetables to use, these all work well:

- 1 pound of bell peppers (red, green, yellow, or purple), seeded and chopped

- 1 pound of sweet onions, peeled and sliced

- 6 garlic cloves, peeled and crushed

- 3 bunches of green onions, thinly sliced

Note: *This same technique makes fruit-flavored vinegars, too. Simply substitute 1 to 2 pounds of ripe fruit.*

That's Historical

In the days of the clipper ships, vessels were often away from their home ports for a year or more at a time—and rarely could they pull into a shoreside town and buy supplies. For that reason, the food they carried had to hold up in long-term storage. One of the onboard staples was hardtack, a rock-solid, far-from-tasty biscuit made of flour and water. To make the stuff at least edible, the sailors soaked it in a mixture of vinegar and water to make a sort of porridge they called skilligalee. Do yourself a favor, and don't bother trying this at home, kids!

In the last chapter, I shared tons of terrific tricks for putting vinegar to work around your kitchen, with a few choice recipes scattered throughout the pages. Well, if those whetted your appetite for more ways to cook with vinegar, you're in for a treat! These pages are chock-full of my, and Grandma Putt's, favorite recipes. Some are brand-new. Others are as old as the hills—and every bit as scrumptious as they were way back when.

SALAD DRESSINGS & MARINADES

▶ *Real* French Dressing

How did that gooey orange supermarket stuff become known as "French dressing"? This classic vinaigrette is the real deal.

> 1 tbsp. of wine vinegar
> Salt and pepper to taste*
> ⅔ cup of extra virgin olive oil

With a wire whisk, beat the vinegar with the salt and pepper until the pepper dissolves. Then whisk in the olive oil a drizzle at a time. Use it as a salad dressing, a topping for lightly steamed vegetables, or a dipping sauce for raw veggies or crusty French bread. *If you like, add mustard, crushed garlic, and/or fresh herbs to taste, too.*
Yield: *About 1 cup*

FOR GOOD LIVING

▶ Balsamic Vinaigrette

While this dressing is delicious on tossed salad, it's also perfect for basting grilled vegetables or fish, or for marinating chicken.

1 cup of balsamic vinegar

¼ cup of sweet vermouth

1 large shallot, minced

2 cups of extra virgin olive oil

Salt and pepper to taste

Mix the first three ingredients together in a bowl, and then slowly whisk in the olive oil. Season with the salt and pepper. Refrigerate the dressing in a tightly closed container for up to 30 days. Shake well before using. **Yield:** *About 3¼ cups*

▶ Mustard-Tarragon Marinade

Around my house, this quick and easy blend is a standby during outdoor grilling season. It's great with chicken, pork, or meaty fish like salmon, swordfish, and halibut.

Word to the Wise

Whenever you make a marinade, multiply the recipe if necessary to ensure that your meat, poultry, or fish is fully submerged in the liquid. Otherwise, you'll need to turn the pieces several times during the marinating process.

1 cup of extra virgin olive oil

¼ cup of Dijon mustard

¼ cup of tarragon white-wine vinegar

1 tbsp. of minced fresh tarragon

2 garlic cloves, minced

Process all of the ingredients in a blender or food processor until the consistency is smooth. Then pour the mixture into a glass or ceramic dish, and set your meat, fish, or poultry into the marinade. Cover the container, and refrigerate it for several hours or overnight. About 30 minutes before grilling time, remove the dish from the fridge, and let it sit at room temperature. **Yield:** *About 1½ cups*

▶ Red-Wine Marinade

This hearty blend is tailor-made for beef or lamb.

- ¼ cup of olive oil
- 1 cup of minced onion
- 2 garlic cloves, minced
- ½ cup of garlic red-wine vinegar
- ¾ cup of dry red wine
- ½ cup of water
- ¼ cup of tomato paste
- 1 tbsp. of minced fresh rosemary
- 1 bay leaf

In a heavy, nonreactive skillet, warm the oil over medium heat. Add the onion and garlic, reduce the heat to low, and cook, stirring, until they're softened (about five minutes). Stir in the vinegar and cook until it's reduced by half. Add the remaining ingredients and simmer for five minutes. Let the blend cool, transfer it to a glass or ceramic dish, and tuck in the meat. Refrigerate, covered, for at least several hours, until 30 minutes before grilling time. **Yield:** *About 2 cups*

OLD-TIME Vim and Vinegar

Early on in my cooking career, Grandma Putt taught me that the key to making a successful vinaigrette dressing is to create an emulsion, which (as I'd learned in chemistry class) is the result of mixing two or more ingredients that don't normally blend together—in this case, oil and vinegar—and making them stay together. The simple secret: First, whisk together all of the ingredients except the oil. Once they're thoroughly combined, slowly dribble in the oil while whisking it into the vinegar mixture.

FOR GOOD LIVING

▶ Zesty Coleslaw

A malt vinegar dressing puts a whole new twist on this classic side dish. Try it—you'll love it!

1 head of green cabbage, shredded*
1 head of red cabbage, shredded
1 large carrot, coarsely grated
1 small red onion, thinly sliced
1 cup of mayonnaise
½ cup of malt vinegar

¼ cup of coarse-grained mustard
2 tbsp. of sugar
Juice of 1 lemon
Salt and pepper to taste

Combine the first four ingredients in a large bowl. In a smaller bowl, whisk together the mayonnaise, vinegar, mustard, sugar, and lemon juice. Toss the slaw with the dressing, and season with the salt and pepper. Cover and refrigerate for at least an hour before serving.
* Instead of the green and red cabbage, you can use two packages of coleslaw blend. **Yield:** 8 servings

▶ Spinach-Apple Salad

Here's a nugget of nutritional trivia for you: The synergistic combo of spinach and apples delivers a jolt of energy to your body and also helps ease any pain in your muscles or joints. But you don't have to be tired or aching to enjoy this scrumptious salad.

2 apples, cored and diced
4 tbsp. of freshly squeezed lemon juice
3 tbsp. of extra virgin olive oil
2 tbsp. of raw honey
1 tbsp. of unfiltered apple cider vinegar

Salt and pepper to taste
8 cups of baby spinach leaves, washed
⅔ cup of crumbled goat cheese
½ cup of walnuts

Toss the apples with 2 tablespoons of the lemon juice. Whisk the remaining juice with the olive oil, honey, and vinegar, and season with the salt and pepper if desired. Combine the spinach, apples, and dressing, and divide among four bowls. Top with the cheese and nuts, and dig in! **Yield:** *About 4 servings*

▶ Sweet Potato Salad

If you only serve sweet potatoes at Thanksgiving and Christmas, give this recipe a try. It'll become a year-round favorite—guaranteed!

3 large sweet potatoes (about 1 lb.), peeled and cut into bite-size cubes

2 tbsp. of apple cider vinegar

2 tbsp. of Dijon mustard*

¼ cup of extra virgin olive oil

¼ cup of diced onion

½ rib of celery, thinly sliced

½ small red pepper, diced

Salt and pepper to taste

Boil the sweet potatoes in a covered pan until they're just tender enough to pierce with a fork (about 8 to 10 minutes—no longer!). While they're cooking, mix the vinegar, mustard, and oil together in a small bowl. Drain the potatoes into a large bowl, and toss them with the onion, celery, red pepper, and dressing. Add the salt and pepper.
* *Or substitute a sharp-sweet honey mustard.*
Yield: *8–12 servings*

> **IF YOU HAVE TROUBLE DIGESTING RAW ONIONS,** marinate them in sherry vinegar for an hour or so before you add them to a salad or sandwich. Your tummy will thank you!

FOR GOOD LIVING

▶ Bean Salad with Balsamic Vinaigrette

Balsamic vinegar gives a taste-tempting surprise to this delicious salad. But besides being absolutely scrumptious, this dish is a standby in heart-healthy diet plans.

2 tbsp. of balsamic vinegar	1 can (15.5 oz.) of black beans, rinsed and drained
⅓ cup of fresh parsley, chopped	1 can (15.5 oz.) of garbanzo beans, rinsed and drained
4 garlic cloves, finely chopped	1 medium red onion, diced
Ground black pepper to taste	6 lettuce leaves
¼ cup of extra virgin olive oil	½ cup of finely chopped celery

Whisk the vinegar, parsley, garlic, and pepper together until well blended. Continue whisking, and slowly drizzle in the olive oil. Mix the beans and onion together in a large bowl, pour the vinaigrette over them, and toss gently until the bean mixture is evenly coated. Cover the bowl, and refrigerate. At serving time, put a lettuce leaf on each plate, top it with the salad, and garnish with the chopped celery. Serve immediately.

Yield: *About 6 servings*

QUICK & QUIRKY

Dandy Dandelion Salad—
For a real change of pace, mix fresh, young dandelion greens with a dressing made from 1 cup of olive oil, ⅓ cup of apple cider vinegar, and salt and pepper to taste. (Just make sure the dandelions have not been treated with any chemicals!)

▶ Italian Gazpacho

Balsamic vinegar gives an Italian kick to this refreshing summertime classic.

3 large, ripe tomatoes (about 1½ lbs.), cut into 2-inch pieces

1 large cucumber, peeled, halved lengthwise, and cut into 1½-inch-thick slices

1 red or yellow bell pepper, cut into 1-inch pieces

1 small red onion, coarsely chopped

1 large garlic clove, finely chopped

1½ cups of tomato juice

⅓ cup of balsamic vinegar

½ tsp. of salt

¼ tsp. of red-pepper flakes

⅓ cup of fresh basil leaves, chopped (for garnish)

Extra virgin olive oil (for serving)

Put the first three ingredients into a food processor, and pulse until they're coarsely chopped. Add the remaining ingredients, except the basil and oil, and process (in batches if necessary) until the vegetables are all finely chopped. Don't overprocess—this soup should be chunky! (If necessary, process it in batches.) Transfer the soup to a large bowl, cover it tightly, and refrigerate overnight, or for at least four hours. Then serve it up in chilled soup bowls, with the basil sprinkled on top. Set out a cruet of olive oil, so diners can drizzle it on their soup to taste. **Yield:** *6–8 servings*

IN 8TH CENTURY SPAIN, gazpacho was made by blending stale bread with garlic and vinegar, then adding any available vegetables.

▶ Kale & Kielbasa Soup

Nothing warms up a cold winter evening like this hearty soup, and this one's an old-time favorite around the Baker house.

1 tbsp. of extra virgin olive oil

8 oz. of kielbasa or Italian sausage, thinly sliced

1 large leek (white and light green part), sliced

1 bunch of kale, rinsed, de-stemmed, and chopped

1 can (15.5-oz.) of white beans, rinsed and drained

3 cups of chicken broth

1 tbsp. of red-wine vinegar

½ tsp. of kosher or sea salt

Freshly ground black pepper to taste

Parmigiano Reggiano cheese, freshly grated

Heat the oil in a large, heavy saucepan over medium heat. Add the sausage and cook until browned (about 5 minutes). Add the leeks and cook for about three minutes, then add the kale and cook until it's wilted (about 3 minutes). Stir in the beans and broth, bring to a boil, then reduce the heat and simmer until the kale is tender (10 to 15 minutes). Stir in the vinegar, season with the salt and pepper, and ladle the soup into bowls. Serve the grated cheese in a bowl, so guests can sprinkle their soup to taste. Better yet, place a chunk of Parmigiano Reggiano on a plate with a hand grater, so guests can grate their own topping. **Yield:** *4 servings*

QUICK & QUIRKY

Hot & Sour Soup—Fast—For two to four servings, heat 2 cups of chicken broth, 2 tablespoons of rice vinegar, 1 tablespoon of chili-garlic sauce, and ½ tablespoon of grated ginger over medium heat. When it reaches a slow boil, mix in a beaten egg, and continue cooking for one or two minutes.

► Turkey Soup

This was Grandma Putt's go-to recipe for the day after Thanksgiving—and it's still mine, too!

1 leftover turkey carcass
2 tbsp. of white vinegar
2 cups of barley
4 carrots, sliced
3 ribs of celery, diced
2 large onions, diced
1 can (28 or 32 oz.) of diced
   tomatoes

VINEGAR IS THE SUPERSTAR in this recipe: It makes the turkey meat easier to remove from the bones and draws body-building calcium from the bones into the soup.

Put the carcass in a stockpot, cover it with water, and add the vinegar. Simmer, covered, for two hours, adding more water as needed. Remove the carcass, pull the meat from the bones, and put it back in the pot. Add the next four ingredients. Cook for 50 minutes, then stir in the tomatoes, and cook for 10 minutes. **Yield:** *6–8 servings*

► Tomato-Potato Basil Soup

America's two favorite vegetables—tomatoes and spuds—team up with basil in this super-simple soup.

1 lb. of tomatoes, peeled,
   seeded, and diced
¾ lb. of potatoes, peeled
   and diced
1 medium onion, diced

3 cups of chicken stock
⅓ cup of basil vinegar
¼ cup of fresh basil, minced
Salt and freshly ground
   black pepper to taste

Combine the first five ingredients in a large nonreactive pan. Cover it and bring the mixture to a boil over medium heat. Reduce the heat to low, and simmer for 30 minutes, or until the potatoes are very soft. Pour the soup into a blender and puree. Stir in the basil, salt, and pepper. **Yield:** *8–12 servings*

FOR GOOD LIVING

▶ Down-Home Ham Loaf

Back in Grandma Putt's day, when nothing went to waste, this was her favorite way to use leftover ham. (If you don't have any on hand, ask your local butcher to grind some for you.)

1½ lbs. of ground cooked ham	½ tsp. of Worcestershire sauce
½ onion, minced	Cooking spray
½ cup of cracker or	1½ cups of brown sugar
bread crumbs	½ cup of apple cider vinegar
½ cup of milk	½ cup of ketchup or chili sauce
2 eggs, beaten	1 tbsp. of Dijon or
½ tsp. of dry mustard	spicy brown mustard

Mix the first seven ingredients together in a large bowl, shape the mixture into a loaf, and set it in a loaf pan that you've lightly coated with cooking spray. Bake it at 350°F for about 40 to 50 minutes, or until the center is no longer pink. If the top of the loaf threatens to burn, cover it loosely with aluminum foil. Meanwhile, make the sauce by mixing the remaining ingredients together in a small pan over medium heat. Bring it to a boil, stirring well to dissolve the brown sugar. Reduce the heat and simmer for five minutes. Remove the pan from the stove and let it cool. When the loaf is done, remove it from the oven, let it sit for about 10 minutes, and transfer it to a serving platter. Cut the loaf into thick slices, and serve them drizzled with the sauce. **Yield:** *4–6 servings*

▶ Lemon Roasted Chicken

Lemon vinegar gives a moist, tender oomph to the classic baked bird. Here's the simple process.

1 whole chicken
(about 4 lbs.)

2 tbsp. of lemon
vinegar*

2 tbsp. of extra virgin
olive oil

½ tbsp. of sea salt

2 onions, quartered

1 bunch of fresh
tarragon, washed
and shaken dry

OLD-TIME
Vim
and
Vinegar

My Grandma Putt made the best-tasting hot dogs in town! And when I was old enough to start cooking them for myself, she let me in on her little secret: She always gave the wieners a few pokes with a fork, and then boiled them for a few minutes in water that had a table-spoon of vinegar added to it. Try it—you'll be amazed at the delicious difference it makes!

Rub the vinegar onto the chicken, inside and out. Follow up by brushing the olive oil onto the interior and exterior, and sprinkle the surfaces with the salt. Stuff the onion and tarragon into the cavity, tie the legs together, and set the bird breast side down on a rack in a shallow roasting pan. Roast, breast side down, at 400°F for 30 minutes. Then turn it breast side up and continue roasting for another 30 minutes or so, or until the skin is dark brown and crisp and the juices run clear when you pierce the thigh with a fork. Move the chicken to a platter, and wait about 10 minutes before carving and serving. * *Use either commercial or homemade vinegar following the basic instructions for making DIY vinegar in Chapter 3.* **Yield:** *4 servings*

► Glorious Beef Stew

This recipe has what Grandma Putt used to call a high glory factor. That simply means that when you serve it up to your guests (or even your picky kids), it rates "oohs and aahs" way out of proportion to the effort it took to make it.

2 lbs. of cubed stew beef, trimmed of fat

2 cups of fresh mushrooms, sliced

2 sweet onions, sliced

1 cup of beef stock

¼ cup of apple cider vinegar*

2 tbsp. of brown sugar

1 cup of sour cream

Chopped parsley for garnish (optional)

Mix the first six ingredients together in a Dutch oven or casserole dish, cover, and bake at 300°F for 1½ hours, or until the beef is fork-tender. Remove the dish from the oven and stir in the sour cream. Sprinkle the parsley on top, if desired, and serve immediately. *Or substitute garlic vinegar.* **Yield:** *6 servings*

► Fresh Trout with Vinegar Sauce

Attention, fly fishermen! This recipe is dedicated to you (but you folks who buy your trout at the local fish market will love it, too).

¼ cup of unbleached all-purpose flour

1 tsp. of salt

½ tsp. of freshly ground black pepper

4 rainbow trout

4 sprigs of rosemary

1 tbsp. of fresh lemon zest

1 tbsp. of extra virgin olive oil

2 garlic cloves, minced

¼ cup of rosemary white-wine vinegar*

¼ cup of dry vermouth

Combine the flour, salt, and pepper, and lightly dredge the trout in the mixture. Tuck a sprig of rosemary and a generous pinch of lemon zest into each fish. Warm the oil on medium heat in a nonreactive skillet, and sauté the trout on both sides until the fish is golden and flakes easily. Remove and set on a platter. Add the garlic and 1 tablespoon of the seasoned flour to the skillet. Cook, stirring constantly, until the garlic and flour are golden. Pour in the vinegar and vermouth, and cook, still stirring, until the mixture is slightly thickened. Pour the sauce over the fish, and serve immediately.

Or substitute rice vinegar. **Yield:** *4 servings*

> **AFTER DEEP-FRYING FISH,** lightly spray each still-hot piece with apple cider vinegar. Why? Because it'll moderate the fishy odor and also add a slightly tangy taste that everyone will enjoy.

VEGETABLES

▶ Roasted Balsamic Onions

Serve these sweet-and-tangy onions as a side dish or as a topping for pasta or baked potatoes.

3 large, sweet white onions, peeled and quartered*
¼ cup of balsamic vinegar
3 tbsp. of extra virgin olive oil
½ tsp. of sugar
Kosher salt and ground black pepper to taste

Mix all of the ingredients together in a large bowl. Spread them out in an even layer in a large, ovenproof skillet. Cover it with aluminum foil, and roast at 350°F for 20 to 25 minutes. Remove the foil, toss the onions to coat them with the sauce, and return the skillet to the oven, uncovered, for another 20 to 25 minutes.

Or substitute red onions. **Yield:** *4 servings*

▶ Dilly-Pepper Potatoes

This side dish may seem simple, but the dill-peppercorn vinegar makes these spuds superstars! Serve them with baked ham and a mixed-greens salad for a dinner your whole family will love.

¼ cup of extra virgin
    olive oil
1 lb. of small new
    red potatoes
3 tbsp. of dill-pepper-
    corn vinegar
3 tbsp. of fresh dill,
    minced
Salt and freshly
    ground black
    pepper to taste

Warm the oil over medium heat in a heavy, nonreactive skillet. Add the potatoes and sauté, stirring frequently, for about 15 minutes, until they're tender and lightly browned. Add the vinegar and cook for another 3 minutes. Sprinkle the dill over the potatoes, and season with salt and pepper. **Yield:** *4 servings*

▶ Grandma's Green Beans

Grandma Putt learned this recipe from her own grandma, and it sure made a vegetable lover out of me and my children—and my grandchildren, too! Trust me: It'll be love at first bite at your dinner table, too.

QUICK & QUIRKY

Marinated Stuffed Peppers— This old-time dish entails some waiting time, but it couldn't be quicker to make! Stuff large green peppers with coleslaw (vinegar-based, not the creamy slaw mixed with mayo). Stack the peppers in a stone crock, and cover them with white vinegar. Let 'em age for four weeks, then dig in!

2 or 3 slices of bacon,
cut into ½-inch pieces

3 tbsp. of chopped onion

2 cups of cooked green beans

2 tbsp. of white or apple
cider vinegar

1 tbsp. of sugar

Fry the bacon until crisp. Drain off the drippings, saving 1
tablespoon of it in the skillet. Sauté the onion in the grease
until tender. Mix in the beans, vinegar, and sugar. Cover and
cook over medium heat, stirring occasionally, until warmed.
Yield: *6–8 servings*

▶ Minty Carrots

Don't be surprised to
find Bugs Bunny himself
knocking on your door
when you whip up this
refreshing side dish!

1 lb. of baby carrots

1½ cups of water

½ cup of mint or
white-wine vinegar*

1 tbsp. of minced fresh
spearmint

½ tsp. of minced fresh thyme

Salt and freshly ground black pepper to taste

Word to 🦉 the Wise

Fortified vinegars are far more
than just flavorful dressings
and toppings (see "Instant
Gratification" on page 134).
These thick, creamy blends also
give you an easy, delicious way
to add more health-building
fruits and vegetables to your
(and your picky kids') diets.

Put the first five ingredients in a nonreactive pan. Bring
to a boil over medium heat, then reduce the heat and cook for
10 minutes, or until the carrots are tender. Serve warm
or chilled, seasoned with salt and pepper.
* *If you don't have mint-infused vinegar on hand, use 1½ tablespoons of minced fresh spearmint.* **Yield:** *4 servings*

FOR GOOD LIVING

INSTANT GRATIFICATION

A fortified vinegar is a thickened blend of vinegar mixed with herbs, spices, fruits, and/or vegetables. You whip it up in a blender or food processor and use it as a dip, salad dressing, or topping for anything from meat, pasta, and baked potatoes to your favorite desserts. As far as ingredients go, the sky's the limit, but these are some of my favorite combos:

Fortified Vinegar	Ingredients
Carrot	1 cup of sliced carrots, ½ cup of apple cider vinegar, ½ cup of water, 3–4 tbsp. of honey (optional)
Cucumber, celery & onion	1 large cucumber, 2 cups of chopped celery, 1 small chopped onion, 1 cup of champagne vinegar, 1 cup of water
Garlic	8 garlic bulbs, peeled, and 1 cup of apple cider vinegar
Honeydew	2 cups of chopped honeydew melon, ¼ cup of champagne vinegar, ¼ cup of water
Kale-mustard	2 cups of kale, ¼ cup of apple cider vinegar, ¼ cup of water, 2 tbsp. of dry mustard
Lemon	1 whole lemon (including peel), chopped; 2 tbsp. of champagne vinegar; ½ cup of water
Mint	2 cups of fresh mint leaves, 1 cup of malt or red-wine vinegar, 2 tbsp. of honey
Parsley	2 cups of fresh parsley, ½ cup of red-wine vinegar, ½ cup of water
Raspberry	1 cup of raspberries (fresh or frozen) and 3 tbsp. of red-wine vinegar
Strawberry	2 cups of fresh strawberries, 1 cup of sugar, ½ cup of champagne vinegar

▶ Classic Coarse-Grained Mustard

Just like ketchup, homemade mustard is better than anything you'll find on store shelves—and it's a snap to make. This full-bodied blend is one of my favorites. It's delicious on burgers and sandwiches of all kinds, and it adds the perfect touch to the Zesty Coleslaw recipe on page 122.

½ cup of white or malt vinegar

¼ cup of beer*

¼ cup of brown mustard seeds

¼ cup of yellow (a.k.a. white) mustard seeds

Pinch of kosher or sea salt

1 tbsp. of brown sugar

In a small nonreactive bowl, combine the first five ingredients. Cover the bowl, and let it sit for about 24 hours. Then add the brown sugar, and blend the mixture in a blender or food processor until combined. Pour it into a sterilized jar, and store it in the refrigerator for at least a day or so before serving so that the flavors can blend. Tightly covered, it'll keep for up to one month. *I prefer a hearty brown ale, but use whatever kind of beer you fancy.* **Yield:** *About 1½ cups*

Word to the Wise

Perk up and personalize commercial mayonnaise and creamy salad dressings by spiking them with herb-infused vinegar—either store-bought or your own homemade creation.

FOR GOOD LIVING

► Big Apple Hot Dog Topping

This classic condiment has been a mainstay of New York City hot dog vendors—and their customers—for a century or more.

2 large onions, thinly sliced (about 2 cups)

⅓ cup of ketchup

1 tbsp. of apple cider vinegar

1 tbsp. of water

¾ tsp. of sugar

Mix all of the ingredients in a pan, and simmer until the onions are translucent. Pour the mixture into a covered container, and store it in the refrigerator. **Yield:** *½ cup*

► Sweet-and-Tangy Barbecue Sauce

If you prefer a barbecue sauce that's zesty rather than steamy hot, then this recipe's for you. It's perfect on beef, pork, or poultry, or even as a topping for baked potatoes.

1 cup of ketchup

½ cup of orange juice

⅓ cup of molasses

¼ cup of balsamic vinegar

Juice of 2 limes

2 tbsp. of brown sugar, lightly packed

1½ tbsp. of minced fresh ginger

1 tbsp. of chili powder

½ tsp. of salt

> **ANY BASTING SAUCE THAT CONTAINS** sugar, honey, molasses, or fruit juice should be applied after the food is partially cooked. Otherwise, the sauce will burn before the vittles are done!

Mix all of the ingredients together in a saucepan over medium heat. Simmer for 15 minutes, stirring occasionally. Remove from the heat and cool to room temperature. Store the sauce, covered, in the refrigerator, where it will keep for about three weeks. **Yield:** *About 2 ½ cups*

▶ Mango Chutney

Talk about versatile condiments! This fruity blend has a sweet-and-savory bite that makes it a perfect companion for seafood, poultry, beef, or pork. It also boosts the flavor of cold cuts in a sandwich, and it's delicious when paired with cream cheese on a toasted bagel.

1 cup of sugar
½ cup of white or
  apple cider vinegar
2 mangoes, peeled,
  pitted, and cut into
  ¾-inch pieces
1 small onion, chopped
¼ cup of golden raisins
2 tbsp. of crystallized
  ginger, finely chopped
2 garlic cloves, minced

Combine the sugar and vinegar in a 6-quart pot, and bring the mixture to a boil, stirring until the sugar has dissolved. Add the remaining ingredients, and simmer, stirring occasionally, for 60 minutes, until it reaches a slightly thickened, syrupy consistency. Pour it into sterilized jars, and store in a cool, dark place, where it should keep for up to 1 year. After the jar has been opened, store the chutney in the refrigerator. It should stay fine for months, but if you detect an "off" odor, appearance, or flavor, toss the jar in the trash. **Yield:** *6 cups*

That's Historical

If you think chutney is a fancy concoction that modern-day foodies came up with, think again. In fact, we owe this sophisticated and versatile condiment to the British troops who extended the Empire into India in the 18th century. Three factors contributed to the development of chutney: the Brits' love of sweet sauces; the presence of foods rarely seen in England, such as mangoes, ginger, allspice, and non-malt vinegar; and the need to preserve food on long sea voyages, with no refrigeration.

SNACKS & PARTY FOOD

▶ **Wonderful Walnut Dip**

Your guests will go wild for this scrumptious (and healthy) dip.

1½ cups of toasted walnut pieces*	1 tsp. of kosher salt
1 tbsp. of olive oil	½ tsp. of pepper
1 tbsp. of sherry vinegar	3–5 tbsp. of water
Juice of 1 small lemon	3 tbsp. of chopped fresh chives
1 tsp. of Dijon mustard	Walnut pieces

Put the first seven ingredients and 3 tablespoons of water in a food processor and process until smooth, adding more water if necessary. Stir in 2 tablespoons of chives, pour the dip into a bowl, and garnish with walnuts and additional chives. Serve with raw vegetables. *Spread the nuts in a single layer on a baking sheet, and bake at 350°F, stirring once, until lightly browned (10 to 12 minutes).* **Yield:** *About 2 cups*

▶ **Avocado-Cucumber Salsa**

Here's a salsa you can't buy in stores, and it makes a refreshing change of pace from the standard tomato-based kinds.

1 ripe avocado, peeled and diced	¼ cup of minced red onion
1 small cucumber, peeled and diced	2 tbsp. of lemon vinegar
	2 tbsp. of minced cilantro
1 chili pepper, seeded and minced (optional)	1 tbsp. of lime juice
	Salt to taste

Toss all of the ingredients together in a bowl. Serve immediately with crunchy tortilla chips (it's especially good with the blue corn variety), or refrigerate until ready to use. It will stay fresh and—thanks to the citrus juice—should keep its color for up to two days. **Yield:** *About 2 cups*

▶ Texas Caviar

No party in the Lone Star State would be complete without this kissin' cousin to bean salsa—and once you've tasted it, you'll know why! As with any folk recipe, there are many variations, but this is one of my favorites.

2 cans (15.5 oz. each) of black-eyed peas, drained and rinsed

2 medium ripe tomatoes, chopped

1 small red bell pepper, finely chopped

1 or 2 jalapeño peppers, finely chopped

¼ red onion, finely chopped

¼ cup of fresh parsley, coarsely chopped

¼ cup of red-wine vinegar

2 tbsp. of extra virgin olive oil

3 garlic cloves, minced

Kosher or sea salt and freshly ground black pepper to taste

> **HAVE A BALL!**
> Namely, this cheese ball. It'll be the hit of any party—guaranteed! To make it, mix 8 ounces of grated Swiss cheese, 3 ounces of softened cream cheese, ½ cup of grated apple, ½ cup of finely chopped pecans, 3 tablespoons of sage apple cider vinegar, and 3 tablespoons of minced fresh sage in a food processor. Then form the mixture into a ball (adding more vinegar if it seems too dry), and roll it in additional finely chopped pecans. Cover and refrigerate for several hours before serving it with crackers, melba toast, or apple slices. **Note:** *If you like, substitute chopped walnuts for the pecans.*

Mix the first nine ingredients together in a bowl, and season with the salt and pepper. Cover with plastic wrap, and refrigerate for at least 2 hours and up to 48 hours (but it'll never last that long). **Yield:** *6 servings*

▶ Marinated Olives

These tasty (and healthy) tidbits beat anything you'll find in a fancy food shop. They're terrific either eaten as snacks or added to recipes—and they couldn't be simpler to make.

4 cups of assorted olives
(such as kalamata,
manzanilla, or
pimiento-stuffed)

1 tbsp. of lemon peel,
cut into thin strips

1 tbsp. of orange
peel, cut into
thin strips

1 tbsp. of red pepper,
cut into thin strips

2 garlic cloves, minced

1 sprig of fresh or 1 tbsp.
of dried oregano

¼ tsp. of dried red-pepper flakes
(optional)

½ cup of balsamic vinegar

½ cup of extra virgin olive oil

QUICK & QUIRKY

Apricot Dipping Sauce—
Looking for an out-of-the-ordinary dip to serve with chicken wings or chicken strips? Look no further! Just mix 1 cup of apricot preserves, 2 tablespoons of balsamic vinegar, and 1 tablespoon of soy sauce in a glass bowl. You won't believe that anything so delicious could be so easy to make!

Drain off any brining liquid, rinse the olives, and put them in a large jar, along with the next six ingredients. Whisk the vinegar and oil in a bowl, and pour just enough of the mixture into the jar to cover the olives. Put the lid on the jar and shake it to mix the contents. Then stash the olives in the refrigerator. You can use them right away if you really need to, but they'll reach their peak of flavor after two weeks or so. **Yield:** *About 1 quart*

▶ **Berry Fine Berry Beverage**

This refreshing drink is a cooling summertime treat served over crushed ice. And minus the ice, it's also delicious poured over fruit salad or brushed onto grilled chicken.

8 cups of ripe blackberries, blueberries, raspberries, or strawberries	1 qt. of apple cider vinegar 4 cups of sugar

Crush the berries and mix them with the vinegar and 1 cup of the sugar in a nonreactive bowl. Cover it and set it in the refrigerator for about 48 hours. Press the berries through a strainer, reserving the juice and discarding the pulp. Pour the liquid into a nonreactive pan, add the remaining sugar, and bring the mixture to a boil. Reduce the heat, and simmer for eight minutes, skimming off any foam. Remove the pan from the stove, let the juice cool, and ladle it into sterilized bottles. Store them in the refrigerator for two to three months. **Yield:** *3 quarts*

▶ **Balsamic Lemonade**

When the dog days of summer are dragging you down, try this new twist on the refreshing summertime classic.

1 cup of freshly squeezed lemon juice (about 10 lemons) ¾ cup of superfine sugar 4 cups of water	1–2 tsp. of balsamic vinegar to taste 1 cup of vodka (optional)

Mix the juice, sugar, and water in a large pitcher. Add the vinegar and stir. Add the vodka, if desired, and pour the lemonade into ice-filled glasses. **Yield:** *4–6 servings*

FOR GOOD LIVING

▶ Peach Shrub Syrup

No, this isn't a stray tip from one of my gardening books. Rather, it's just one example of a libation that dates back to Colonial times, when our ancestors used vinegar to preserve seasonal fruits. Like many old-time treats, shrubs went out of vogue early in the 20th century, but in the past few years, they've staged a big-time comeback in trendy cocktail bars from coast to coast.

>   1 cup of fresh, ripe
>   peaches, peeled,
>   chopped, and mashed*
>   1 cup of sugar
>   1 cup of white balsamic
>   vinegar*

Mix all of the ingredients together in a pan, bring them to a very brief boil, then simmer for at least 10 to 20 minutes, stirring frequently. Once the sugar has melted, and the vinegar has a very strong peach flavor, remove the pan from the heat. Strain it two or three times through a sieve or cheesecloth. Let the syrup cool, pour it into a sterilized bottle, and store it in the refrigerator, where it'll keep for a month or so. Use it in shrub cocktails (see "A Peach of a Pair," above). Or simply put a tablespoon or so of the syrup into a tall glass, and fill it up

A PEACH OF A PAIR

Here are two ways to serve peach shrub syrup at your next neighborhood get-together—or simply enjoy it as you relax on your deck on a summer evening.

▶ **Peach & bourbon cocktail.** Mix 2 ounces of bourbon, ¾ ounce of cherry liqueur, ¾ ounce of peach shrub syrup, and a dash of absinthe in an ice-filled cocktail shaker. Shake well, and strain into a chilled cocktail glass.

▶ **Peach mocktail.** Put 3 key limes (quartered) and 8 fresh mint leaves in a cocktail shaker, and muddle them. Add 1 ounce of peach shrub syrup and ice,  and shake, shake, shake. Strain into a tall, ice-filled glass, and top with ginger ale.

with fizzy water and ice.
*Substitute any fruit and
vinegar combo you fancy.*
Yield: *About 2 cups*

▶ Chocolate Cooler

What do you serve to a
lactose-intolerant child
(or grown-up) who loves
chocolate milk? This yummy
stand-in—that's what!

> ¼ cup of balsamic
>   vinegar
> 1 cup of dark chocolate
>   chips
> Sparkling water
> 1–2 oz. of vodka
>   (optional)

Combine the vinegar and
chocolate chips in a small
saucepan, and warm the
mixture over medium heat
until the chocolate melts.
Then whisk the mixture
until it's smooth. Put 2 to
3 tablespoons of the blend
into each tall glass, mix it
with sparkling water, and
add ice. For the adult version, add vodka to taste, if
desired. **Yield:** *4–6 servings*

OLD-TIME Vim and Vinegar

Long before commercial
sports drinks came along,
folks quenched their hot-
weather thirst with a DIY
beverage called summer
switchel. To make it, put 1
cup of apple cider vinegar,
1 cup of honey or pure
maple syrup, ¼ cup of mo-
lasses, and 1 tablespoon
of ground ginger (or less
to taste) in a 1-gallon jar
or jug. Add 2 or 3 cups
of warm water to dissolve
the honey and molasses.
Then fill the balance of the
container with cold water.
Stir or shake vigorously to
combine the ingredients,
and pour the libation into
ice-filled glasses. Garnish
with fresh lemon slices,
and drink a toast to the
good old summertime!
Note: *With a shot of dark
rum added, switchel makes
a dandy cocktail—in sum-
mer or winter.*

FOR GOOD LIVING

▶ Vinegar Pie Crust

Although this flaky, delicious pastry shell is "camped out" with the desserts, it works just as well for quiches and other savory pies.

2 cups of all-purpose flour	¼ cup (scant) of water
1 ½ tbsp. of sugar	½ tbsp. of white or apple
1 tsp. of salt	cider vinegar
½ cup of vegetable oil	1 egg

In a medium-size bowl, combine the first three ingredients thoroughly. Form a well in the center. Then add the remaining ingredients to the well and stir vigorously, moving outward from the center until they've all been incorporated. Crumble the pastry* into an ungreased metal (not glass) pie plate and press it into place with your fingers or the back of a spoon. Prick it well on the bottom and sides with a fork, then bake it at 325°F for five to seven minutes. Remove it from the oven, add your filler of choice, and continue baking according to your recipe instructions. * *It's impossible to roll this dough out, so you need to treat it as you would a graham cracker or cookie-crumb crust.* **Yield:** *1 pie crust*

▶ Old-Time Vinegar & Molasses Taffy

Taffy pulls were popular forms of entertainment back in the Roaring Twenties—which is when this recipe originated.

2 cups of molasses	1 tsp. of white or apple
1 cup of sugar	cider vinegar
1 tbsp. of butter	

Mix all of the ingredients together in a saucepan and boil for 20 minutes, stirring constantly. Then beat the mixture by hand until it's smooth and creamy, and pour it into a buttered 8- by 8-inch pan.

When the batter is cool enough to handle, pull it into long strips until the candy is satiny and light-colored. Cut the strips into desired lengths. Wrap individual pieces in wax paper and store them in an airtight container. **Yield:** *About 1 pound*

▶ Very Fine Vinegar Fruitcake

If you consider traditional fruitcake to be a Christmastime menace, give this version a try. Everyone on your gift list will love it, and so will you—guaranteed!

1 cup of milk
3 tbsp. of white or
    apple cider vinegar
1 tsp. of baking soda
¾ cup of butter, softened
¾ cup of brown sugar
1 cup plus 2 tbsp. of flour
1 cup of candied cherries
1 cup of candied mixed
    fruit or pineapple
1 tsp. of cinnamon

Mix the milk and vinegar together in a large bowl. Then stir in the baking soda. In another bowl, combine the butter, sugar, and flour. Add the fruit and cinnamon and stir. Fold in the milk and vinegar mixture and beat thoroughly. Pour the batter into a greased 8- by 8-inch pan and bake at 350°F for 60 minutes.
Yield: *9–12 servings*

A LIGHT AND SWEET HOLIDAY TREAT

It seems that between Thanksgiving and New Year's Day, the heavy, calorie-laden desserts never stop coming. So at your next winter holiday gathering, offer your guests a change of pace with a seasonal fruit salad featuring pears, tart apples, and grapes topped with a dressing made from 2 parts honey to 1 part balsamic vinegar. It makes an especially useful addition to a buffet because—thanks to the vinegar—it can sit on the table without the fruit turning brown.

FOR GOOD LIVING

▶ Strawberry-Balsamic Pie

When it comes to super-star combos, balsamic vinegar and strawberries rank right up there with Fred Astaire and Ginger Rogers. And the duo turns out a mighty fine perfor-mance in this variation on the classic custard pie.

⅓ cup of butter

2 eggs

½ cup of water

¼ cup of balsamic vinegar

1 cup of sugar

3 tbsp. of flour

10–12 firm, ripe strawberries

8- or 9-inch prepared pastry shell*

OLD-TIME
Vim and *Vinegar*

Rats! You cut into a melon only to find that its flavor was not quite up to snuff. Well, don't toss it out! Grandma Putt would have thrown a major hissy fit even thinking about that kind of waste. Here's what she would do instead: Put some life back into that fruit by dousing each slice with honey-sweetened thyme vinegar. Your fami-ly's taste buds will leap to attention!

Melt the butter over low heat and set it aside to cool. In a small bowl, beat the eggs until they're frothy. Add the butter, water, and vinegar, and stir until thoroughly blended. Mix the sugar and flour in another bowl, then add the liquid ingredients and beat well. Fold in the strawberries, and pour the whole thing into the pie shell. Bake at 325°F for about 60 minutes, or until a knife inserted in the center comes out clean. Serve warm or at room temperature, and refrigerate any leftovers. *See the recipe for Vinegar Pie Crust on page 144.* **Yield:** *1 pie*

▶ Bread & Butter Pickles

This is *the* classic American pickle. And like just about any other taste treat, your own homemade version beats store-bought brands hands down.

1 ½–2 lbs. of pickling cucumbers, cut into ¼-inch slices

1 ½ tbsp. of pickling or kosher salt

1 large onion, thinly sliced

1 cup of sugar

1 cup of white vinegar

½ cup of apple cider vinegar

1 ½ tsp. of mustard seeds

½ tsp. of celery seeds

⅛ tsp. of turmeric

Toss the cukes and salt in a large, shallow bowl, then cover and refrigerate it for about 90 minutes. Rinse off the salt. Drain the cucumbers, and mix them with the onions in a nonreactive bowl. Combine the remaining ingredients in a saucepan, and bring the mixture to a simmer over medium heat. Stir to dissolve the sugar, then pour the hot mixture over the vegetables, and let them sit at room temperature for 60 minutes. Cover and refrigerate overnight. Store the pickles in airtight, sterilized containers in the refrigerator for up to four weeks.

Yield: *About 2 quarts*

Word to the Wise

If you see bubbles in any pickled or canned food, it means that the jar contains either air or bacteria, and the contents are not safe to eat. So toss the vittles in the trash, and sterilize the jar before you use it again, even for dry storage.

TROUBLESHOOTING PICKLES

Pickling foods is just like anything else in life: The more you do it, the better results you'll have. Use this handy guide to diagnose any problems that crop up:

If the Pickles Are...	The Problem Is...
Tough	You used too much salt.
Shriveled	You used too much sugar.
Tough and shriveled	You used too much vinegar.
Soft	You used too little salt.
Cloudy	You used table salt, which contains starch.*
Hollow	The cucumbers were too old.
Off-color	Water has a high mineral content, or you used a copper kettle.
Slippery	The pickles spent too little time in the brine solution.
Mushy	The pickles were cooked too long.

To keep the brine clear, always use either pickling, kosher, or sea salt.

▶ Cooling Pickled Chard Stalks

Before summertime sets in, make up a batch or two of these ultra-simple pickles and keep them in the fridge. They'll cool you down fast when the weather turns steamy and also give you a healthy dose of probiotics that'll help keep your digestive system running smoothly.

1 bunch of Swiss chard stalks

2 cups of hot water

1 cup of unfiltered
   apple cider vinegar

3 tbsp. of raw honey

3 tbsp. of Sriracha sauce*

Glass canning jars

Cut the stalks about an inch shorter than the depth of the jars, and pack them in tightly. Mix the remaining ingredients together in a bowl, stirring until the honey dissolves. Pour the mixture over the stems so they're completely covered. Close the jars tightly, and store them in the refrigerator for at least a week to let the flavor develop fully. These pickles will keep in the fridge for up to a year as long as the stems are completely covered with vinegar. *Available in the Asian-food sections of most supermarkets and online. Or substitute your favorite hot sauce.* **Yield:** *About 3 one-quart jars*

▶ Pickled Sliced Onions

These savory rings are classic British pub fare. They're delicious on burgers and all kinds of hearty sandwiches, and they make an amazingly flavorful topping for baked potatoes or cold pasta salad.

1 ½ tsp. of whole mustard seeds	2 lbs. of sweet or red onions, thinly sliced and separated into rings
1 ½ tsp. of whole peppercorns	
1 bay leaf	
3 cups of malt vinegar*	

Simmer the spices in the vinegar for 20 minutes, and then strain them out. Blanch the onion rings in a pot of boiling water for 20 seconds. Strain, and let the onions sit until they're cool enough to handle. Pack them firmly into sterilized glass jars, and pour in the warm, strained vinegar so that it completely covers the onions. Put the lids on the jars, and stash them in the refrigerator for at least a week so that the onions develop their full flavor. They'll keep in the fridge for at least a year, as long as they're completely covered with vinegar. *Malt is the traditional choice, but if you prefer another type of vinegar, go for it!* **Yield:** *About 2 quarts*

FOR THE LONG HAUL

To store condiments or pickled foods at room temperature almost indefinitely, use the boiling-water canning method. This may sound intimidating if you've never done it before, but don't worry—it's actually quite easy! Here's all there is to it:

▶ Ladle, pour, or pack the prepared ingredients into hot, sterilized canning jars, leaving ¼ inch of space at the top.

▶ Wipe the jar rims with a damp cloth, and attach the two-piece lids.

▶ Put the jars on a rack in a large, deep pot that's no more than 4 inches larger in diameter than the stove burner. If you don't have a canning rack, don't fret. Just DIY with some unused canning jar rings held together with plastic zip ties.

▶ Pour in enough boiling water to cover the lids by 2 inches, and add a tablespoon or two of white vinegar to keep hard-water deposits from forming on the jars' sealers.

▶ Cover the pot, bring it to a hard boil, and boil for 15 minutes, lowering the heat if necessary to keep the water from overflowing. Then carefully remove the hot jars and set them on a rack or dish towels to cool. Again, it's fine to improvise if you don't have a jar lifter. Just wrap some rubber bands around the ends of your kitchen tongs.

▶ Wipe the jars with white vinegar to remove any food residue. Then label them, and store them in a dry place that's well removed from any heat source, such as a furnace, water heater, or hot-water pipes.

▶ Wait at least 30 days before using, so the flavors can blend, and refrigerate after opening.

 **Note:** *Always use either Mason or Ball® jars that are specifically designed for home canning. Commercial-food jars can't handle the necessary heat, and their mouths will not generally accept the two-piece sealing lids.*

part TWO
Inside Your Home

Judging from all the hoopla you see on TV, you'd think that nobody could possibly survive without cupboards full of special "miracle" products that do everything from scrubbing floors to polishing furniture, washing clothes, and deodorizing our homes from top to bottom. Well, I have news for the folks who make and sell all that stuff: Long before chemists started dreaming up these expensive, and often noxious, concoctions, people were using good old vinegar to spruce up the whole house and just about everything in it. And that's what this part of the book is all about. But the focus isn't only on work—far from it! You'll learn how vinegar can play a key role in home-decorating projects and holiday celebrations, as well as fun times and special treats for the kids and critters in your life.

chapter five ▶ KITCHEN & BATHROOM

If your home is like most, it's a sure bet that the kitchen and bathroom pose some of the most daunting cleaning challenges of all. Well, never fear: No matter what kind of grease, grime, or grit you're dealing with, vinegar can rise to the occasion. In this chapter, I'll remind you of some of the ways that your grandma—and her grandma—put this powerhouse to work. You'll also learn some terrific tips for using vinegar to solve problems that didn't even exist in the days when those wise and lovely ladies were ruling the roost!

KITCHEN APPLIANCES

Potent Porcelain Stove Cleaner

Here's an all-purpose potion that's so darn good, it'll spiff up your entire porcelain stove—including the oven! To put it to work at your place, follow this process:

Fill a spray bottle with 2 teaspoons of white vinegar, 1 teaspoon of borax, ½ teaspoon of baking soda, a squirt of grease-cutting dishwashing liquid, and 2 cups of water. Shake it well to blend the ingredients.

Spray and wipe your porcelain stove top, drip pans, gas burner grates, oven, and even the glass windows in your oven door. (Make sure all the surfaces are cool first!)

For dried-on spills, soak the spots with the potion, and wait about 15 minutes or so before wiping it off.

Shake the bottle frequently as you work, and store it in a cool cabinet between uses.

STAINLESS STEEL APPLIANCES WILL STAY SPOTLESS and gleaming if you wipe the surfaces periodically with a sponge or soft cloth dampened with a little vinegar.

Note: *Do not use this formula on stainless steel appliances or smooth-surface cooktops because it could scratch them.*

Smooth-Top Stove Cleaner

If you have a smooth-top range, you know that these glass or ceramic surfaces seem to pick up scratches if you even come close to them with a commercial cleanser—much less use it! So how do you keep your old (or new) smoothie clean and bright without risking damage to the surface? Here's how:

- Mix ¼ cup of white vinegar and 2 to 4 drops of lemon oil in a small spray bottle. (You can find essential oils of all kinds in health-food stores or the health-food section of most supermarkets.)

- Sprinkle baking soda over the dirty areas of the stove top, and spray the vinegar and oil over the soda. (It will fizz.)

- Wait for 5 to 10 minutes until the mixture becomes pasty, and wipe it away with a soft, damp cloth. The dirt will go with it, but your stove top's sparkly shine will stay!

Vim *and* Vinegar

There are scads of commercial degreasers on the market—but not one of 'em cuts through grease and oil splatters any better—or faster—than Grandma Putt's favorite formula. To make it, mix 2 cups of white vinegar and ½ cup of lemon juice together in a spray bottle. Keep it in the kitchen, and the minute any grease spills onto your stove, in your oven, or on any other surface, spritz it with the solution and wipe it away with a paper towel. (Wait until the stove top or oven has cooled down first!)

Range Hood Degreaser

Oily molecules that go airborne when you're cooking invariably crash-land on the range hood, where they harden into a layer that takes a ton of elbow grease to remove. So to keep the crud (and your workload) to a minimum, wipe your hood down every week or so with a spray made from 1 cup of white vinegar and ½ cup of baking soda per 2 cups of hot water. Simply spritz the potion onto the hood, inside and out, and wipe the greasy film away. Rinse off the residue with a damp cloth, and the hood will be ready to ride the range again!

The Flame Won't Light!

When you push the ignition button on your gas stove and nothing happens, don't panic. There's a good chance that the problem is merely a clogged igniter head. When dirt builds up—as it always does over time—it blocks the spark between the burner and an electrode that kicks it into action. The simple solution: Turn off the gas and remove the burner head. Dip the head of a retired toothbrush in white vinegar and scrub until the crud washes away.

Oven Bath Time, Over Easy

There's no doubt about it: Commercial oven cleaners rank among the nastiest, smelliest chemical concoctions on the planet. But you can breathe easy because here's the good news—you don't need the foul things! This simple process will get that old (or new) baker spic-and-span with no unpleasant side effects.

STEP 1. Heat the oven to 350°F and leave it on for about five minutes. While it's warming up, mix 5 tablespoons of baking soda, 4 tablespoons of white vinegar, and a few drops of dishwashing liquid to make a thick paste. (Multiply the recipe if necessary to cover an extra-large or extra-dirty oven.)

STEP 2. When the five minutes are up, turn the oven off, and carefully spread the paste across the floor and walls of the oven, concentrating on any especially grimy spots.

STEP 3. Wait 60 minutes or so, and then scrub with a sponge or plastic scouring pad. Wipe the crud away, and rinse thoroughly with clear water.

STEP 4. Dampen a clean sponge with full-strength vinegar, and wipe down the whole oven to prevent future greasy buildup.

Word to the Wise

If you have a newer oven that has concealed heating elements, be aware that (according to appliance repairmen) using the ultra-hot self-cleaning feature can—and frequently does—result in expensive damage to the oven. Fortunately, it's a snap to clean the free and clear interior using old-fashioned vinegar and baking soda.

INSIDE YOUR HOME

Rack 'Em Up

Whether you clean your oven the old-fashioned way, or let the appliance do the honors itself, you still need to tackle the racks. That's because if you leave them in the oven while the self-cleaning process is under way, the ultra-high heat could easily warp the metal. So after you've removed those grates, give them a no-mess bath this way:

- Put each rack in a large, heavy-duty plastic trash bag.

- Add 1 cup of white vinegar, ⅓ cup of dishwashing liquid, and enough hot water to almost fill the sack.

- Then seal the bag tightly and put it in a bathtub full of warm water for 60 minutes or so.

- Remove the rack from its bag and scrub it with a scouring pad or brush. Then rinse the rack with clear water and let it air-dry.

And there you go—spankin' clean oven racks with no greasy bathtub or mess to clean up!

QUICK & QUIRKY

Deal with the Door—To clean the grease-splattered window on your oven door, simply open the door and saturate the glass with full-strength vinegar. Let it sit, open, for 10 to 15 minutes, and then wipe the grease away with a damp sponge. If necessary, repeat the process until you can see through the glass clearly.

Mop Up Microwave Messes

When food grime builds up in your microwave, here's an almost effortless way to clear it out: Pour 2 cups of water and ½ cup of vinegar into a microwave-safe bowl, and put it in the heating chamber. Nuke it on high for three to four minutes, or until the water starts to boil. Let it sit for another three to four minutes, with the door closed, so the steam can loosen the food gunk. Then open the door, remove the bowl, and wipe the compartment clean with a damp sponge.

Focus on the Fridge

To keep your refrigerator clean and odor-free, simply wipe the shelves and walls every week or so with a half-and-half solution of vinegar and water. This same mixture should work just fine outside the fridge, too—except for the top, which always seems to collect a solid coat of grime no matter how often you wipe it off. For that grubby surface, use paper towels or a cloth dipped in full-strength vinegar.

Sack Sticky Spills

To loosen up food residue that's stuck to the inside of your refrigerator, heat ½ cup of white or apple cider vinegar in the microwave or on the stove top. Then pour it into a small, heat-proof bowl, and set it in the fridge for about five minutes. The steaming vinegar will unstick the gunk, and you can just wipe it away. The inside of the appliance will look like new again, and any lingering odors will be gone!

Withdraw Your Deposits

A lot of water runs through the average dishwasher, and the minerals in that fluid can make a mess of your dishwasher's heating element—and leave you with a hefty repair bill if you don't take action. So hop to it this way: Make a paste of white vinegar and baking soda, and wipe it generously onto the area. Rinse with full-strength vinegar, and your cleanup helper will be back in business.

When the Spray Arm Simply Sputters...

It's probably jammed with mineral deposits and food residue. To clean out the crud, first remove the dish racks, and then take out the screws that hold the arm in place. Lift it off, and lay it flat on a counter. Then poke a strand of thin wire into each hole. When you're through, give the arm a gentle shake to make sure nothing else is caught in there, and then scrub away the mineral deposits with a solution of vinegar and hot water.

Wash Your Dishwasher

A couple of times a year, stand 1 cup of vinegar in the upper rack and 1 cup of vinegar in the lower rack, along with a full load of dishes. Run the machine as usual. The vinegar will be dispersed throughout the mechanism, removing any mineral deposits and soap residue. Think of this routine as the equivalent of

That's Historical

In olden days, commercial vinegars didn't look anything like the clear, filtered, pasteurized versions sold in the supermarket today. In fact, they were so thick with sediment and sometimes flavorings that they were often dehydrated and sold as vinegar sticky balls. Travelers took these dried globs on their voyages and tucked them away on cupboard shelves. Then, when the need arose, they mixed the balls with water to make—voilá—instant vinegar!

your car's 15,000-mile checkup—it's just what your dishwasher needs to keep on truckin' for miles.

Ice Is Nice

Here's an icy-hot tip for you: Always keep a tray of vinegar ice cubes in your freezer, and use them once a week in these two ways:

- Run three or four cubes through your garbage disposal, and let the cold water flow for a minute or so afterward. The grinding of ice on blades will remove any clinging food particles, and the vinegar will eliminate odors.

- Pop a couple of cubes into the dishwasher just before you start a cycle. The vinegar will keep the machine's interior both stain- and odor-free.

Unlock Your Disposal

Drat! Your garbage disposal won't dispose of anything because the mechanism is clogged. Well, before you do anything drastic, try this simple remedy: Just mix up equal parts of vinegar, salt, and baking soda. Pour the concoction directly into the drain, and let it sit for 10 to 15 minutes. Then rinse with 2 cups of boiling water to clear things up.

And from now on, kick the habit that probably gummed up the works to begin with—namely, using hot water when you run your garbage disposal. Why? Because no matter how careful you are to avoid sending grease into the unit, some of the foods that you do

TO REMOVE THE CHALKY DEPOSITS THAT A DISHWASHER OFTEN DELIVERS, put the "victims" on the lower rack, and run the machine for about five minutes with 1 cup of vinegar. Follow up with a complete cycle using your regular detergent. Your dishes will come out sparkling clean with no elbow grease needed!

grind up are bound to contain certain amounts of fat, and the hot water will melt it. Eventually, it will harden way down inside and block the mechanism. So always run cold water when you're grinding up your dinner remains, and keep that chilly stream flowing for at least 60 seconds after you flick off the switch.

Give It Lip Service

How often do you clean the underside of the rubber lip that guards the opening to your garbage disposal? If you answered "Huh?" then this tip's for you: Once a week or so, reach under there, and wash the rubber with the rough side of a scrubbing sponge dipped in vinegar. It'll eliminate odor-causing crud and bacteria that build up in that out-of-sight, out-of-mind spot. **Note:** *Needless to say (I hope!), make sure the disposal is turned off before you even touch that lip!*

Rejuvenate the Java Flava!

If your electric coffeemaker is producing java that tastes bitter or sour, here's your quick fix:

- Fill the well to capacity with a half-and-half solution of water and white vinegar.

Word to the Wise

If you have a new, upscale coffeemaker, consult your owner's manual before you run vinegar through the machine. If the technique is not approved, you could void the manufacturer's warranty.

- Install an empty filter to catch any crud that comes out, and run the machine through a normal brewing cycle.

- "Brew" three or four batches of clear, fresh water to remove all traces of vinegar.

As you might expect, how often you need to perform this purifying routine depends on the quality of your water and how much coffee you make—so just trust your taste buds to tell you when it's time.

Caring for Your Keurig

Keurig® brewers have attracted a large and loyal following because of their ability to produce a single cup of coffee, tea, or hot chocolate at the press of a button (provided, of course, that you've inserted the appropriate "pod" containing your beverage of choice). One key to keeping your Keurig crankin' out cuppas is to de-scale it on a regular basis. To do that, fill the water reservoir halfway with white vinegar and run the brewer (minus K-Cup®) through several brewing cycles until the container is empty. Then rinse it, fill it with clear water, and run it again until all the water is gone. As with regular coffeemakers, how often you need to perform this chore depends on how much you use the machine and how hard your water is. Some models have an indicator light that goes on when it's time for de-scaling. If your machine is lightless, let your taste buds be your guide.

FANTASTIC FORMULA

DIY Do-It-All Cleaner

Who needs those expensive "miracle" spray cleaners? This old-time recipe cleans floors, greasy countertops, kitchen and bathroom fixtures, as well as appliances—both large and small. It even kills mildew. What's more, there's no need to rinse!

1 cup of clear ammonia

½ cup of white vinegar

¼ cup of baking soda

1 gal. of hot water

Mix all of the ingredients together in a bucket. Then pour the solution into a spray bottle and go to town. Or, if you'd prefer, mop or sponge it on straight from the pail.

Do a Clog Dance

No matter how careful you are, your kitchen drain is bound to get clogged up now and then. Here's a simple way to clear out the blockage in three simple steps—without resorting to caustic drain cleaners:

STEP 1. Pour about ⅔ cup of baking soda into the drain.

STEP 2. Follow that with about the same amount of white vinegar, and cover the drain with a bowl or a plate.

STEP 3. While that soda-vinegar mixture is doing its thing, put a kettle of water on to boil. Once the water is boiling, uncover the drain and pour in the water. The bubbling action of the vinegar and baking soda dissolves many clogs, and the boiling water usually gets the rest of the gunk that's down there.

To prevent future buildups—and keep unpleasant odors at bay—pour a cup of white vinegar down the drain every month or so.

Note: *Do not use this method if you've already tried a commercial clog cutter. The vinegar can react with the drain cleaner to create dangerous fumes.*

QUICK & QUIRKY

Fresh out of Baking Soda? No worries! Drop in three antacid tablets followed by a cup of white vinegar to clear a clogged drain. Give it a few minutes, and run the hot water for three to four minutes. The pipes should be free and clear again!

Funky Fixture Fixes

A whale of a lot of water passes through—and over—every kitchen and its fixtures. So it's no wonder those spigots and faucets wind up with water splotches and mineral buildup. In most cases, you can make those marks meander by wiping them with a paste made from 2 tablespoons of salt and 1 teaspoon of vinegar. For stubborn stains, use one of these more intensive treatments:

- Soak a cloth in white vinegar and lay it on the stained area for 60 minutes or so. Then scrub with the salt-and-vinegar paste described above.

- Heat a cup or two of vinegar just to the boiling point, and pour it over the fixtures. That should soften the deposits enough so that you can just wipe them away with a sponge.

CABINETS & COUNTERTOPS

Say Good-Bye to Grease

Every time you cook with oil, fat, or grease of any kind, tiny bits of the stuff escape into the air and settle on your cabinets. In a surprisingly short time, an oily coating builds up on the surface, where it acts like a magnet for dust, hair, and other airborne gunk. There are potent commercial cleansers that can clear the crud off your cabinets, but they can easily damage the delicate surface. The simple—and safe—solution: Fill a 1-gallon bucket almost halfway with water. Then add ½ gallon of white vinegar and 1 cup of baking soda, and stir well to blend the ingredients thoroughly. Dip a sponge in the solution, and scrub your cabinets, moving with the grain of the wood. Rinse with a soft, clean cloth moistened with warm water. Then dry the surface with another soft, clean cloth. Whatever you do, never let your cabinets air-dry; the water can leach into the wood and ruin the finish.

OLD-TIME
Vim and *Vinegar*

With the popularity of preservative-free bread on the rise, bread boxes are back! So do what Grandma Putt always did to control the mold in your freshness preserver: Wash it out every week or so with a mild solution of vinegar and water (about 2 teaspoons of vinegar per quart of water will do the trick).

Kitchen Cupboard Cleanup Formula

For routine cabinet cleaning, mix up a solution of 1 cup of ammonia, 1 cup of white vinegar, and ⅓ cup of baking soda per gallon of water. Then use a sturdy sponge to wash your cupboards—inside and out. Rinse the sponge in clear water between swipes so that the potion in your bucket stays potent.

Polish Your Kitchen Cabinets with Malt Vinegar

Yep, you read that right. This easy-does-it formula is the best friend a wooden cabinet ever had. To make it, mix ½ cup each of malt vinegar and linseed oil in a small jar or bowl, and then stir in 1½ teaspoons of lemon juice. Apply the polish with a soft, clean cloth, adding a little elbow grease, and your cabinets will be the talk of the town (or at least your house).

Hold On to the Hardware

Thinking of giving your kitchen cabinets a facelift? Well, whether you plan to paint or reface the surfaces, don't automatically rush out and replace the hardware. How come? Because, depending on its age and material, there's a good chance that your current "crop" is better made by far than comparable new versions. Plus, at today's prices, replacing dozens of pulls, handles, and hinges of even decent quality will cost you a pretty penny. So unless you simply can't live with the look of your old cabinet appendages, consider sprucing up and reinstalling those venerable veterans using (you guessed it) vinegar. Of course, how you go about it depends on the condition they're in. Here's the deal:

Simple wear, tear, and grime. Fill a sink or bucket with hot water and a few squirts of dishwashing liquid (enough to make a nice crop of suds). Add ½ cup of white vinegar, and swirl the solution around with your hand. Drop the dingy pieces into the drink, and let them soak overnight. Then pull 'em out, one by one, and scrub them with a soft toothbrush. Rinse with clear water, dry with a soft towel, and they should look as good as new.

Rusty patches. If the metal is *not* chrome-plated, mix 2 tablespoons of salt with 2 tablespoons of white vinegar to make a paste. Rub it onto the rusty spots with a

---

VINEGAR AND GRANITE DON'T MIX!
If you have granite countertops in your kitchen or bathroom, never—and I mean never—clean them with vinegar or any DIY formula that contains vinegar or any other acidic substance, including lemon and other citrus juices. Instead, for routine cleaning, wipe the countertop with denatured alcohol or cheap vodka. If you prefer a commercial cleanser, use one that's specially made for granite, not a general all-purpose product. **Note:** *This no-acid rule also applies to marble and other types of stone. When in doubt, contact your stone supplier for guidance on the best cleaning products to use.*

soft, dry cloth. Then rinse with clear water, and dry thoroughly.

Tarnish on uncoated brass. Dip a soft, clean cloth in hot vinegar, then sea salt or kosher salt, and rub the tarnish away.

Tarnish on copper or lacquered brass. Rub the surface with a paste made from equal parts of salt, flour, and white vinegar.

Rust from chrome. Rub the surface with a balled-up piece of wet aluminum foil. The aluminum will combine with the rust (a.k.a. iron oxide) to form a slimy brown layer of aluminum oxide. Wipe it off with a soft, clean cloth, and bingo—clean, shiny chrome!

COOKWARE & TABLEWARE

A Glass Act

Pyrex® ovenware has been a staple in American kitchens since 1915, and for good reason. Make that plenty of good reasons. It's sturdy, inexpensive, and readily available. It reduces cooking time and distributes heat evenly. It's both stick- and odor-resistant. It comes in every size and shape imaginable. And with just a brief thawing-out period, it goes from freezer to oven without missing a beat. There's just one minor problem: It and newer brands of glass bakeware invariably collect brown food stains. This is strictly a cosmetic issue, but if the marks bother you, you don't have to grin and bear 'em. This simple trick will send the marks packing pronto:

- Fill the dish with 1 part vinegar and 4 parts water, and heat the mixture to a slow boil in the oven.

- Let it boil on low for five minutes, then carefully pull the pan out of the oven. Wait until it's cooled down and then scrub the surface lightly with a plastic scouring pad. Those unsightly splotches will be splitsville!

Unstick Stuff from a Nonstick Surface

Most of the time, nonstick cookware lives up to its name. But when food gets left in a pan for too long and ends up burning, you'll wind up with a nasty mess no matter how slick the surface is. Here's how to remove charred food and its accompanying odor—without damaging the pan's delicate coating:

STEP 1. Put 1 cup of water, ½ cup of white vinegar, and 2 tablespoons of baking soda in the stricken pan. Stir the mixture with a wooden spoon until the baking soda is dissolved. Then heat the solution to boiling and let it boil for 10 minutes to loosen the burned-on food.

STEP 2. Remove the pan from the stove, pour the vinegar mixture down the drain (carefully!), and let the pan cool until it's just warm to the touch.

STEP 3. Scrunch up a pair of retired panty hose, dampen the fabric, and squirt on a few drops of dishwashing liquid. Then scrub-a-dub-dub the surface crud away, rinsing the panty hose frequently and adding more dishwashing liquid as needed.

OLD-TIME Vim and Vinegar

When you need to tackle extra-greasy pots or pans—especially big ones—take a tip from Grandma Putt: Spray the surfaces with full-strength white vinegar. Let the cookware sit for a few minutes, and then wash it as usual. You'll save time, labor, *and* soap.

INSIDE YOUR HOME

STEP 4. Rinse your now-spotless pan with warm water, and dry it as usual.

From now on, when something's cooking on the stove, keep an eye on it to make sure it doesn't burn!

Make Your Stainless Pots Spotless

Contrary to its name, stainless steel can be—and frequently is—stained by any number of foods. The most effective way to get them off depends on the nature of the marks. Here are your choices:

Routine food stains. Pour in enough white vinegar to cover the marks, and let it sit for 30 minutes. Then wash the pan with hot, soapy water and rinse with cold water.

Burned-on grease and food. Mix 1 cup of vinegar in enough water to cover the stains. If the splotches are near the top of a large pot, add another cup or so of vinegar. Bring the liquid to a boil, continue boiling for five minutes, and remove the pan from the heat. When the metal is cool enough to handle safely, empty the vinegar water, and wash the pot as usual. With just a little light scrubbing, the gunk should come right off.

A First-Class Copper Cleaner

If you're a real cooking enthusiast, you know that nothing beats copper pans when it comes to conducting heat evenly. What's more, it looks as good as it cooks, as well it should, considering what it costs. To keep your cookware looking like all it's worth—or to spruce up copper that's gotten tarnished and dingy—simply fill a spray bottle with vinegar and 3 tablespoons of salt, shake until the salt dissolves, and give the copper a good spritzing. Let the pots sit for 10 to 12 minutes and then scrub them clean with a soft cloth. **Note:** *Never use scouring powders or abrasive cleaning pads on copper because they can leave fine scratches in the metal.*

The End of the Rainbow(s)

We all know how aluminum pots get those annoying rainbow marks inside. But maybe you don't know how easy it is to get rid of them. Just fill the pot with a solution of 1 tablespoon of vinegar per quart of water, and heat the concoction on low for three or four minutes—but no more! Then rinse it with clear water. You'll get a shine you can see yourself in!

2 CLEVER CUTTING BOARD CAPERS

Day after day, cutting boards pick up food residue and odors galore. Here are two simple ways to get rid of them both:

▶ **Slower version.** After you use the board for the last time at night, spray it with full-strength vinegar. Overnight, the potent acid will work its cleansing magic. Come morning, rinse the board with clear water, and you'll be good to go.

▶ **Faster action.** Give the board a good rubdown with baking soda. Then spray the surface with full-strength vinegar  (the mixture will bubble up for a moment or so and then subside). Let it sit for 5 to 10 minutes and then rinse it off with clear water.

Retract the Reaction

Aluminum pans are just about the most reactive kind under the sun. When you use them to cook acidic foods of any kind, not only will metallic particles be released into your vittles, but you'll also be left with unsightly dark stains on the cookware. To give 'em the heave-ho, simply mix 1 teaspoon of white vinegar for every cup of water needed to cover the marks. Boil the blend for a couple of minutes, then rinse with cold water.

Rout Out Rust

There's nothing more frustrating than reaching for a favorite tool, kitchen knife, or cast-iron pan and finding that it's splotched with rust. Well, don't fret—and don't rush out and buy a corrosive commercial rust remover. Use one of these ultra-safe kitchen-counter "cures" instead:

The quick method. Make a paste from 1 part vinegar and 2 parts salt. Rub the paste onto the metal until the spots vanish, and rinse with clear water.

The slower, easier way. Soak your stricken pieces overnight in full-strength vinegar. The rust will dissolve like magic.

Word to the Wise

It's fine and dandy (and effective, too!) to clean an aluminum pan with vinegar. But never leave the vinegar in the pan for more than a few minutes. If you do, the acid will corrode the metal.

So Long, Side Effects

To my way of thinking, coffee and tea are two of life's greatest pleasures. But there's nothing pleasing about the ugly brown stains they leave on ceramic cups, mugs, and teapots. Fortunately, wherever the hangers-on have settled, it's a snap to get rid of them. Here's how:

Cups and mugs. Just mix equal parts of salt and white vinegar, and scrub the marks away.

Teapots. Rub the insides with a half-and-half mixture of salt and vinegar, then rinse with warm water.

3 Mighty Anti-Mineral Maneuvers

Mineral deposits in a teakettle can be the very dickens to remove. But they're no match for vinegar. Depending on how extensive the buildup is, one of this trio of tactics should clear 'em out:

Minor low-down deposits. For a fairly light buildup on the bottom and lower sides, pour 3 or 4 tablespoons of baking soda into the kettle, and follow up with enough vinegar to cover the stained area. Let the mixture bubble for at least 30 seconds, then swirl it around inside the kettle. Dump the solution down the drain, rinse thoroughly, and wipe out the interior with a

FANTASTIC FORMULA

Amazing Aluminum Cleaner

This simple DIY cleanser will keep your aluminum pots and pans looking brand-spankin' new. (It'll also work its magic on your aluminum outdoor furniture!)

> ½ cup of baking soda
>
> ½ cup of cream of tartar
>
> ½ cup of white vinegar
>
> ¼ cup of soap flakes (such as Ivory Snow®)

Combine the baking soda and cream of tartar in a bowl. Add the vinegar, and mix to form a paste. Stir in the soap flakes, and transfer the mixture to a glass jar with a tight-fitting lid and label it. Apply the paste with a plain steel wool pad, and rinse.

clean dishcloth. If any spots remain, pour more vinegar into the kettle and let it sit for at least five minutes before rinsing.

All-over deposits. Pour 1 part vinegar and 4 parts water into the kettle so you have about 2 inches of liquid. Heat the kettle and let it steam for three to four minutes. (Boiling isn't necessary; the water just needs to be hot enough to generate steam. So if you have a whistling model and can't remove the whistle, it's okay to keep the heat low enough to ensure a bearable noise level.) Swirl the mixture around in the kettle—carefully! Then let the liquid cool to room temperature, dip a dishcloth into the drink, and sprinkle it with baking soda. Empty the kettle into the drain, and use the soda-topped cloth to wipe away any remaining deposits. Rinse thoroughly with clear water.

{ EITHER WHITE OR APPLE CIDER VINEGAR will work like a charm for removing mineral deposits. }

Thick, stubborn deposits. Pour 1 cup of vinegar, 1 cup of water, and 2 tablespoons of salt into the kettle. Swirl it around, then heat the mixture to boiling. Let it boil for 15 minutes—noise or no noise—checking occasionally to make sure the liquid hasn't evaporated away (add more if needed). Let the filled kettle sit overnight, or for at least eight hours, then empty it out. Wipe the inside with a damp dishcloth, adding baking soda if any residue remains in the kettle. Then rinse with clear water.

Make Cloudy Glassware Sparkle

It's a bummer, all right: You're getting ready for your big New Year's Eve bash, and you discover that your wine and cocktail glasses are all looking hazy and dull. Not to worry! Just fill a pan with vinegar, and heat it until it's almost—but not quite—too hot to put your finger in. Soak the glasses for about three hours, and then wash them as usual. (Depending on the depth of the "cloud cover," you may need to scrub with a plastic scouring pad.) They'll sparkle like stars!

Be Kind to Your Crystal...

And other treasured glassware—including vintage jelly glasses or souvenir shot glasses that you've gathered over the years. Here's your two-part TLC plan:

Dodge the dishwasher. Over time, minerals in the hard-hitting spray will etch the glass and wear away any painted designs. So play it safe, and wash the glasses in a sink filled with hot water, 1 cup of vinegar, and a few drops of dishwashing liquid.

Spray and rinse. Spritz each glass with full-strength vinegar, and then rinse it quickly in hot water. After that, you can

OLD-TIME *Vim and Vinegar*

If your household is anything like mine, your teakettle spends a lot of time on top of the stove, where it picks up splatters and splotches galore. So get 'em off the way Grandma Putt taught me to do: Spritz the outside with apple cider vinegar. Then sprinkle baking soda on a soft, damp cloth, and wipe the marks away. Just make sure you follow the grain of the metal to avoid scratching the surface.

either dry it with a soft, clean dish towel, or simply let it drip dry on a rack or mat.

Note: *This same dishwasher-avoidance policy applies to glass plates, bowls, and other tableware—for instance, the popular and highly collectible Depression glass.*

Send the Stink Out for Lunch

Back in the days when I toted my lunch to school, Grandma Putt relied on vinegar to keep my lunch box and thermos bottle odor-free—and it works just as well today. Here's all there is to it:

Lunch box. Saturate either a clean sponge or a slice of bread in white vinegar, tuck it into the box, snap the lid shut, and leave it overnight. Come morning, rinse the box out and dry it thoroughly.

Thermos bottle. Pour ¼ cup of vinegar into the bottle, and fill 'er up the rest of the way with hot tap water. Then whisk the inside with a bottle brush, and rinse with clear water.

Bingo—in both cases you'll have no telltale reminders of yesterday's lunch!

A CUNNING CAN OPENER CLEANER

Got a manual can opener that's so rusty you're tempted to toss it in the trash? Well, don't do it! Instead, soak the tool overnight in full-strength vinegar. Come morning, rinse the opener thoroughly, and dry it with a hair dryer, making sure to get the hot air into all the tiny nooks and crannies. When the dried metal has cooled enough to touch, lubricate the moving parts with a

few drops of mineral oil. That handy gadget will look—and work—like new!

BATHROOM SURFACES

Scrub Softly

If you're concerned that harsh abrasive cleansers could damage the surfaces of your bathroom fixtures, you could buy one of those ultra-gentle commercial products. Or you could make your own version by mixing ½ cup of liquid castile soap, ½ cup of water, and ¼ cup of vinegar in a spray bottle. Spray it on your sink, tub, or toilet; wipe with a damp sponge, and rinse with a second sponge or cloth. Ta-da! You'll have sparkling clean fixtures with no marks—at a fraction of the price you'd pay for a commercial no-scratch cleanser. **Note:** *You can find liquid castile soap in the cleaning or body-care section of your local supermarket or any large pharmacy.*

Clear the Air...

But get rid of those big cans of chemical deodorizers. The fact is that just about all they do is clutter up your bathroom counters and cabinets. You may think they make the air cleaner and fresher. Actually, though, they fill it with chemicals that cover up the unpleasant aromas and also interfere with your sense of smell so you don't notice the odors as much. So can the cans! Instead, pour some white vinegar into bowls, and set them around the bathroom. The acidic liquid will banish the unwanted smells pronto.

TO CLEAN HARDENED MINERAL DEPOSITS FROM AROUND FAUCETS, cover them with paper towels saturated with vinegar. Leave the towels in place for about two hours. The ugly white splotches will wipe right off.

FANTASTIC FORMULA

All-Around Antibacterial Cleaner

Who needs cupboards full of toxic (and expensive) cleaning products? This formula combines the work-horse power of vinegar and baking soda with the antiseptic and clarifying properties of witch hazel and tea tree oil. The result: a super-strength, antibacterial cleanser that wipes up cleanly—no rinsing needed.

½ cup of baking soda

½ cup of water

½ cup of white vinegar

¼ cup of witch hazel

1 tsp. of tea tree oil*

Mix all of the ingredients together in a spray bottle, and use the formula to clean bathroom fixtures as well as kitchen appliances (inside and out), countertops, and ceramic-tile surfaces all through your house.
* Available in health-food and herbal-supply stores, both online and brick-and-mortar versions.

2 Ways to Conquer Clogged Showerheads

When you step into the shower, turn on the faucet, and get a drowsy drizzle instead of a wake-up cascade, don't rush out and replace the head. Just clear out the mineral deposits that are blocking the water from getting through. You can do that in one of two ways:

- Unscrew the head, and soak it for 10 to 15 minutes in a mixture of 1 quart of boiling water and ½ cup of white vinegar. (If your showerhead is plastic, use hot, not boiling, water.)

- If you can't unscrew your showerhead—or you'd rather not bother—just fill a plastic bag halfway with white vinegar, and then slide the open end up over the head so that it's completely submerged.

Secure the bag with duct tape or a twist tie, and leave it in place overnight. Then remove the bag and rinse the fixture in water. (This also works to clean the aerator on your kitchen spigot.)

Whichever method you use, your shower will flow as freely as the mighty Niagara Falls (well, more or less).

Slip Off the Nonslip Strips...

Or maybe flowers, polka dots, or puppy dogs. There's no doubt about it: Whatever shape or color they are, nonslip decals are a boon to bathroom safety, providing tub-bottom traction through shower after shower and bath after bath. There's just one downside: When it's time for a change in decor, the same super-strong adhesive that provides such staying power makes these clingers challenging to remove. And once you do get them off, they often leave a sticky residue behind. Well, never fear—vinegar (what else?) is here! Just grab your jug and proceed as follows:

STEP 1. Fill the tub or shower stall with an inch of very hot water and 1 cup of white vinegar. Let the mixture sit until it's cool enough to stick your hand in.

STEP 2. Grab an edge of one of the stickers, and try to peel it back. If it doesn't come all the way off, slide a plastic scraper, silicone spatula, or expired credit card under the decal, and pry it up. Once you've removed all of them, drain the tub.

STEP 3. To clean off any remaining adhesive, soak cloths or paper towels in hot vinegar, and lay them over the

Word to the Wise

Shower curtains and liners are major mildew magnets. To stop spores in their tracks, keep a spray bottle of undiluted vinegar near the tub. Then once or twice a week, spray the fabric from top to bottom.

**Stop Scrubbing
the Bathtub Ring—**
Instead, soak paper towels
in white vinegar, and press them
in place over the unlovely line.
When the towels have dried,
remove them and spray the
area with vinegar. The ring
will wipe right off.

gooey residue. Wait 10 minutes
or so for the acid to penetrate
the glue, and then scrape
it off with the same tool
you used to remove the
stickers.

STEP 4. Thorough-
ly rinse your newly
stripped tub with clear
water. Wait until the
surface is completely dry
before applying another type
of anti-slip material.

Face Up to Fiberglass

Fiberglass tubs and shower stalls may have their advantages—
but repelling dirt isn't one of them. To make your cleaning labor a
whole lot lighter, sprinkle the surface generously with baking soda,
then wipe it with a cloth soaked in vinegar. Rinse with clear water,
dry with a second clean cloth, and admire your spankin' clean tub.

Do the Soap Scum 2-Step

It's an ugly fact of bathroom life: Anyplace soap has been used
there's bound to be soap scum—on sinks, tubs, walls—you name it.
And removing that stubborn goo can give you one heck of a headache, unless you try this simple two-part removal process:

- Spray straight vinegar onto the surfaces covered in soap scum.

- Once the vinegar has dried, spray again with a fresh supply,
  and wipe the area with a damp sponge.

Repeat the process if necessary—as it may be on extra-thick scum.

Prevent Smears

If you think that streaky glass shower doors are an inescapable fact of bathroom life, think again! You can kiss those smears good-bye with this simple tactic: Pour ⅓ cup of vinegar, 3 cups of distilled water, and 5 drops each of eucalyptus and sage oils into a spray bottle. Spritz the solution onto the glass, and polish with a clean, dry cloth. Any leftover mixture will last for six months. **Note:** *This fabulous formula also works wonders on frequently fogged bathroom windows.*

That's Historical

Although vinegar is mentioned numerous times throughout the Bible, the word plays its most visible role—purely by accident—in the 1717 edition published by John Baskett, the official printer for England's King George II and Oxford University. The volume is beautifully designed and illustrated, but the proofreader failed to catch a glaring typo in the page heading for Luke Chapter 20. Somehow, the line that should have read "The Parable of the Vineyard" came out "The Parable of the Vinegar." That whopper earned the book the nickname Vinegar Bible. Today there are only 11 known copies in existence and, as you might expect, whenever one of them changes hands, it's highly sought after by collectors with mighty deep pockets.

Stay on Track

For as narrow and shallow as they are, shower door tracks collect an amazing amount of crud. Fortunately, there's a simple way to clear the stuff out: Just fill the channels with white vinegar and let it sit for a few hours. Then pour hot water into

INSIDE YOUR HOME

the tracks, and use a brush to scrub the scum away. **Note:** *Make sure you put old towels on the floor first to catch any overflow that doesn't go into the tub.*

Toil-less Toilet Cleaning

It's probably safe to assume that cleaning a toilet bowl does not rank among your favorite pastimes. Well, nothing will make it as much fun as a three-ring circus, but either one of these methods will get the job done as quickly, easily, and pleasantly as possible:

- For routine cleaning, simply sprinkle ¼ cup of baking soda into the bowl and drizzle ¼ cup of vinegar over the soda. Add a few drops of your favorite essential oil if you like (any scent that suits your fancy is fine). Then grab a long-handled brush and scrub-a-dub-dub!

- To remove unsightly mineral deposits, make a paste of 3 parts borax to 1 part white vinegar, slather it on the marks, and leave it for three to four hours. Then rinse it away with clear water.

WHEN A TOILET TRICKLE HAS YOU IN A PICKLE . . .

The most likely cause is mineral deposits that have built up on the flapper valve and the valve seat. The quick fix: Shut off the water, flush the toilet to empty the tank, and scrub off the pesky crust with a plastic scouring pad dipped in white vinegar. (If your valve  seat is made of brass, as older models are, use fine-grade steel wool.) When you're finished, turn the water back on and flush the toilet a few times to clear out the residue.

---

2 Secrets to an Odorless Toilet

I kid you not. Performing these two tricks on a regular basis will keep the bowl free of unpleasant aromas:

- Pour 3 cups of white vinegar into the bowl, let it sit for 30 minutes or so, and then flush.

- Spray full-strength white vinegar on the toilet rim, as well as inside the rim of the bowl. Don't rinse or wipe the vinegar away, though. As the vinegar evaporates, it'll take the offensive odors right along with it.

Note: *How often you need to repeat these chores depends (of course) on how much use the toilet gets, so let your bathroom's traffic pattern be your guide.*

> **TO FRESHEN THE AIR IN YOUR BATHROOM,** fill a spray bottle with vinegar and add a few drops of your favorite perfume, extract, or essential oil. Then spritz the air whenever you feel the need.

FLOORS & WALLS

Clean Your Floor the Classic Way

And what way is that? The same one my Grandma Putt used: Mop or scrub it with a solution made from ½ cup of apple cider vinegar per gallon of warm water. This stuff will cut right through the toughest grease and dirt—and leave the whole room smelling sweet, too. It works like a charm on any resilient floor covering, including vinyl, ceramic tile, cork, or (Grandma's favorite) linoleum.

Put a Shine on Linoleum

If you want your linoleum floor to look as though you've just waxed it—but you're in no mood to do the job—buff it up instead using this simple three-step trick:

STEP 1. Squeeze non-gel toothpaste onto an old toothbrush or a dry cloth, and wipe away any scuff marks.

STEP 2. Mix 1 cup of white vinegar and 1 gallon of water in a bucket, and use it to rinse the whole floor clean.

STEP 3. Wrap an old—but clean—towel around each foot and scoot yourself around the floor. In the process, you'll buff the floor to a high shine and get a little workout at the same time!

TLC, Ceramic Tile Style

By and large, glazed ceramic tile is what my Grandma Putt called an "easy keeper." But if you want it to last and keep its good looks for the long haul, you need to treat it gently at cleaning time. In particular, never clean ceramic-tile floors or walls with abrasive scouring pads or powders because they will dull the finish. Instead, use either a commercial tub and tile cleaner or (Grandma's cleaner of choice) ½ cup of white vinegar mixed in a gallon of warm water.

Word to the Wise

Never use vinegar or any formula that contains vinegar on a no-wax vinyl floor. The acid could damage the tile's top layer. Instead, use a commercial product that's especially made for no-wax vinyl.

True-Grit Grease Cutter

Even in the best-kept homes, the kitchen floor can pick up more than its share of greasy dirt. But here's a superpowered cleaner that'll cut right through the grease and grime, leaving your linoleum or vinyl-tile floor shiny and spotless. To make it, pour ¼ cup of washing soda, ¼ cup of white vinegar, 2 tablespoons of dish-washing liquid, and 1 gallon of very warm water into a bucket. Mix until the solution is sudsy, and then mop the floor as usual. **Note:** *Don't use this cleaner on a waxed floor because it could make the wax sticky.*

Winning the War on Mold and Mildew

Mold and mildew spores can develop in any place that has high humidity, constant moisture, or the presence of potentially leaky or dripping pipes. Because your kitchen and bathrooms are prime suspects, it's important to keep a constant lookout for signs of trouble. If you find any, launch whichever of these two battle plans suits the problem areas:

Nonporous surfaces. These include ceramic tile, painted walls, or varnished floors, as well as pipes and bathroom fixtures. Wipe

OLD-TIME *Vim and Vinegar*

When you've got an extra-grubby floor that cries out for intensive care, use this DIY cleaner that Grandma Putt swore by—and I still do. It leaves even the dirtiest floor as clean as a whistle and as shiny as a new penny—without waxing. To make it, put 2 gallons of very hot water in a bucket, and stir in 2 cups of white vinegar, ¼ cup of washing soda, and 2 tablespoons of liquid castile soap. Mop the solution onto the floor, and let it air-dry. Then stand back and admire the shine! **Note:** *You can find washing soda in hardware stores and the laundry section of many supermarkets.*

Fragrant Floor Cleaner

This delightfully aromatic (and thoroughly nontoxic) potion works equally well on ceramic tile, rubber, vinyl, cork, and linoleum floors.

> **1 cup of white vinegar**
>
> **1–2 tbsp. of liquid castile soap (optional)**
>
> **1 tsp. of lavender or eucalyptus oil**
>
> **1 tsp. of rosemary oil**
>
> **1 gal. of hot water (at least 130°F)**

Mix all of the ingredients together in a bucket, and mop your floor as usual. If you've used the castile soap, rinse with clear water. Otherwise, you can skip this step.

them down thoroughly with straight white vinegar. To help the drying-out process, open as many windows as possible throughout your house, and, especially in the bathroom, keep the fan running. Also, clean all shower and tub drains using the procedure in "Do a Clog Dance" (see page 162).

Grout between ceramic tiles. Soak three or four paper towels in white vinegar, and lay them over the grout. Press the towels firmly to ensure full contact, and leave them in place for about eight hours. If the paper begins to dry out, spray or splash it with more vinegar to keep it saturated. When time's up, remove the towels, and use an old toothbrush to scrub away any remaining crud. Then rinse with cool, clear water. **Note:** *Unfortunately, when mold and mildew have invaded porous surfaces such as carpets or wallboard, you'll need to remove, discard, and replace the "victims" immediately (or have a pro do the job).*

Along about the same time our ancestors discovered that vinegar could add flavor and zest to their food, they found that it could also perform miraculous cleaning feats. They didn't know the reason, but we do, and it boils down to two words: acetic acid. And you know what? Here in the 21st century, good old vinegar can still go head to head with just about any newfangled formula you can name.

FLOORS, WALLS & WINDOWS

Wooden You Know It

Has your finished wood floor lost its luster? This remarkable remedy will bring back the shine in a flash. Mix equal parts of white vinegar and vegetable oil in a pump-style spray bottle. (About a pint of each, thoroughly mixed, should cover two 11-by 14-foot floors.) Apply a thin mist to the floor, and rub it in well with cotton rags or a wax applicator you can get from the hardware store. Remove the excess with clean cotton rags, and buff to a shine.

Baseboard Cleaning: An Upright Solution

Even if you don't use a sponge mop to scrub your floors, pick one up the next time you're out and about, and use it to spiff up your baseboards. Mix ½ cup of vinegar per 3 cups of warm water in a bucket, dip the mop into the solution, and wipe down the trim. It'll clear away dust, pet hair, and other crud without the normal backbreaking, knee-crushing effort. In fact, you'll barely have to bend over to get the job done!

Clean Mops Mop Cleaner

You wouldn't paint your walls with an old paint-encrusted brush or roller, would you? So don't even think of using a dirty old mop to "clean" your floors! If you're lucky, it'll do a less-than-stellar job. If you're not so lucky, any gritty particles of dirt will scratch the finish on your floor. The good news is that it's easy to keep that essential cleaning tool in tip-top shape. Here's all there is to it:

- After every few times you use the mop, shake it outdoors to remove the dust. If you don't live in a place where you

FANTASTIC FORMULA

Baseboard Bonanza

Once grime builds up on baseboards, it can be the very dickens to deal with. But if you routinely tackle those vertical surfaces at the same time you scrub your floors, the job is a snap. Start by vacuuming the baseboards with a soft brush attachment. Then wipe 'em down with this DIY spray.

1 tbsp. of cornstarch

2 cups of boiling water

⅓ cup of white vinegar

Measure the cornstarch into a spray bottle, then carefully add the water through a funnel, and stir until the cornstarch has dissolved. (Chopsticks and shish kebab skewers make good stir-sticks.) Add the vinegar, and stir again. Then take aim and fire the spray on the baseboards, wiping them clean with a soft cloth or damp sponge.

can give your mop a brisk shaking in the great outdoors without disturbing the neighbors, give the business end a good going-over with your vacuum cleaner.

- When your mop gets really grungy, detach the head and toss it in the washing machine with a little bleach and detergent; when it's done washing, put it in the dryer.

- Once it's dry, lightly mist it with a solution made of 2 parts white vinegar and 1 part vegetable oil.

Note: *Before you use your spanking-clean mop, wait until it has completely absorbed the solution. Otherwise, instead of collecting dust, you'll be spreading oil!*

Road Salt Rides Again...

Right into your home sweet home. The salt crystals that you pick up on your feet and track indoors act like sandpaper, dulling the surface of your floor and damaging its finish—whether the covering is wood, vinyl, linoleum, cork, or ceramic tile. Your best defense is fast action: The second that any potentially salt-bearing water drops from your

TO ADD A FRESH-SMELLING and streak-reducing kick to any vinegar-water cleaning formula, simply mix in 5 to 10 drops of lemon oil.

or anyone else's shoes, wipe it up immediately.

When you don't reach the scene until after the salt has dried, spray the stricken area with a solution of roughly ½ teaspoon of vinegar per cup of warm water. Let it sit for a minute or two, and then wipe it up with a clean, dry towel.

Burn Unit 911!

Oops! You accidentally bumped a lighted candle, and it toppled onto your hardwood floor. Or maybe a party guest missed the ashtray with a cigarette. Whatever caused the burn on your floor, this three-part process will get rid of the mark fast:

● Mix equal parts of white vinegar and baking soda to make a paste, spread it over the burned spot with your fingers or a soft cloth, and use a pencil eraser to rub the paste into the wood.

● Wipe off the residue with a damp sponge, and let the spot dry thoroughly.

● Use a wood-stain marker to color the blemish until it blends right in.

And from now on, be more careful with candles and cancer sticks!

Erase Muddy Footprints

Muddy footprints make a mess of your carpet—but they'll "walk" off into the sunset when you go at them with this five-step routine:

STEP 1. Mix 2 tablespoons of dishwashing liquid per ½ cup of warm water, stirring gently to minimize suds. Then dab the solution sparingly onto the spots with a sponge or clean cloth. Don't rub!

STEP 2. Wait for a few minutes, then lay a clean, dry cloth on the area, and blot up the soap solution.

STEP 3. Pour a little white vinegar onto the stain, and blot again with a clean, dry cloth.

STEP 4. Sponge on the soap solution again, blot once more, and rinse by sponging with clear water.

STEP 5. Blot with a clean towel to remove as much moisture as possible, and let the carpet dry completely. Then fluff up the fibers with your fingers, and that carpet will look as good as new!

Rev It Up

Carpet looking dull and dreary? Or smelling less than fresh? If so, then bring that floor covering back to its youthful glory with this simple trick: Mix up a solution of 1 cup of white vinegar per gallon of water, and pour it into a handheld spray bottle (or, if the area is large, a pump sprayer). Spritz the

OLD-TIME
Vim
and
Vinegar

Don't make a sour face at that carpet stain! This old-time trick will make your rug look sweet again in no time flat! Here's how: Mix ⅓ cup of white vinegar with ⅔ cup of warm water, sponge it onto the soiled spot, and blot with a clean, dry cloth. Repeat as needed until the blemish is a bygone.

carpet with the mixture, and immediately wipe it off with a soft, absorbent cloth. The colors will glow, and the musty odors will vanish. **Note:** *As always, play it safe and test an inconspicuous patch of carpet first.*

An After-Shampoo Shampoo

Shampooing your own carpet costs less than hiring a pro to do the job, and as long as you're not dealing with major, set-in stains, it can be just as effective. There's only one problem: DIY shampooing can leave a sticky residue that attracts dirt like a magnet. So whenever you give your rug a bath, follow up with this procedure: Fill the shampooer tank with a solution of 1 cup of white vinegar per 2 ½ gallons of water. Then run the machine over the floor, and let the vinegar lift out the soap that's built up on the fibers. Empty the reservoir and fill it with clear, warm water, and make another pass to be sure that all of the soapy residue is gone.

Divert a Paint-Spill Disaster

You're almost finished painting the living room when down goes the

FANTASTIC FORMULA

Carpet Scorch Lifter

Light scorch marks on carpet will come right out when you treat them with this fantastic formula.

1 cup of white vinegar

½ cup of unscented talcum powder

2 onions, coarsely chopped

Mix all of the ingredients in a pot, and bring the mixture to a boil, stirring constantly. Let it cool to room temperature, then spread it over the stain with a sponge. When the spot is dry, brush or vacuum away the residue. Your carpet should look as good as new!

paint bucket, splashing latex paint onto your carpet. Well, don't panic, but do act fast as follows:

- Fill a bucket with 2 tablespoons of white vinegar and 2 table-spoons of dishwashing liquid per 2 quarts of warm water.

- Fill another bucket with clear water.

- Tackle the spill using a clean sponge dipped in the vinegar solution, then between wipes, rinse the sponge in the clear water.

In no time at all, you'll have freshly painted walls *and* a nice clean carpet!

Window Wonderland

To keep your windows crystal clear, mix ½ cup of white vinegar and 2 table-spoons of lemon juice per quart of warm water. Pour the solution into a spray bottle, and spritz the glass. Then wipe the surface clean with a squeegee or a sponge—forget the time-honored advice to go at the glass with a fistful of paper towels or scrunched-up newspaper. According to professional window cleaners, that simply moves the dirt around from one place to another. **Note:** *If your windows—indoors or out—are really grimy, see "Window Washing 101: What the Pros Know" on page 296.*

Word to the Wise

Never clean stained glass with vinegar or any formula (store-bought or DIY) that contains vinegar or another acidic substance. Likewise, avoid ammonia, as well as abrasive cleansers and scrubbing pads of any kind— even the gentlest plastic versions. All of these cleaners will severely damage the surface of the glass.

Clean Textured Plaster...

Without losing your mind. If you've got textured plaster walls, you know that it's all but impossible to clean them without ripping rags, shredding sponges—and leaving bits and pieces of the stuff behind. Well, stop fretting and launch into action this way:

- Round up some scraps of low-pile carpet, and cut them into hand-friendly pieces. (If you don't have any remnants on hand, check with a local carpet shop for outdated samples.)

- In a bucket, mix up a solution of ½ cup each of white vinegar and liquid laundry detergent per gallon of warm water.

- Dip a piece of carpet into the solution and scrub the wall as usual. The rug chunk will glide right over the jagged plaster without leaving pieces of itself behind.

- When you're finished, rinse the wall with a clean piece of carpet dipped in water, and blot it dry with a terry-cloth towel.

QUICK & QUIRKY

Try a Super Stripper—New wallpaper is a cinch to strip off walls, but older wallpaper is a much tougher customer. To loosen it, mix ½ cup of white vinegar in a bucket of hot water. Then just paint the solution onto the wall, let it soak in, and scrape the paper right off. (If the paper is especially stubborn, add more vinegar to the water.)

Wonderful Wood-Paneled Wall Cleaner

An occasional dusting will usually keep paneled walls looking great, but when they demand a more thorough cleaning, reach for this DIY formula: Mix 1 cup of white vinegar and ¼ cup of lemon juice per 2 cups of water in a pail (multiplying the formula as needed to suit the size of your room). Then bunch up a handful of old panty hose, dip the wad into the solution, and wipe the paneling clean. For best results, work from the bottom of the wall upward to avoid messy runs, drips, or errors. **Note:** *The texture of panty hose or other nylon stockings provides the perfect abrasive, yet gentle, scrubbing action for this job.*

FURNITURE

Pulverize the Polish

You've found a terrific table for peanuts at a flea market. There's just one problem: There's a thick buildup of polish on the wood. How do you get the old stuff off? Simple: Wipe it with a half-and-half solution of white vinegar and water, and rub it off immediately. Repeat if you need to (but you probably won't).

Drink a Toast to Beautiful Furniture

Your fine furniture will look its elegant best when treated with this easy-to-make polish—with a kick. To whip it up, mix ¼ cup of linseed oil, ⅛ cup of vinegar, and ⅛ cup of whiskey in a glass jar. Wipe the mixture onto your wooden furniture with a soft, clean cotton cloth. Then buff with a second cloth. Store any leftovers at room temperature in the tightly capped jar.

Ring around the Table

It happens to all of us: No matter how often we remind our nearest and dearest to use coasters and napkins, those white circles always seem to appear, as if by magic. Well, if the rings were made within the past week or so, you can make them disappear like magic, too. Simply mix equal parts of olive oil and white vinegar in a bowl, and rub the blend into the marks with a soft, clean cloth, using a circular motion. Then buff the wood with a second cloth. Those blasted blemishes will be gone in no time!

OLD-TIME *Vim* and *Vinegar*

This DIY furniture polish is as old as the hills, but it cleans and shines wood as well as any newfangled product on the market. And I ought to know because I use it all the time, just as my Grandma Putt did. To make the polish, mix ½ cup of malt vinegar, ½ cup of linseed oil, and 1½ teaspoons of either lemon or lavender oil in a clean glass jar with a screw-on plastic lid. Wipe the formula onto the wood with a soft, clean cotton cloth and buff with a second cloth. You'll have a shine you can see yourself in! **Note:** *You can buy standard-size plastic lids in just about any place that sells canning supplies as well as from online retailers.*

Black Ring Remedy

Finding white water rings on your wooden furniture is disheartening enough (see "Ring around the Table" on page 193). But if you spot a black ring, it means that water has worked its way through the varnish and into the wood—and to prevent permanent damage, you'll need to act fast. So drop whatever you're doing, and proceed as follows:

STEP 1. Gather your gear. You'll need fine-grit sandpaper, rubber gloves, chlorine bleach, white vinegar, a wax-filler stick, wood stain (to match the original color), varnish, extra-fine steel wool, and furniture wax (optional).

STEP 2. Very lightly sand away the finish over the black ring. Then give the mark itself a light sanding. If it's stubborn, put on rubber gloves and bleach the wood.

STEP 3. When the stain has

faded enough to match the original wood color, thoroughly rinse off the bleach with clear water. Then wipe the area with a sponge dampened with vinegar to neutralize the wood. (Make sure every trace of bleach is gone!)

STEP 4. Fill any dents or scratches with the wax filler, and follow up with wood stain, if necessary, for a perfect match.

STEP 5. Apply a few coats of varnish, using the steel wool to gently blend it in.

STEP 6. Finish with the furniture wax, if desired, and you're done.

Word to the Wise

If your blemished (or otherwise damaged) piece of furniture is a valuable antique or artisan-made item, don't try any DIY tricks. Instead, ask a reputable antique dealer to recommend a professional furniture restorer who can get your treasure back in shape. In the case of a contemporary gem, if at all possible, have the item's creator perform any repairs. An original, one-of-a-kind piece of furniture can plummet in value (for both insurance and resale purposes) if anyone other than the originating artisan works on it. The same goes for original works of art and high-end crafts such as wood carvings or textiles.

A Winning Way to Nix Nicks

When a tabletop, dresser, or any other piece of wooden furniture picks up a shallow scratch, dust the piece off and then reach for this down-home remedy: Mix ¾ cup of olive oil and ¼ cup of vinegar and wipe the formula onto the surface with a soft, clean cloth. The kind of vinegar you need depends on the color of the wood. Either white, apple cider, or balsamic vinegar could work, so start with whichever seems most likely, and test it in a hidden spot to make sure the color blends in nicely.

Remove Dripped Wax from a Tabletop

It's probably safe to say that for most folks, glowing candles are a homey, comforting sight—until they drip all over one of your favorite tables. The good news is that waving wax on its way is as easy as 1, 2, 3!

Soften the wax by blowing it with a hair dryer set on low.

Slide the softened wax away with paper towels.

Wipe the surface with a half-and-half solution of vinegar and water to remove any remaining traces of wax.

Tickle the (Faux) Ivories

To clean plastic piano keys (which are found on all the instruments made in the last 40 years or so), wipe them with a chamois dampened with a solution of warm water and white vinegar. About 1 tablespoon per quart of H_2O should do the trick. No rinsing needed.

Vibrant Vinyl Revitalizer

If you have vinyl-covered furniture, then you know that dirt and grime galore gravitate to the surfaces. Well, here's a fabulous—and fabulously simple—way to clean that crud off lickety-split: Mix ½ cup of water, ½ cup of white vinegar, and 2 tablespoons of dishwashing liquid in a bowl or small pail. Wipe the solution onto the dirty spots with a clean cloth or sponge. Then wipe it off with a soft, clean cloth or chamois. Your vinyl will be clean as a whistle and rarin' to steal the limelight in a 1950s sitcom!

Very Fine Vinyl Upkeep

For general maintenance, just damp-wipe vinyl surfaces with full-strength white vinegar on a soft, clean cloth. Then dip another cloth in warm water and wipe the vinegar off. Make this chore a part of your weekly cleaning routine, and the vinyl will stay nice and soft—even in spots that tend to turn brittle from heavy use, like headrests, armrests, or the seats on retro kitchen chairs.

That's Historical

Have you ever wondered how medieval knights kept their chain mail armor clean, rust-free, and flexible? I'll tell you how: They—or more often, their squires—put the intricately pieced garments in barrels half-filled with a mixture of sand and vinegar, and rolled the casks down the side of a hill. Then Sir Galahad and his cohorts donned their protective finery, and charged into battle! (For all you historical reenactment buffs, this trick works just as well today.)

Simple Saddle Soap

Despite its name, saddle soap is the bee's knees for cleaning anything that's made of leather, including car and furniture upholstery, home accessories, footwear, and even leather-bound books. There are many brands on the market, but this is a dandy DIY version.

2 tbsp. of beeswax*

¼ cup of white vinegar

⅛ cup of linseed oil (not boiled)

⅛ cup of vegetable-based dishwashing liquid (such as Seventh Generation™ Free & Clear Natural Dish Liquid)

Put the beeswax and vinegar in a small pan and heat on low until the wax has melted. In a small bowl, mix the linseed oil with the dishwashing liquid. Add the solution to the wax mixture, stirring until all of the ingredients are thoroughly blended. Pour the mixture into a shallow, heat-resistant container with a lid (such as a candy tin or a glass jar that once held shoe cream). That's all there is to it!

* *Available in craft-supply stores.*

3 Steps to Lovely Leather

Nothing destroys the luxurious look and feel of leather upholstery like a waxy buildup of dirt. Fortunately, it's a snap to get rid of that gunk. Here's all you need to do:

- Mix ½ cup of water and ¼ cup of white vinegar, and rub the solution onto the leather with a soft sponge or cotton cloth.

- Wash the piece with saddle soap and water, and apply a high-quality leather conditioner.

- Finish by buffing the leather with a soft cotton cloth to bring out its natural shine.

Note: *You can find saddle soap in tack shops, feed and grain stores, and shoe-repair shops. But it's easy to make your own "home-cooked" version (see Simple Saddle Soap, at left).*

Shore Up Sagging Seats

Over time, the seats of cane and wicker chairs tend to sag. Well, don't fret—and don't rush 'em off to a repair shop—at least not until you've tried this DIY fix: Wash down the seats with a half-and-half solution of white vinegar and hot water. Then set the chairs outside to dry in the sun on a hot day. As the cane dries, it'll tighten right up.

> **IF THE MANEUVER** (at right) doesn't work to your satisfaction, take your wicker chairs to a repair shop that specializes in cane and wicker. (Ask an antique dealer to recommend one.)

Vomit Stain Vanishing Spray

This routine will quickly remove most "recycled food" residue from carpet, furniture, or mattresses (for treating vomit on clothes, see "Big and Simple Solutions" on page 220). Here's all you need to do: Mix equal parts of white vinegar, rubbing alcohol, and water in a spray bottle. Lightly spritz the affected area, wait a few minutes, and blot the stain. Repeat until all traces of the foul stuff are gone.

Beat the Brewski Spill Solution

It can be mighty relaxing to kick back with a cold beer—that is, unless you kick back a little too quickly and the brew winds up on your couch. Well, never fear. You can still salvage your evening. First, sponge up as much as you can, then saturate the area with a half-and-half solution of white vinegar and water. Blot the area with an absorbent towel, and the scene should be clean and clear. So grab a fresh beer and toast your success. But this time, sit down slowly and gently. **Note:** *This beer-removal trick works just as well on carpet as it does on upholstery fabric.*

Vinegar: The Drink of Air-Moisturizing Champions

There are several kinds of humidifiers on the market. Each performs its work in a slightly different way, but in order to function at peak efficiency—without spewing germs into the air—they all need regular, thorough cleaning with vinegar. The exact procedure depends on the type of mechanism. Here's the deal:

Rotating. Most portable humidifiers work by slowly rotating either a permanent sponge or a disposable filter through a water reservoir and then past a fan that blows air through the wet object, thereby sending moisture into the room. In either case, you need to clean the water reservoir every day to keep mold from growing. To do that, first turn off the unit, empty the reservoir, and wash it with hot, soapy water. Then rinse it thoroughly with clear water. Every third day, follow up by wiping the container with white vinegar to break up any mineral deposits. Then rinse and dry the container before you fill 'er up with fresh water. If your humidifier has a disposable filter, check it every three days, and replace it as soon as it turns gray.

DEGREASE GRATES, GRILLES, AND BLADES

Heating grates, air-conditioner grilles, and ceiling-fan blades all tend to attract more than their fair share of greasy dust. And that grime not only looks unsightly, but it can also significantly reduce airflow from the devices. Your one-stop cleaning solution: full-strength white vinegar. Simply wipe it onto the surfaces with a soft cotton cloth, and the gunk will come right off. To get inside tight spaces, dip a retired toothbrush into the vinegar, and scrub-a-dub-dub.

Ultrasonic. As the name implies, these babies use a metal diaphragm (a.k.a. nebulizer), which vibrates at an ultrasonic frequency to create a mist that's released into the air—accompanied by bacteria and other crud if the water's not crystal clean. So each time you fill the reservoir, wash it out with white vinegar. And at least once a week, remove any clogs in the diaphragm by soaking it in vinegar for 20 minutes or so, and then rinsing it with clear, cool water.

Steam-powered. This type boils water and mixes the resulting steam with air that cools it, in the process releasing a warm, gentle mist. It's the safest system from a health standpoint because the heat kills germs lickety-split. On the downside, mineral deposits tend to build up in the boiling chamber, decreasing the unit's efficiency (and therefore its life span). The simple solution: Clean that cavern every week or so with a soft brush dipped in a half-and-half mixture of vinegar and water.

OLD-TIME *Vim and Vinegar*

The marketing hype for commercial air fresheners would have you believe that these things actually remove unpleasant odors from the air. Baloney! All they do is cover up the aromas and dull your sense of smell with fake fragrances and other (sometimes dangerous) chemicals. Fortunately, you have a safe alternative that actually *does* banish unwanted smells—and folks like Grandma Putt used it for centuries. Just pour white vinegar into bowls, and set them around the problem areas. If you like, add a few drops of scented extract or essential oil. With or without the additional scent, the acidic liquid will make short work of even the nastiest smells.

Debug Your Dehumidifier

A dehumidifier can prevent a whole lot of household problems, ranging from musty smells to structural damage caused by mold and mildew. But if you're not careful, that dandy drying device can turn into a breeding ground for bad bacteria—as well as the mold and mildew you're trying to prevent. For that reason, you need to stay on top of some crucial maintenance chores—namely these:

- If your unit has a washable filter, give it a bath periodically in a half-and-half solution of vinegar and water. The exact timing varies from one model to another, as well as the machine's workload, so consult your owner's manual or the manufacturer's website for guidance. (Disposable filters should be changed as needed, again according to the manufacturer's recommended timetable.)

- Empty the water-collection bucket frequently, and wash it in hot, soapy water with a splash of white vinegar added to it. Then rinse and dry the container thoroughly before putting it back on the job.

- When the reservoir shows any signs of mold or mildew, fill it with a half-and-half solution of vinegar and water. Let it sit for an hour or so, then empty it out, rub the interior with straight vinegar, and don't rinse.

Word to the Wise

In the case of all filters, the timing is approximate. If you have heavily shedding pets on the scene, or if you're cooling or heating a room where dust flies frequently (such as a workshop), you should clean or replace your filter more often. Conversely, if you spend a lot of time away from home, or you live in a mild climate that doesn't demand everyday cooling or heating, you can go longer between changes. Just take a gander now and then, and let your eyes be your guide.

- Before you put a dehumidifier into storage, or when you won't be using it for a while (for example, during the dry winter months), wash and dry the bucket extra thoroughly.

Evict AC Algae

The condensation drain line in your home's central air-conditioning system may look like any other piece of PVC pipe, but it's actually the perfect place for algae to grow. And grow. Over time, the slimy stuff can completely block a drain, causing water to overflow the drain pan and seep into ceilings and walls. Fortunately, if you catch a blockage in its early stages, there's a good chance you can clear it out before it causes major trouble. And it just so happens that (surprise!) vinegar makes the job a snap. Here's all there is to it:

{ **IN THE SUMMERTIME,** you'll probably want to perform the AC algae eviction chore (at left) early in the morning to dodge extreme heat in the attic. }

Assess the situation. A condensate drain that's working properly drips whenever the AC is in use. If your drainpipe is not dripping, that probably means that the drain is blocked. (You'll generally find the drainpipe attached to the wall of your house near the outdoor compressor.)

Another clue: If your drain pan has an alternate pipe under the eaves (as many do so that water can escape outside rather than overflow indoors), it should *not* be dripping. If it is, that's another indication that the main drain is clogged.

Clear the drain. On the pipe in the attic that leads away from the drain pan, you should see a tee with a threaded plug. Remove it (it should twist off easily), and slowly pour ¾ cup or so of white vinegar into the hole. That's all there is to it—although if the blockage is major, it could take several hours for the vinegar to clear it out.

Keep it up. After that, to keep the drain free and clear, pour ¾ cup of vinegar into the line every few months.

Finesse Your AC Filter

A room air conditioner delivers more chilling power and lasts longer when it has a spanking-clean filter. If your wall or window AC has a disposable filter, simply replace it with a new one every 30 days. To keep a foam or metal mesh version in tip-top shape, follow this procedure at least once a month:

OLD-TIME *Vim and Vinegar*

Whenever Grandma Putt found burn marks on her brick hearth, she'd sponge them off with white vinegar, and rinse with clear water. For routine cleaning of brick or stone, she used 1 cup of white vinegar in a bucket of warm water.

STEP 1. Put the filter in a basin filled with a half-and-half solution of white vinegar and water. Make sure the container is large enough for you to completely submerge the filter, allowing the vinegar to kill all of the allergens and bad bacteria that may be present.

STEP 2. Let the filter soak. If your AC sees only moderate use, or if you've cleaned it within the past few weeks, a one-hour bath will do fine. But if it's been more than a month since you've done the job, give it about four hours in the drink to get fully sanitized.

STEP 3. Fish the filter out of the water, and lay it on an old clean towel to drain—outdoors in the sun if possible. Do not rinse! You want the vinegar to remain so it can continue counteracting the foul stuff in the incoming air.

STEP 4. Let the filter dry completely before reinstalling it. Whatever you do, don't use the air conditioner until the clean filter is back in place!

HOME FURNISHINGS & ACCESSORIES

A Sure Cure for Bronze Disease

Despite its name, this ugly green corrosion can attack both bronze and copper when moisture reacts with the metal. Fortunately, in its early stages, it's a snap to halt the chemical reaction that's causing the color change. At the first sign of greenish patches or speckles, stop trouble in its tracks this way:

- Soak a soft, clean cloth in 1 cup of hot vinegar with ¼ cup of salt mixed into it.

- Lay the cloth on the affected area(s) and let it sit for about 15 minutes.

- Wash the "patient" in soapy water, rinse with clear water, and dry the metal thoroughly before you put it back on display or into storage.

Don't Moan Over Lost Lacquer

You hauled your favorite brass candlesticks out of storage and discovered that the lacquer finish is damaged. No problem—just strip off the old coating by rubbing it with nail polish remover on a soft cloth. Then, if you don't care to have the pieces professionally relacquered, leave the brass in its natural state and keep it shiny and bright by rubbing the surface periodically with a soft cotton cloth moistened with white vinegar and sprinkled with salt. Follow up by rinsing the brass with a cloth dipped in warm water, and then buff it dry with another soft cotton cloth.

Copper Shine Solution

Copper accessories can get dingy over time, just like everything else in your house. But you have to tread lightly when you clean them because scouring powders and other abrasives can leave fine scratches in the metal. So to get a nice sleek shine, try this gentler trick: Put your copper item in a large pot on the stove, and pour in enough water to cover the object. Add 1 cup of vinegar and 1 tablespoon of salt, and bring the water to a boil. Then turn down the heat, and let it simmer for a few hours so the acid can go to work on the tarnish. Let the water cool to a comfortable temperature, fish your treasure out of the drink, and wash it in soapy water. Dry it thoroughly, and put it back in its decorative duty station.

That's Historical

When the first cannons rolled onto the battlefield in 1346 during the Hundred Years' War, vinegar went with them. From then, well into the 1800s, troops used it to cool down the hot iron and also inhibit rust. The French, in particular, used lavish amounts of vinegar. In fact, legend has it that during just one of his many battles in the 1600s, Louis XIII paid 1.3 million francs for cannon-cooling vinegar. (In today's currency, that's a little over $500,000 in U.S. dollars.)

Perfectly Pleasing Pewter Polish

Pewter may look tough and sturdy, but it's actually pretty darn delicate. Abrasive pads or cleansers will deliver major scratches to it in a New York minute, and the heat of a stove or a dishwasher can actually destroy a pewter object. (The metal begins to melt at a mere 450°F!) Fortunately, there's a simple, safe way to clean this wimp—and here it is:

Mix 1 cup of white vinegar with 1 teaspoon of salt, and add enough white flour to make a smooth paste.

Smear the mixture generously onto the object, and let it dry for 30 minutes or so.

Rinse off the paste with lukewarm water. (If necessary, use a

FANTASTIC FORMULA

Bravo Brass Cleaner

This marvelous mixture will keep your brass accessories and hardware shining like the morning sun. And, unlike commercial formulas, it contains no harsh chemicals. (It works the same magic on copper cookware.)

- ½ cup of all-purpose flour
- ½ cup of dry laundry detergent (without bleach)
- ½ cup of salt
- ¾ cup of white vinegar
- ½ cup of hot tap water
- ¼ cup of lemon juice (freshly squeezed or bottled)

Mix the flour, detergent, and salt in a bowl. Add the remaining ingredients, and blend thoroughly. Dip a soft, clean cotton cloth into the mixture, and rub it onto the brass, taking care to get into all the nooks and crannies. Buff with a second cloth. Store any leftover cleaner in a jar with a tight-fitting lid.

INSIDE YOUR HOME

Word to  the Wise

cotton swab to get the paste out of nooks and crannies.)

Note: *As you apply the polish, rub back and forth in one direction, not in circles or patterns, so your strokes match those of the metal.*

Here's to Glorious Globes!

Light-fixture globes are intended to let the light shine through clearly. But to ensure that a friendly glow keeps beaming down on you and yours, you need to clean the glass periodically. The ultra- simple method: Turn the light off. Once the globe has cooled to room temperature, submerge it in a sink full of warm water mixed with ¼ cup of white vinegar and a squirt or two of dishwashing liquid. Wipe the glass, inside and out, with a clean dishcloth, then rinse with cool, clear water. Dry it with a clean dish towel or let it air-dry. Then, to help repel dust, rub the outer surface with a dryer sheet.

2 Ways Vinegar Keeps Vases Vivacious

When it comes to getting—and keeping—glass clean, good old white vinegar is the heavyweight champ of the world. Here's how it can solve two of your most vexing vase problems:

Dull-looking vases, decanters, or decorative bottles. Toss a handful of salt and 2 teaspoons of white vinegar into the bottom, and give it a few good shakes. Then rinse it with clear water. Your treasure will sparkle like a metallic Christmas tree!

TO MAKE CUT FLOWERS STAY FRESH LONGER—whether they came from a florist or your own garden—mix 2 tablespoons of vinegar and 1 tablespoon of sugar with the water that you pour into the vase.

Water lines on the glass. Saturate a towel or washcloth (depending on the size of the container) with white vinegar, and stuff it in so it has contact with the sides. Let it sit overnight, and by morning those unsightly marks will wash right off.

Can the Clingers!

Glue may be one of the most useful inventions that ever came down the pike, but there are times when it's a royal pain in the neck—namely, when you want to remove something that's tightly stuck to its "home base." The good news is that vinegar can conquer two of the most common clinging conundrums.

Stick-on wall hooks. Simply saturate a sponge or cloth with vinegar, and squeeze it behind the hook so that the vinegar drips down and makes contact with the adhesive. Wait a few minutes, and then gently pull the hook away from the wall, or slip a putty knife behind the base and pry it off.

Price tags and other labels. Paint or sponge several coats of vinegar over the sticker. Give it three or four minutes to penetrate the paper. Then scrape it away with a fingernail, a plastic scraper, or an expired credit card.

Mirror, Mirror on the Wall

To clean mirrors, spray them with a solution of ¼ cup of vinegar per cup of water. Wipe with a sponge or squeegee, moving away from the frame on all sides so that water doesn't get under the edge. You'll get a spot-free, streak-free shine every time!

Save the Ashtrays!

Smoking may be a big no-no from a health standpoint, but vintage ashtrays are hot collectibles these days. If you're lucky enough to have your parents' collection (or your own discards) stashed in the attic, don't hesitate to haul 'em out. You can simply put them on display, or use them to contain all kinds of tiny essentials, from pushpins and paper clips to keys and everyday jewelry. To make those holdalls clean and fresh—without harming their value—wipe them with a half-and-half solution of vinegar and warm water. If the butt bearers are badly stained, soak them in full-strength vinegar until all the tobacco residue is gone. **Note:** *In this case, either white or apple cider vinegar will work fine.*

Move Out, Minerals!

Minerals in your water can accumulate in your washer's hoses, inlet valves, and pump. Over time, the buildup restricts water flow, increases friction, and shortens the life of the machine. To fend off trouble, periodically fill the drum with cold water, add 1 cup of vinegar (no soap and no clothes), and run the washer through a complete cycle. Performing this ploy about every three months should keep your machine's mechanism free and clear, but do the job more frequently if your water is hard and/or you average more than 8 to 10 loads of laundry a week. **Note:** *Besides eliminating trouble-causing minerals, this treatment will help keep your washer's drum clean.*

Don't Let Detergent Be Your Downfall

Using more detergent will not get your clothes any cleaner—but it could cause major damage to your washing machine. The damage could come in one (or both) of two ways: An overload of detergent will send the water spilling over the rim of the tub and into the drive motor, causing it to burn out. What's more, the suds can push socks or other small items over the top of the drum, where agitation will pull them into the outer tub and from there quite possibly into the water pump. Either scenario could land

Word to the Wise

For laundry, stain-removal, and other clothing care, use only white vinegar. Apple cider vinegar, red-wine vinegar, or any other kind with a tint to it will create stains rather than remove them!

Wash Your Washer—Every washing machine needs an extra-thorough washing every now and then. To get rid of built-up soap scum, hair, lint, and heaven knows what else, pour 1 gallon of white vinegar into the drum, and run the washer through a regular full cycle.

you with a bill for major repairs or a new washer.

So what do you do when you accidentally put too much laundry detergent in the washing machine? It's simple: Add 2 tablespoons of vinegar to the water. It'll counteract the overkill of suds so your machine will live to wash another day—or even for many more years.

The Dastardly "Dry-Clean Only" Lie

When you see the words *dry-clean only* on a garment's label, it's only natural to think that if you ignore that admonition you'll wind up with a wardrobe that would fit a two-year-old. Not so! If you follow these guidelines, you can do the job yourself, and your clothes will come out just fine—without the use of harsh chemicals that could potentially hasten the demise of your duds. Here's the simple three-step process:

- Gently hand-wash the garment in lukewarm (100°F) water with mild soap.

- Rinse it thoroughly in cool water with a teaspoon or so of white vinegar added to it.

- To dry the garment, lay it flat, and stretch it to its original shape and size.

Note: *These instructions apply to critter-derived fabrics, including alpaca, angora, cashmere, mohair, and wool.*

Preserve the Color

Modern-day fabrics tend to be a lot more colorfast than they were in days gone by. Still, unless you're absolutely sure the dye will stay put, it doesn't pay to take chances. So before you wash a new, bright-colored garment for the first time, soak it for about 15 minutes in a solution made from ⅔ cup of white vinegar per gallon of cold water. Then wash and dry the article according to the guidelines on its care tag.

Sack the Smell!

It might be fun to get new clothes. But there's nothing enjoyable about the telltale chemical odor that often comes with them—or with the "has-been" kind of aroma that can linger on vintage or thrift-store finds. Fortunately, there's a simple way to send the smell packing: The first time you wash your new garments, pour 1 cup of white vinegar into the wash cycle. They'll come out smelling better than new!

Wash Up Whiter Whites

We all know that white clothes tend to take on a dull, grayish tone over time. Chlorine bleach can restore the brightness—but it also weakens the fabric, thereby (of course) shortening the life of the garment. To accomplish

KEEP YOUR DENIM DARK

Some folks (yours truly included) like blue jeans best when they're comfortably soft and faded. But if you want yours to stay their original shade of deep indigo, this tip's for you: Before you wash the pants for the first time, soak them for an hour or so in a solution of ½ cup of vinegar per 2 quarts of water. Then toss 'em into the washer on a normal cycle.

the same objective with no nasty side effects, simply add 1 cup of white vinegar to your washer's rinse cycle.

Safer Ways to Soften

Both liquid fabric softeners and dryer sheets have been shown to be highly toxic. They're also entirely unnecessary. Here are a couple of safer—and less expensive—ways you can make your laundry soft and static-free:

- Add ½ cup or so of vinegar to each wash load.

- Spray vinegar on a piece of all-cotton cloth, and toss it into the dryer with the load.

Hair's the Fabric Softener

This DIY fabric softener will make your laundry soft and smelling as clean and fresh as just-shampooed hair. Plus, it can work its magic in your washing machine or your dryer. All you need to do is mix 1 cup of white vinegar, ¾ cup of hair conditioner (any kind will do), and 2 cups of water in a bowl. Pour the mixture into a clean bottle with a tight-fitting lid. Then, come laundry day, use your super softener in one of these two ways:

- Add ¼ cup of the softener to your washing machine's rinse cycle.

- Sparingly spray some of the liquid onto a washcloth and toss it into the dryer along with your freshly laundered clothes.

Note: *For the sake of convenience, you might want to make two batches. Keep one of them in a regular, open-neck bottle for easy pouring, and the other in a spray bottle for convenient spritzing.*

A Trick for Terrific Towels

How long even premium bath towels stay on the job depends on how you treat them on laundry day. Specifically, always remember this little secret: Every time you wash your towels, add 2 cups of white vinegar to the rinse water. Or, if you find it easier, keep a tray or two of vinegar ice cubes in the freezer, and toss three or four of them into the washer. Either way, your towels will stay as soft and fluffy as almost anything this side of a five-star hotel! **Note:** *This ploy works just as well to keep cotton and washable wool blankets feeling fresh and soft as new.*

What's *That* I Smell?!

A slight stench coming from your laundry room generally means one thing: You forgot about a load of laundry that you left in the washing machine, and now the wet clothes are on the high road to Mildewville. Well, whatever you do, don't toss 'em in the dryer in that condition! Even a handful of dryer sheets won't be able to erase the aroma. Instead, revive the just-washed scent this way:

{ **WHENEVER YOU WASH** a vinyl tablecloth, shower curtain liner, or similar waterproof wonder, add a cup of vinegar to the rinse water. The plastic fabric will be soft and supple when it dries. }

Pour 2 cups of white vinegar into the machine, set it on the hottest temperature the fabric will tolerate, and run the load through a full cycle. Once it's done...

Wash the load again, this time with your regular detergent and no vinegar. Then immediately pop the duds in the dryer, and they should come out smelling as fresh as daisies.

Sputter Busters

Hard water can leave mineral deposits that clog vents in a steam iron, causing it to sputter and possibly stain whatever you're ironing. Here's a duo of dandy ways to prevent this annoying problem:

- Fill the water holder with white vinegar, set the dial on "high steam," and go about your business while the appliance cleans itself. When the reservoir is dry, flush it with distilled, bottled, or otherwise filtered water. (How often you need to perform this maneuver depends on how much ironing you do; let your eyes be your guide.)

- Every now and then, augment that heat treatment by cleaning out the holes with a wooden toothpick—while the iron is turned off and unplugged, of course!

Look Sharp

To make creases in freshly ironed clothes come out a lot spiffier (as Grandma Putt would say), spray them lightly with a 50-50 solution of vinegar and water before you iron them. For extra-

QUICK & QUIRKY

Spray Wrinkles Away—Oops! Your cotton chinos came out of the dryer looking like a wrinkled mess. Well, don't bother ironing them. Instead, fill a spray bottle with 1 part vinegar to 3 parts water, and mist-spray the pants all over. Then hang 'em up to air-dry. It's easier and gentler than ironing!

sharp creases in dress slacks and shirts, first dampen the garment with a clean cotton cloth moistened with a solution of 1 part vinegar and 2 parts water. Then lay a clean brown paper bag over the crease, and iron away! **Note:** *Make sure the bag is plain brown. If it has any lettering or other designs, you'll press them right into your clothes.*

Remove Scorch Marks

Steam irons have gotten a lot fancier than they were in Grandma Putt's day, but one thing hasn't changed: When the iron gets hot, or you leave it in one place too long, you can wind up scorching the fabric. Unfortunately, serious burns are usually fatal, but you can often erase light scorch marks the same way Grandma did: Rub the spot with a soft, clean cloth dampened with white vinegar, then blot it up with a clean towel. Repeat if necessary until the brown spots vamoose.

Defeat Set-In Stains

The longer any stain has time to sit, the harder it is to get out. In fact, sometimes it's downright impossible! But don't give up. Here's how to attempt removal:

- Saturate the mark with white vinegar, and then rub it vigorously with a paste made from equal parts of vinegar and baking soda.

INSIDE YOUR HOME

- If the stain won't budge, mix 2 tablespoons each of white vinegar and laundry detergent per gallon of cool water. Submerge the blemished part(s) of the item, and leave it overnight. Then rinse the spot with clear water and toss the garment in the wash.

Out, Danged Spot!

Some of the most common clothing stains are also among the hardest to remove. But if you've got a bottle of white vinegar on hand, you've got it made. To banish each of the blemishes below, simply follow the simple directions and then immediately wash the garment as usual.

OLD-TIME
Vim and *Vinegar*

To remove just about any non-oily stain, do what folks did before fancy spot removers came along: Mix 1 teaspoon each of white vinegar and liquid detergent in 2 cups of warm water. Apply the mixture to the spot with a brush or sponge, and then launder the garment as usual.

Blood. Pour full-strength white vinegar on the spot. Let it soak in for 10 minutes, then blot with a clean cloth. Repeat as necessary.

Coffee and tea. Continuously flush the soiled area with straight vinegar until the stains are gone.

Crayon. Brush the colorful marks away with an old toothbrush dipped in straight vinegar.

Deodorant. Rub straight vinegar into the fabric until the stains vanish.

Grass. Just sponge the streaks with white vinegar. If the stain persists, make a paste of vinegar and baking soda, and brush it into the stain with an old toothbrush.

Ink. Dampen the stained area with vinegar. Then rub with a paste made of vinegar and baking soda, and let it dry.

Mildew. Moisten the spots with a half-and-half mixture of vinegar and water. Then spread the item out in the sun until the marks vanish.

Mustard. Soak the stain in a half-and-half solution of white vinegar and water until the spot disappears. Blot with a soft cloth.

Perspiration. Sponge the stain with a solution made of 1 cup of water and 1 tablespoon of white vinegar.

Soda pop. Pour vinegar over the stain, and let it sit for 10 minutes or so.

KEYS TO SUCCESSFUL STAIN REMOVAL

No matter what kind of messy marks you're dealing with, follow these guidelines for best results:

▶ Act fast. The fresher any stain is, the more likely it is that you'll get it all out.

▶ Always use cold water on any protein-based stain, including blood, gravy, meat juices, eggs, vomit, urine, or fecal matter. Hot or very warm water will cook the offending substance right into the fabric.

▶ Make sure any stain is completely gone before you toss the treated item into the dryer. Otherwise, the heat will set the marks in for good.

▶ After you've treated severe stains, add 1 to 2 cups of vinegar to the follow-up wash cycle.

Bust the Rust

It's a wash day nightmare all right: Your freshly laundered clothes and bed linens are all decked out in orangey streaks and splotches. Most likely that's because the enamel coating inside your washing machine or dryer drum has gotten chipped, and rust spots have formed on the bare metal. Fortunately, they're easy to fix (see A Word to the Wise, below). But first, tackle the rust stains this way:

Mix white vinegar and salt to make a thin paste, spread a thick layer of it over the rusty spots, and go about your business for 30 minutes or so.

Lay the stained part of the fabric over a large pot or tub.

Pour 4 cups of boiling water through the rusty area.

Let the fabric dry (in the sun, if possible). If any marks remain, repeat the process.

Once all traces of rust are gone (and your washer or dryer has also been de-rusted), run the clothes and/or linens through a complete wash cycle.

Big and Simple Solutions

When some substances go "splash," they tend to cover a fair amount of space on garments, tablecloths, or bed

Word to  the Wise

As soon as you notice rust stains on your laundry, trot down to your local hardware store and buy some porcelain enamel touch-up paint. Pinpoint the dings (they may be tiny, so use a flashlight and look carefully—you don't want to miss any). Dab some paint onto each chipped spot and let it dry, following the manufacturer's instructions. While you're at it, touch up any chips that you find around the machine's door, too, because rust can set in there when you move damp laundry. Once you've done a thorough cover-up job, you can kiss your orange-streak woes good-bye!

linens. For example, beer, fruit juices, black coffee or tea, and vomit all fall into these categories. The simplest first response: Soak the stricken fabric overnight in a solution of 3 parts vinegar to 1 part cold water. Then take a look. If the stains are still present and accounted for, repeat the process as many times as you need to until they're gone. Then toss the item into the washing machine with your usual detergent.

Ring Out Ring around the Collar...

Or cuffs. How? Grab a retired toothbrush, dip it in a paste made from 2 parts white vinegar to 3 parts baking soda, and scrub-a-dub-dub. Let the paste set for 30 minutes or so, and then toss the shirts in the wash. **Note:** *This trick also works to remove light mildew stains from washable linens.*

FANTASTIC FORMULA

All-Around Stain Zapper

Stains are one of life's little gotchas. And while many colorful blotches should generally be treated according to their individual nature, this basic formula can effectively tackle most smears, splotches, and blobs.

- **¼ cup of ammonia**
- **¼ cup of white vinegar**
- **2 tbsp. of baking soda**
- **1 tbsp. of dishwashing liquid**
- **1 qt. of water**

Pour all of the ingredients into a spray bottle, put the lid on, and shake the bottle to mix well. When a stain appears, spray the pretreater onto the spot, and work it into the fibers with an old clean toothbrush. Wait a minute or two, and if the mark is still visible, repeat the process. Once the item is stain-free, drop it into the washer with the rest of the load, and run the machine as usual.

MY CLOTHES WEREN'T ICY!

Road-salt damage isn't limited to floors (see "Road Salt Rides Again..." on page 187). The nasty stuff can also take its toll on clothing and footwear. Fortunately, if you act fast, vinegar can often save the day. Your modus operandi depends on the nature of the victim. Here's the deal:

Weather-resistant fabric. Snow boots and water-repellent coats are common victims. Wipe the spots with a soft, clean cloth dipped in a water-vinegar mixture. Start with 1 tablespoon of vinegar in a quart of water, and if that doesn't do the trick, gradually add more vinegar. When the marks are gone, wipe the area(s) with a clean, dry cloth.

Nonwashable fabrics. Let the salt dry and then brush it off with either a clothing brush or a soft-bristled, off-duty hairbrush. (If there is mud on the garment, make sure it's also completely dry before you start brushing, or you'll work it into the fibers.) If any salt and/or mud splotches remain, sponge them with a cloth dipped in the vinegar-water solution described above. Then dab off the dirty water with a dry cloth.

Leather. Dip a soft, clean cloth in a half-and-half solution of vinegar and water, and wipe the marks away. And be quick about it because salt can damage leather in the blink of an eye!

Suede. Blot (don't rub!) the spots with a soft, clean cloth dipped in undiluted white vinegar. Then blot again, using a soft, dry cloth until the surface is dry. Follow up by brushing with a soft  suede brush or a clean terry-cloth towel. Work in circular motions to raise the nap until the surface looks clean and new.

Tough Treatment for Stubborn Ink Stains

Got an ink stain that just won't budge? Well, don't keep scrubbing at it—that's likely to drive the ink even deeper into the fabric. Instead, switch gears and try this much stronger solution:

STEP 1. Mix 1 tablespoon of milk, 1 tablespoon of white vinegar, 1 teaspoon of borax, and 1 teaspoon of lemon juice in a bowl.

STEP 2. Place the stained area of the item between two clean cloths, so the solution doesn't directly touch the fabric. Then dip a sponge in the liquid and gently pat the cloth that's on top of the stain for about three minutes.

STEP 3. Remove the top rag and use a clean sponge to blot the stain with cool water.

Repeat steps 2 and 3 until the stain is completely gone, then launder the item as usual.

Give a Hemline Hangover the Heave-Ho

It's annoying all right: Your new skirt was a tad too short, so

OLD-TIME Vim and Vinegar

Grandma Putt never had a problem with clothes moths—and her closets always smelled as fresh as the great outdoors. Her secret: her special lavender vinegar (moths *hate* lavender!). To make it, she steeped two heaping handfuls of new lavender leaves per quart of white vinegar for 10 days. Then she strained out the leaves and used the infused vinegar to wash down the walls of all her closets. Try it—you'll love it!

INSIDE YOUR HOME

you let down the hemline. The new length looks much better—but now you've got needle marks where the old thread used to be. The simple solution: Dampen a clean cloth in a half-and-half solution of vinegar and water, and spread it out on your ironing board. Then lay your garment over the cloth, and iron over the hem. Those needle perforations will be gone with the wind, er, steam.

QUICK & QUIRKY

Perfect Patent Ploys—Patent leather shoes, purses, and belts are known for their glossy shine. So when your patent accessories lose their luster, brighten them up by wiping them with a little vinegar on a soft, clean cloth. Wipe the surface dry with another soft cloth.

Toss the Smoke Smell

When you've been to a gathering in a smoke-filled room, or around a fire pit or campfire, your clothes are bound to pick up the aroma. But don't fret. It's a snap to remove l'eau de smoke. Simply fill your bathtub with very hot water, and pour in 2 to 4 cups of apple cider vinegar. Hang your odoriferous duds on the shower rod overnight, and by morning, they should be back to their usual clean-smelling selves.

Reshape a Warped Purse

Leather shoulder- and handbags tend to get bent out of shape when they sit on a shelf for too long. If that carryall is unlined, this three-step procedure will put it back in business fast:

- Make the leather more flexible by wiping down the bag's interior with a solution of 5 parts white vinegar to 1 part water.

- Stuff the purse with tissue paper until it's back to its shape.

- Let the bag sit for a couple of days, and then air it out to remove the vinegar smell.

Then, to prevent future warping, keep the purse stuffed with acid-free tissue paper between uses—or simply carry it more often.

To reshape a lined bag, forget the vinegar and water treatment and just pack the interior tightly with tissue paper. The process will take longer, but eventually the leather will regain its original contours.

Save Your Saturated Footwear

If stepping in a puddle leaves your leather shoes or boots saturated, dump out the water and remove any unattached insoles. Then rub castor oil or a commercial conditioner into the leather so it doesn't stiffen up. Finally, stuff the shoes with crumpled newspaper, and let them dry naturally, away from heat sources (direct heat could do more damage than water could). **Note:** *If the mishap occurred in the winter, when the puddle may have contained salt-induced snowmelt, attack the deposits following the guidelines in "My Clothes Weren't Icy!" on page 222.*

TO REMOVE GREASE SPOTS on suede bags, shoes, or jackets, brush the marks with a soft toothbrush dipped in white vinegar. Let them air-dry, then brush with a suede brush. If necessary, repeat the process a time or two.

Shape Up!

When your panty hose get baggy, don't relegate them to your cleaning kit—at least, not before you try this clever caper: Soak them for 15 minutes in a sink or basin filled with lukewarm water with 2 teaspoons of vinegar added to it. Rinse in water and hang the hose up to dry, and they should be as good as new! If, by chance, they were too far gone for anything to shrink them into shape, put 'em to work as gentle scrubbing "pads," floor polishers, or the gazillion other household tasks that nylon hose can perform so well.

End Your Jewelry's Film Career

When you see the words *24-carat gold* on a piece of jewelry, you know it's made of gold and nothing but gold. Lower carat numbers like 10K, 14K, and 18K indicate that the item has other metals mixed in. And those additives make it react with your body oils, hair spray, perfume—and even the air itself—to produce a dull film on your bracelet, necklace, or other adornment. When that haze appears, clear it away with this simple four-step procedure:

STEP 1. Find a glass container that's the right size to contain your treasure, and pour in enough salt to fill it about three-quarters of the way up.

Word to the Wise

Never use vinegar—either straight or in a formula—to clean softer stones such as emeralds, opals, pearls, turquoise, or jade. The acetic acid will destroy them. Likewise, don't try to spruce up any silver object with vinegar. While your treasure will survive, the acid will darken, rather than brighten, the metal.

STEP 2. Slowly pour in white vinegar almost to the top.

STEP 3. Drop in your golden goodies, and set the glass aside. Give it a shake several times a day so that the salt can gently scrub off the discoloration.

STEP 4. After seven days of shaking things up, empty the container and rinse your bauble with clear water. Then enjoy it to the hilt!

Note: *This technique also works like a charm to clean diamonds.*

Back when my Grandma Putt was raising her family, vinegar played a key role in the work—and the fun. And that versatile, vivacious fluid is every bit as helpful here in the 21st century. In these pages, we'll take a gander at some of the ways this lusty liquid can lend its star power to your child- and pet-care chores, and also help keep your four-legged and fine feathered friends in tip-top shape. As for the fun angle, just wait till you see the ways you can use vinegar in creative projects and kid-pleasing games!

BABY & CHILD CARE

Make Baby Gear Mouth-Worthy

As all you parents and grandparents know, tiny tykes require a lot of equipment that needs to be kept clean—and a whole lot of it winds up in baby's mouth at one time or another. So forget toxin-laden chemical cleaners. Good old vinegar can produce the same results with none of the harmful side effects. Here's a trio of examples:

Baby bottles. Soak 'em in full-strength vinegar for an hour or so to remove stains and hard-water marks. Scrub with a bottle brush to remove any stubborn film left by formula or milk. Then rinse thoroughly with clear water.

INSIDE YOUR HOME

Baby toys. Add 1 cup of white vinegar and 1 tablespoon of dishwashing liquid to a sink of hot water. Slosh the playthings around, wipe off any surface dirt, and then rinse thoroughly with cool, clear water.

Vinyl, cloth, or board books. Dampen a cloth with a solution of 1 part white vinegar and 2 parts water, and wipe the covers and any pages that are made of the sturdy, baby-resistant material. Do not use vinegar on any thin paper!

Diaper Duty

Plenty of parents and grandparents still use old-fashioned cloth diapers—at least part of the time. So if you're among those traditionalists, vinegar can be your best friend on laundry day. Put it to work this way:

- After you rinse dirty diapers in the tub or toilet, soak them in a solution of 1 part vinegar to 10 parts water before you toss them in the wash.

- Always add 1 cup of white vinegar to the final rinse cycle. It'll break down both uric acid and soap residue, leaving the fabric softer and more comfortable on baby's tender skin.

OLD-TIME *Vim and Vinegar*

How'd you like to learn a simple old-time trick that'll deodorize and humidify your baby's room and make it safer at the same time? Well, here it is: Just take a damp towel out of the washing machine, spray it with white vinegar, and hang it over the top of the door to the nursery. As the vinegar-soaked fabric dries, it'll control odors, add moisture to the air, and keep the door from closing all the way—so the little one won't be accidentally locked in the room.

Deal with the Diaper Pail

Nothing will make it smell like a bed of roses, but this simple routine will help keep the odor to a minimum: After you remove the dirty diapers, wash the pail with hot, soapy water and then rub the inside with full-strength white vinegar. It'll eliminate the unpleasant aroma—at least until the container gets filled up again.

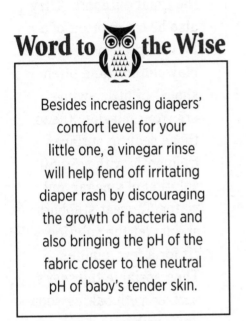

Word to the Wise

Besides increasing diapers' comfort level for your little one, a vinegar rinse will help fend off irritating diaper rash by discouraging the growth of bacteria and also bringing the pH of the fabric closer to the neutral pH of baby's tender skin.

What a Doll!

Spruce up plastic dolls by wiping them from head to toe with full-strength vinegar. To wash Dolly's clothes, soak them in a quart of warm water with 3 tablespoons of vinegar and 2 tablespoons of baking soda mixed into it. (The soaking time depends on how dirty the duds are, so let your eyes be your guide.) Then rinse with clear, cool water and let the little garments air-dry. **Note:** *Before you wash doll clothes for the first time, test an inconspicuous area for colorfastness.*

Help for the High Chair

To clean and disinfect this much-used piece of furniture, spray or wipe the whole thing with a half-and-half solution of vinegar and water. Pay special attention to the tray, where a lot of food spends time before finding its way into your baby's mouth.

FANTASTIC FORMULA

Homemade Baby Wipes

Why buy expensive baby wipes when you've probably got everything you need to make your own? Here's how it's done.

- **1 roll of soft, absorbent paper towels***
- **1 plastic container with a tight-fitting lid to hold the paper towels**
- **2 tbsp. of baby oil**
- **2 tbsp. of liquid baby bath soap**
- **1 tbsp. of white vinegar**
- **2 cups of water, boiled and cooled to room temperature**

Cut the roll of paper towels in half with a serrated knife, and remove the cardboard tube. Place half the roll, cut end down, in the plastic container. Mix the liquid ingredients, pour the solution into the container, and close the lid. The towels will absorb the liquid. As you need them, pull the wipes up from the center of the roll.

A premium paper towel brand like Viva® works best.

Get in the Swing

The seats of swing sets—whether they're made of plastic, wood, or metal—spend all of their time in the great outdoors. They also bear the brunt of a lot of dirt deposited by play clothes (and often shoes) of little swingers. Your mission: Clean those seating surfaces frequently with a 50-50 solution of vinegar and water. To treat stubborn stains, let the solution sit for a few minutes. Then sprinkle the seat's surface with baking soda, and scrub with a rag or brush. Rinse with clear water, and you're ready for action! **Note:** *The same routine that makes swing seats sparkle works just as well on outdoor action toys like pedal cars and tricycles.*

Be a Sport

Remove ground-in dirt

and mud from plastic, aluminum, or fiberglass sports equipment with this simple routine:

- Rub the dirty surfaces with a paste made from 1 part vinegar to 3 parts baking soda.
- Wash the paste off with soapy water.
- Rinse with clean water and dry with a soft, clean cloth.

Then let the games begin!

Don't Cry over Misguided Crayons

Let's face it: Where there are small children, there are crayons. And the young artists don't always confine their creative efforts to paper. So if your creative children or grandchildren left a colorful masterpiece where they shouldn't have, don't panic. Simply remove the wayward strokes from fabric, painted walls, and just about any other surface under the sun by moistening an old, soft toothbrush with vinegar and gently scrubbing the marks away.

OLD-TIME *Vim and Vinegar*

Throughout this book, I've been singing the praises of good old-fashioned vinegar as a superstar cleaning agent. But if you have small children or pets on the scene (even if they're only frequent visitors), you have an especially important reason to make vinegar a major part of your cleaning arsenal: Even the "greenest" commercial products can cause big-time trouble if they wind up in the hands (or stomach) of a curious child or pet. But if your nearest and dearest should take a swig of vinegar, the only consequence will be an unpleasant jolt to the taste buds!

Bouncing Apple Seeds

Kids of all ages—and grown-ups, too—never fail to get a kick out of this simple, natural magic trick: Pour ½ cup of water into a tall, thin drinking glass, then add ⅔ teaspoon of baking soda, and stir until it's dissolved. Drop in the seeds from one or more apples, pour in 1 tablespoon of white vinegar, and stir gently. The seeds will rise up to the surface, carried by carbon dioxide bubbles, then fall back down as the bubbles burst.

Blow Up Balloons—Without Blowing

For this trick, you need a balloon, 2 tablespoons of water, 1 teaspoon of baking soda, 1 clean empty soda-pop bottle, and 4 tablespoons of white vinegar. Once you've rounded up your supplies, proceed as follows:

- Gently stretch the balloon a few times to make it more flexible.

- Add the water and baking soda to the bottle.

- Pour the vinegar into the bottle and very quickly fit the balloon over the top of the bottle.

The carbon dioxide released from the vinegar-soda combo will inflate the balloon in a flash.

QUICK & QUIRKY

Bubble-Blowing Seashells—Tiny tykes love this simple trick: Fill a glass bowl one-quarter of the way with vinegar. Then gently drop in two or three seashells. They'll release a fountain of bubbles. The reason: The acetic acid in the vinegar reacts with the limestone in the shells to form carbon dioxide—the same stuff that gives soda pop its fizz.

Thar She Blows!

This outdoor adventure was not part of my childhood playtime because one of the key ingredients—ziplock plastic bags—didn't exist back then. But all the kids I know in the under-10 set today think it's a blast. Literally. Here's your action-packed plan:

STEP 1. Gather up a sandwich-size ziplock bag (freezer-strength), ¼ cup of warm water, ½ cup of vinegar, 3 teaspoons of baking soda, and a facial tissue. Then take it outside.

STEP 2. Pour the water into the bag, followed by the vinegar.

STEP 3. Put the baking soda in the middle of the tissue, and fold the sides up over the soda.

STEP 4. Now act fast! Zip the bag almost

FANTASTIC FORMULA

Homemade Plastic

Well, sort of plastic. Using this ultra-simple recipe—and with a little adult help—kids can turn milk into moldable blobs. They'll learn a little chemistry and have a lot of fun at the same time.

1 cup of whole milk

4 tsp. of white vinegar

Heat the milk until it's hot, but not boiling, and carefully pour it into a heat-proof bowl. Add the vinegar, and stir it with a spoon for about 60 seconds. Then carefully pour the mixture through a strainer into the kitchen sink. Inside the strainer will be a mass of lumpy blobs. Let them cool down until they're comfortable to the touch. Then rinse them in clear water as you press them together to form a single lump. Mold it into whatever shape you like. In a few days, it will harden into a piece of sculpture. **Note:** *What you've actually produced is a substance called casein, which is a type of protein found in milk. When it meets the acid in the vinegar, the two substances don't mix, so the casein forms blobs.*

INSIDE YOUR HOME

closed, leaving just enough space to insert the baking soda packet. Pop it through the opening, and *quickly* zip the bag up tight.

STEP 5. Set the bag on the ground and step back—pronto.

The plastic pouch will start to expand...until suddenly—*POP!*

Play Rocket Scientist

So what made the plastic bag burst open in our "Thar She Blows!" trick above? The same thing that makes apple seeds bounce and balloons inflate by themselves: the carbon dioxide (CO_2) that's created whenever you mix vinegar and baking soda together. In the case of the popping bag, the gas continuously expands until the bag can't hold it any longer, and *BAM*! It's quite a sight to see. But it's even more fun when you expand the demonstration into a real scientific experiment. How? Simply stage repeat performances, each time changing what scientists call the independent variables, to answer questions like these:

- Will higher or lower water temperatures affect how fast the bag inflates?

That's Historical

The quasi-plastic that you learned how to make using vinegar and milk (see Homemade Plastic on page 233) is nothing new—and it's certainly not limited to experimental blobhood! In fact, some of the earliest plastics were based on casein. Casein-based paint has been around since the days of ancient Egypt (it's still a favorite choice of theatrical-scene painters). Casein-based glues were popular in the aircraft industry as recently as the late 1930s, when they were used in Britain's famous de Havilland Albatross transport planes. Today, while casein is best known as a food additive, it's also used in such far-flung fields as the fabrics industry, transformer manufacturing, and the lamination of fireproof doors.

- Does adding more baking soda create a bigger or faster pop?

- What happens when you use more vinegar?

- If you use a larger bag, will you get a louder bang for your buck?

Someday, you may be sending real rockets into space!

Bend a Bone

If you have trouble getting your youngsters to drink their milk, having them perform this trick just might convince them to guzzle more moo juice. Here's all there is to it: The next time you have chicken for dinner, rinse off a leg bone, and try to bend it (gently, so it doesn't break). Of course, it won't give an inch. Then put the bone into a jar with a tight-fitting lid. Pour in enough white vinegar to completely cover the bone, put the lid on the jar, and let it sit for three days. When time's up, remove the bone, rinse it off, and try again to bend it. This time, it will bend—almost as though it's turned to rubber.

So what the heck happened in that jar? The acid in the vinegar dissolved the calcium in the bone—that's what! The moral of the story, kids: Strong bones and calcium go hand in hand.

CRAFTS & PROJECTS

DIY Decorative Paint

This formula is perfect for adding colorful touches to picture or mirror frames, furniture, or anything else that's made of wood, either finished or unfinished. Here's how to make and use it in five simple steps:

STEP 1. Round up your supplies. You'll need two containers, white vinegar, granulated sugar, clear dishwashing liquid, powdered poster paint, a texturizing tool, a clean rag, a paint-brush, and clear polyurethane.

STEP 2. In the first container, mix ½ cup of vinegar, 1 teaspoon of sugar, and a squeeze of dishwashing liquid.

STEP 3. Put 2 tablespoons of the powdered poster paint into the second container, and stir in enough of the vinegar mix to make a solution that's thick enough not to run when it's brushed on a vertical surface.

DEPENDING ON THE LOOK YOU'RE AFTER, there's almost no limit to the texturizing tools you can use with your decorative paint. But good, easy-to-come-by choices include combs, feathers, sponges, or crumpled pieces of paper.

STEP 4. Use your texturizing tool to brush the paint onto the wood, creating whatever effect you desire. Erase any mistakes by wiping the surface with a rag moistened with vinegar.

STEP 5. When the job is done to your satisfaction, let the paint dry thoroughly, and then brush on several coats of clear polyurethane.

Stain Wood with ACV

Looking for a simple, natural way to stain or age wood on small pieces of furniture or for use in craft projects? Well, look no further! Just gather up six 0000 grade steel wool pads, 1 gallon of apple cider vinegar, a big bucket with a lid, a sturdy pair of gloves, and a paintbrush (it doesn't have to be a good one). Then:

- Put the steel wool pads and vinegar in the bucket, pop the lid on top, and let it sit for four to five days. Check it every 24 hours or so until the solution reaches the shade you want. The longer you wait—of course—the darker the stain will be.

- When the concoction has reached your desired color, give it a quick stir and strain out whatever steel wool is left (there won't be much). The vinegar smell will be powerful, but by the time the stain on your project has dried, the odor will have vanished.

- For ease of use, transfer smaller amounts of the stain to a smaller container.

- Pull on gloves and thoroughly cover your work surface because this stuff will stain anything it touches.

- Working outdoors if possible, brush the stain onto the wood in the usual way. Once it's dried, you can rinse it or not, as you prefer. It's your call—rinsing will remove any rusty residue from the steel wool and will also slightly lighten the color of the end product.

Note: *For this purpose, you don't need the health-giving properties of unpro-cessed ACV, so feel free to use the cheapest stuff you can find.*

> **BROADEN YOUR PALETTE**
>
> Your vinegar stain choices are not limited to ACV. Balsamic vinegar also produces a lovely tint—but for the sake of your pocketbook, you'll probably want to buy the cheapest stuff you can find and limit its use to very small projects. Red-wine and colorful infused vinegars can also produce creative results on small projects. To make your own versions for a lot less money than even the cheapest commercial brands will cost, see  the "Making Your Very Own Vinegar" section in Chapter 3, starting on page 109.

Terrific Tie-Dyed Easter Eggs

I don't know anyone—child or adult—who doesn't enjoy the spring-time ritual of dying Easter eggs. Here's a vinegar-intense variation on the theme that'll give your creative juices free rein:

Lay a sheet of plastic wrap or (better yet) a plastic trash bag on a table, and top it with several layers of paper towels.

Spray the paper with a 50-50 solution of white vinegar and water.

Dribble food coloring all over the paper towels to make assorted-colored blobs.

OLD-TIME

Vim and *Vinegar*

Before commercial egg-coloring kits came along, folks made their own dyes using food coloring and vinegar. The basic formula is 1 tablespoon of white vinegar and ¼ teaspoon of food coloring per ¾ cup of hot water. Then you simply dip a hard-boiled egg into the mixture, wait until it reaches the shade you want, and pull 'er out.

Set a hard-boiled egg in the center of the paper towel, and gather the edges toward the egg.

Holding the towel snugly around the egg, spray it with the vinegar solution until the paper is soaked.

Gently squeeze out any excess vinegar solution, then wrap the covered egg in plastic wrap, and secure the top with a rubber band.

Let it sit for at least 60 minutes so the food coloring can soak into the egg. The longer it sits, the deeper the colors will be.

Note: *For the best, most colorful results, limit the palette to two or three colors. Otherwise, you'll end up with much less vibrant—and even muddy—mixtures.*

PRODUCE TO DYE FOR?

Dye with, I should say. Grandma Putt went all out for holidays, and Easter was no exception. Every year, we colored dozens of eggs to put in baskets for family, friends, and neighbors. The eggs came from Grandma's hens—and the dyes came right from her yard and garden. In case you'd like to try your hand at making natural dyes, see "Old-Time Easter Egg Dye" (below). Here's your color palette:

To Get This Color	Use These Materials
Blue	Blackberries, blueberries, chestnuts, red cabbage leaves
Green	Bracken, coltsfoot, spinach
Purple	Blackberries or purple grapes
Orange	Yellow onion skins
Red	Beets, cranberries, frozen raspberries, red onion skins
Yellow	Shredded carrots, carrot tops (the green part), lawn grass, lemon or orange peels

Old-Time Easter Egg Dye

Every year, when it was gettin' on time for Peter Cottontail to come hoppin' down the old Bunny Trail, Grandma Putt and I would gather our dye makings from the garden, and spend a Saturday coloring eggs. Here's the simple formula:

- Put the eggs in a single layer in a pan with just enough water to cover them completely.

- Add 1 teaspoon of white vinegar and 2 ½ cups of your

chosen fruits, vegetables, or leaves (see "Produce to Dye For?" on page 239).

- Bring the water to a boil, reduce the heat, and simmer for 15 to 20 minutes. Remove the eggs promptly if you want lighter shades. For darker colors, strain the dye into a bowl with the eggs, and let it sit in the refrigerator overnight.

Then turn 'em over to the Easter Bunny to stash in the kids' baskets, or hide them around the yard for the annual hunt.

Paint with Paper...

And vinegar, of course. This is a super-fun project for children or crafty grown-ups—and a great way to make greeting cards for birthdays and holidays. All you need are a brush, a bowl of white vinegar, white construction paper, and tissue paper in your choice of bright colors. (When you buy it at the craft store, make sure it's the non-colorfast kind because you want it to bleed.)

First, cut whatever shapes you desire from the tissue paper—say, Christmas trees or Santa Claus hats for Christmas, hearts for Valentine's Day, eggs or bunnies for Easter, and so on. Next, brush vinegar all over the white paper, and immediately lay the tissue-paper shapes on top. As the vinegar dries, the tissue paper will fall off, leaving a colorful design behind.

DOGS & CATS

Urine—You're Out!

Even the best-trained dog or cat has an accident every once in a while. Before sophisticated enzyme cleaners came on the scene, pet owners used this down-home routine to clean critter urine from their carpets. In a pinch, it works just as well today.

Blot up as much of the urine as you can with paper towels or old rags. (If the deed has just been done, this step alone will take care of 90 percent of the problem.)

Flush the spot with club soda, let it sit for a minute or two, and blot again.

Mix equal parts of vinegar and cool water, and scrub the solution into the rug with a stiff brush. Blot up the excess liquid, rinse with cool water, and let the spot dry.

If a stain remains, reapply the vinegar and water solution, wait 15 minutes, then rinse and blot again.

OLD-TIME *Vim and Vinegar*

If you're using vinegar to deodorize your pet, but your dog or cat simply won't tolerate being sprayed, try this technique: Dip a sponge or washcloth in the vinegar, and gently wipe it onto your pet's coat to keep it smelling fresh.

The Nose Knows

While it is true that vinegar can remove any urine or feces odor you can detect, it can't fool canine noses, which, depending on the breed, are anywhere from 1,000 to (yes, you're reading this right) 100 million times more sensitive than ours. To prevent future mishaps, you need to use a modern enzyme-based cleaner that's specially formulated to break down the biochemicals in the waste product. Otherwise, your pal, and any other dog who ventures near that spot, will continue to smell the enticing "Y'all come!" residue. **Note:** *You can find enzymatic cleaners at* *pet-supply stores and in the cleaning-supply sections of large supermarkets. There are numerous brands, including Nature's Miracle®, Simple Solution® Oxy Charged™, Fizzion®, and PetZyme®.*

More Anti-Aromatic Answers

Vinegar can bring its odor-busting powers to more than just your pet's potty indiscretions. For example:

- To get an unpleasant smell out of your dog's coat, spray on full-strength vinegar and let it air-dry. As an added bonus, this trick will make his coat shiny, relieve hot spots, and help repel fleas and ticks.

WHENEVER YOU USE VINEGAR as a topical treatment—alone or in a formula—be careful to keep it away from your pet's eyes and from any open sores or wounds. While it won't cause permanent harm, it will sting like crazy!

- Deodorize bedding by spraying it with a half-and-half solution of vinegar and water.

- To keep washable bed covers, comfort "blankies," and dog coats fresh-smelling, add ½ cup of baking soda to the wash cycle and ½ cup of white vinegar to the rinse cycle.

Super-Strength Dog-Deodorizing Bath

What do you do when Spike has gotten into who-knows-what, he's covered in greasy dirt, and he reeks to high heaven? Launch into this rapid-response plan—that's what!

STEP 1. Open a kitchen cupboard and pull out a box of baking soda, a jug of vinegar, and a bottle of Dawn® dishwashing liquid (preferably the lavender-scented type).

STEP 2. Mix 1 part baking soda with 4 parts water to make a thin paste. Gently but thoroughly rub it all over the dog's body, making sure that it penetrates to his skin.

STEP 3. Combine ½ cup of vinegar, 2 cups of water, and ¼ cup of Dawn in a large spray bottle or a jug (multiplying the quantities, if necessary, to accommodate the size of your dog). Shake the container until bubbles form, then let them recede.

GETTING SPECIFIC

So why do I specify Dawn dishwashing liquid in the deodorizing bath at left? Simply because it's formulated to cut through tough kitchen grease. And those same hard-hitting ingredients are just the ticket for washing away built-up oils and any newly acquired gunk on your dog's hair and skin. The classic variety will work fine for this purpose, but the lavender-scented type will go a step further and help repel fleas.

STEP 4. Spray or sponge the potion over the baking soda mixture, and use your fingers to work up a thick lather. Then massage it into his coat, being careful to keep the suds away from his eyes.

STEP 5. Rinse with warm water until all the soap and soda are gone. Then dry Spike with a towel, and brush or groom him as needed.

Deep-Clean a Litter Box

If you use one of the modern, clumping brands, Fluffy's bathroom can go for quite a while between litter changes. The timing can vary greatly, depending on how many cats use the box, how diligent you are about scooping out the clumps, and (of course) the sensitivity of your family's noses. But whenever the job needs to be done, here's a thorough way to go about it:

- Remove and dispose of the old litter. Then pour ½ inch of vinegar into the box, and let it sit for 15 minutes or so.

- Pour out the vinegar, then rinse and thoroughly dry the pan.

- Sprinkle the bottom generously with baking soda, and add fresh litter. Now take a deep breath of clean-smelling air!

Note: *This method works just as well for cleaning litter boxes (and cages) used by pet rabbits, puppies, or toy breeds of dogs.*

Word to the Wise

Whenever you use vinegar as an indoor critter repellent—either straight or mixed with water—always take these precautions: Use only white vinegar. ACV could stain the material you're trying to protect. Also, before you spray, test your target for colorfastness by spritzing a hidden spot, like the back side of a sofa skirt or drapery hem.

That Is *Not* Your Scratching Post!

Does your resident feline have a habit of sharpening her claws on your draperies or upholstered furniture? Well, you can stop those shenanigans in a shake. A spray, rather. Just mix equal parts of white vinegar and water in a spray bottle, and lightly spritz Fluffy's target areas. The obnoxious (to her) odor will keep her away, but once the vinegar has dried, you won't notice any aroma at all.

Break It Up, Guys!

All animals need to play. But, as you know if you have more than one cat or dog in your household, there are times when the action gets a tad too rough. When that happens, especially indoors, bad—and expensive—things can happen. But never fear: You and vinegar can call a halt to the havoc. Simply mix a 50-50 solution of white vinegar and water in a spray bottle, and keep it close at hand. Then, whenever your critters get carried away, aim the bottle in their general direction, and squeeze the trigger. The sudden release of the aromatic fluid should send them their separate ways. Just be sure to keep the spray away from their eyes!

A Panacea for Itchy Pets

Got a cat or dog who's scratching up a storm from allergies or other skin irritations? If so, deliver instant comfort this way: Mix equal parts of water and vinegar and a few drops of lavender oil in a covered container, and apply the mixture generously to the affected areas two or three times a day. You can either spray or gently dab it on—whichever is less stressful for your pet.

The secret to success: Vinegar will deliver its potent antibacterial and antifungal properties and will also help restore the proper pH to your pal's skin. The lavender oil offers additional analgesic, antihistamine, and anti-inflammatory properties. And, as mentioned earlier, it also helps repel fleas.

OLD-TIME *Vim and Vinegar* Long before newfangled (and toxic) flea collars and chemical repellents came on the scene, Grandma Putt used vinegar to keep her cats and dogs free of the tiny menaces. It works just as well today. You can either add ACV to your pet's food or drinking water or use an after-bath rinse made from equal parts of vinegar and warm water. **Note:** *If your dog or cat already has fleas, use the Fabulous Flea Shampoo on page 246.*

FANTASTIC FORMULA

Fabulous Flea Shampoo

Lots of commercial shampoos (as well as sprays, powders, and pills) can kill fleas, all right—but these products are also loaded with toxic chemicals that may actually cause more trouble than the little bugs can. On the other hand, this dynamic DIY potion will annihilate the mini vampires and soothe your pet's irritated skin.

1 8-oz. bottle of pet shampoo

1 tbsp. of aloe vera juice or gel

10 drops of tea tree oil

Vinegar

Water

Add the aloe vera and tea tree oil to the shampoo and shake well. Wash and rinse your pet as you would normally, but don't dry him. Wait for 6 to 10 minutes (doing whatever it takes to keep him from rolling on the ground!). And while you're waiting, mix 1 tablespoon of vinegar per pint of lukewarm water. Either spray or sponge it on as a final rinse, and let it air-dry.

Itchy Feet Feats

Canine skin allergies almost always result in itchy feet. You can find numerous safe, gentle remedies in books on natural pet care and (of course) on the Internet. Unfortunately, most of them have you soak all four paws in a footbath for 30 seconds or so. Depending on the size and temperament of the dog, that process can range from messy to downright impossible. Plus, many of these formulas contain taste-tempting ingredients that encourage dogs to start licking, thereby raising the risk of infection. Enter this neater, foul-tasting treatment. It'll remove pathogens, pus, loose skin, and any other troublesome residue—and leave your pup's skin with a pH that fends off both bacteria and foul fungi. Here's the routine:

Mix up a solution of 1 part white vinegar to 1½ parts filtered or distilled water in a glass container.

Pour a small amount of the mixture into a sturdy but pliable plastic bag. Then, one by one, dunk Fido's feet into the bag and massage them from the outside. (Depending on how much dirt comes off, you may need to use a fresh bag of fluid after each paw.)

Squeeze excess liquid from each paw as you remove it from its bag, then wrap it in a towel and squeeze again to dry it as much as possible.

Don't let him lick his feet! Once his paws are thoroughly dry, he'll be less inclined to go after them. In the meantime, distract him with toys, treats, tummy rubs, a walk—whatever it takes. If necessary, use a plastic cone (a.k.a. Elizabethan collar) to keep his mouth well away from his tootsies. Don't bother with topical deterrents. In this case, they're rarely effective.

> **FOR INTERNAL HEALTH-CARE PURPOSES,** always give your pets and livestock the same kind of raw, organic, unfiltered apple cider vinegar that you'd use for human consumption. But don't use apple cider vinegar for this treatment! Few dogs can resist zeroing in on its lightly sweet flavor.

The Critter-Color Conundrum

When you're using vinegar for topical purposes, the kind to reach for depends on the color of your pet's fur. To be specific:

White or light colors. Always use white vinegar because ACV could stain pale hair.

Black or other dark tones. Because white vinegar sometimes bleaches dark-colored fur, play it safe and go with ACV.

Combination coats. If your pal sports large, individual patches of white and dark colors, simply use the appropriate type of vinegar to spot-treat problems such as hot spots and insect bites. Avoid vinegar altogether for whole-body rinses and baths—unless, that is, your pal suddenly has a widespread rash eruption and you have no other remedy at hand.

Darn That Dandruff!

While dandruff does not pose a health problem, it's no more fun for your dog than it is for you. The simple way to bring relief: Pour full-strength vinegar directly on his coat after bathing and rinsing. Fido's flakes will flee fast!

THE FINE PRINT

While it is true that vinegar is one of the most potent healers on the planet, there are some points you need to keep in mind:

▶ If your cat or dog is getting along in years, has sensitive health, is taking medications of any kind, or is pregnant, check with your vet before using any vinegar treatments—even topically, because what goes onto the body goes into the body.

▶ The dosages recommended in this chapter are estimates, based only on the animal's weight. Many other factors can influence the optimum dose for any individual critter. So regardless of your pet's age or state of health, ask your vet how often you should give vinegar to your pal and in what amounts.

▶ Finally, if your pet shows any adverse reactions to vinegar, either internally or externally, go cold turkey immediately and ask your vet for alternate options.

No More Tears

If your dog has reddish-brown tear stains under his eyes or on his muzzle, he's not alone. Scads of canines have them, and the reason can be any of this trio:

- Physical traits such as deep facial wrinkles, long hair on the muzzle or surrounding the eye area, or bulging eyes

- Systemic conditions such as a pH imbalance, red yeast infections, or eye or ear infections

- Environmental factors such as plastic food or water bowls, or minerals in the drinking water

The good news is that, while the marks are unsightly, they pose no health risks and they're a snap to remove using (surprise!) vinegar. Start by putting a few drops of ACV in your dog's water each day. After three or four days, increase the amount to 1 teaspoon per day for small dogs and 1 tablespoon for larger canines. Within a few weeks, the stains should be gone once and for all!

Word to the Wise

To use ACV as a nutritional supplement for dogs, holistic vets generally recommend a daily dose of 1 teaspoon for canines weighing up to 14 pounds, 2 teaspoons for dogs weighing between 15 and 34 pounds, and 1 tablespoon for pooches 35 pounds and above. For cats, mix 1 teaspoon of ACV with 1 or 2 teaspoons of water, and dribble it onto Fluffy's food.

An Equal Opportunity Healer

Back in Chapter 1, we cast the spotlight on the ways humans have used vinegar and vinegar-based tonics for thousands of years to keep themselves in the pink of health. Well, guess what? Holistic vets tell us that ACV can work the very same health-care wonders for your four-legged and two-winged family members as it can for you. Here's just a sampling of what a daily dose can do when you mix it into your pets' food or water:

FANTASTIC FORMULA

After-Bath Comfort Rinse

This potion can soothe your dog's itchy skin, clear up rashes, and restore the skin's natural pH. It also helps fend off flies, fleas, and gnats.

½ cup of brewed green tea, cooled

½ cup of vinegar

1 cup of distilled water

Pour the ingredients in a glass bottle or jar, fasten the cap securely, and shake well. After bathing Fido, apply the rinse generously to his coat and massage it into his skin. Then either rinse with clear water and pat dry, or—for the added benefit of bug relief—let the rinse air-dry. **Note:** *This blend is also good for treating bug bites and stings. Refrigerate in a tightly capped glass container. It should keep for one to two weeks—but pitch it immediately if you detect any sign of mold.*

- Clear up existing urinary tract infections and help prevent the formation of bladder and kidney stones

- Create an internal environment that discourages fleas, ticks, and flies, as well as bad bacteria and foul fungi, including the ones that cause ringworm and mange

- Improve digestion, boost metabolism, and help maintain a healthy weight

- Lower bad (LDL) cholesterol levels

- Combat allergies of all kinds

- Keep internal "plumbing" on an even keel, helping to prevent constipation and diarrhea

- Ease depression and fight fatigue

- Relieve arthritis, stiff joints, and muscle cramps

- Boost the immune system—thereby helping your pal fend off every disease under the sun, as well as external parasites like fleas and ticks

Restore Balance

A dog's internal pH should be between 6.2 and 6.5. To find out where your pooch ranks, just buy some pH strips at the drugstore, and test Fido's urine following the directions on the package. A number below 6.2 means his system is too acidic—but adding ACV to his diet should restore a healthy balance in a hurry. **Note:** *If your dog simply refuses to accept vinegar in his food or water, try serving his daily ration stirred into a spoonful of plain yogurt. Most canines find the stuff irresistible!*

TO EASE THE PAIN OF ARTHRITIS OR SORE MUSCLES, soak a soft cotton cloth in warm (not hot!) vinegar, and hold it on the affected area(s) several times a day for as long as Fido or Fluffy will tolerate it.

Let's 'Ear It for Vinegar!

Vinegar is just what the doctor ordered for fending off or clearing up ear infections in cats and dogs (they are especially prevalent in floppy-eared canines). Here's the simple R$_x$:

To treat an existing infection, put 5 to 10 drops of vinegar (either white or ACV), as needed, into each ailing ear.

To keep ears clean and free of infections, you (and Fido) have two choices: Either dip a cotton pad or piece of cotton gauze in full-strength vinegar and use it to clean out wax, dirt, and other debris. Or put several drops of vinegar into each ear, and gently massage the base of the ears for a few minutes.

Note: *Never use a cotton swab to clean a dog's, cat's—or child's—ears. That small, firm tip could easily puncture an eardrum.*

SMALLER PETS

Did Walt Have This Problem with Mickey?

Mice, hamsters, guinea pigs, and other small rodents can make great little pets. There's just one problem: No matter how often you clean their cages, the little guys' lodgings always seem to give off a distinctive odor. To absorb the aroma, just put a bowl of vinegar next to the cage (but not in it). Replace it with a fresh supply every few days, and the breathin' will be free and easy!

Give Them a Clear View

As you know if you have pet fish—whether they live in a simple bowl or a fancy aquarium—it's important to keep those quarters pristine. Of course, you also want to see through that glass clearly. You'll accomplish both objectives with this simple routine: Every time you take the little swimmers out to clean their home, wipe the sides of the tank with white vinegar. Then rinse the glass very thoroughly with

QUICK & QUIRKY

Caution: Bunnies Ahead—Normally, rabbits breed like, well, rabbits. But if you're trying to increase your brood and the future mama is reluctant to engage in the process, add 1 tablespoon of white vinegar to her fresh water. After 24 hours, she'll be ready to make whoopee—and daddy bunny will be happy, too!

clear water to remove every trace of the vinegar before you refill the tank. Otherwise, your beloved fish will be dead ducks.

Vinegar's for the Birds

Vinegar can pack the same health-giving firepower for your fine feathered friends as it does for all other critters (see "An Equal Opportunity Healer" on page 249). Here's a roundup of ways to use it in the old avian neighborhood:

Word to the Wise

When vinegar is heated, it produces fumes that are toxic to birds—and can even be fatal. So when, for example, you heat vinegar on the stove or nuke it in the microwave, add it to a dishwashing cycle, or use it to clean a coffeemaker, keep your winged wonder(s) in another room, far away from the action.

Spray before you serve. Before you give fresh produce—organic or otherwise—to your bird, spray the fruits and vegetables with apple cider vinegar. Wait about five minutes, and rinse thoroughly with clear water. This shower will remove any bacteria as well as lingering pesticide or fertilizer residue, which (chemically based or not) could harm your bird.

Protect Polly's produce. Whenever you put fresh fruits or vegetables in your bird's food bowl, spray them with apple cider vinegar to reduce the chance of fungal or bacterial growth. (But sprayed or not, don't leave fresh foods out any longer than four to six hours.)

Grow safe sprouts. If you sprout seeds for your bird to eat (as holistic avian specialists highly recommend), mist the seeds with ACV every time you water them. This will prevent bacteria and fungi from getting a toehold.

Good Housekeeping, Avian Style

Wild birds flit around too much to be harmed by mold spores, bacteria, and other foul stuff that builds up on their droppings and food residue. A pet bird, on the other hand, spends most of his life behind bars. If his cage and its furnishings are not kept spotlessly clean, big trouble will come barrelin' around the bend in a hurry. Here's your problem-prevention to-do list:

Every day, while your bird is out of his quarters playing, spray a half-and-half solution of white vinegar and water on the cage bars and grates. Wait until any droppings have softened (five minutes or so should do it), and then wipe off the wires with damp paper towels.

Once a week, thoroughly wash the cage and everything in it with hot, soapy water.

At least once a month— and immediately after the outbreak of any illness— disinfect the whole abode following this routine:

- Remove your bird, along with all perches, food dishes, and toys. Then pull out and discard the floor liner.

That's Historical

Remember the old riddle that asks "How do you fit six elephants into a Volkswagen?" (In case you're too young to recall the heyday of elephant jokes, the answer is "Three in the front and three in the back.")

Well, here's another riddle for you: How do you move dozens of elephants over steep, narrow, rock-rimmed passes in the Alps? The answer: The same way Hannibal did in 218 BC. He built bonfires to heat up the boulders, then immediately poured vinegar over the steaming surfaces. The huge rocks crumbled into sharp gravel that could be easily moved out of the way—thereby allowing General H. and his pachyderm-mounted troops to invade Italy.

- Put the cage in the bathtub (it'll make the job a whole lot easier), and spray it from top to bottom with a half-and-half solution of white vinegar and water. Let it soak in until all the debris softens (if you've been lax in your daily maintenance, it could take 10 minutes or more). Then blast all the crud away with hot water from the shower.

- While the cage is air-drying, clean all the perches, food dishes, and toys with the same 50-50 vinegar-water solution.

- Then put it all together again, and let your pal move back into his happy, healthy home.

LIVESTOCK

Don't Let Weather Woes Get Your Goat(s)

Whether you have a single pet goat or a whole dairy herd, spike their water with apple cider vinegar all year round. During the heat of summer, it'll help repel pesky flies, and in the winter, it'll keep the water from freezing as fast as it otherwise would. The recommended dose: About 2 tablespoons of vinegar per 5-gallon bucket of H_2O. **Note:** *Don't worry that the vinegar might give the goats' milk an "off" taste. Folks who use this trick say it has no effect on the flavor at all.*

More Milk, Please!

Just 4 to 6 ounces of apple cider vinegar per day, added to food or water, will increase a cow's milk production. But

MANY FEED STORES SELL PURE, unprocessed ACV in bulk. But if your local establishment doesn't carry it in livestock-appropriate quantities, you can order it online in 2.5- and 5-gallon containers.

that's not all! ACV can also help prevent or treat mastitis, itchy skin, influenza, and respiratory diseases. Plus, it'll make whelping easier and fend off after-birth complications. (Consult your veterinarian about precise doses.)

Here, Chick-Chick!

Whether you keep exotic chickens as pets, or you raise them as livestock, vinegar belongs in your henhouse care kit. Just 2 or 3 tablespoons of ACV, added to your waterers every few days, will encourage healthy digestive systems, boost your flock's immunity, and help fight dehydration during hot spells.

Horsing Around

Holistic equine vets and experienced horsemen swear by ACV as an all-around health tonic, with all the same benefits it has for humans. The R$_X$ for a healthy horse: ¼ cup of pure, unprocessed ACV mixed with an equal amount of water, added to Dobbin's feed grain once a day. Because of vinegar's potassium and trace mineral content, this tonic is especially helpful for pregnant mares and for older horses with arthritis or digestive trouble. **Note:** *This same daily dose of ACV will help deter potentially death-dealing horseflies. (For a potent topical repellent, see Super-Safe Horsefly Spray on page 258.)*

Forestall the Stones

Studies at the University of California at Davis have shown that horses who ingest vinegar regularly—in either their food or water—are

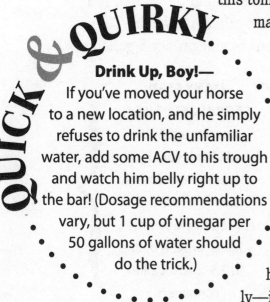

QUICK & QUIRKY

Drink Up, Boy!— If you've moved your horse to a new location, and he simply refuses to drink the unfamiliar water, add some ACV to his trough and watch him belly right up to the bar! (Dosage recommendations vary, but 1 cup of vinegar per 50 gallons of water should do the trick.)

less likely to develop enteroliths. These stones, which can cause serious intestinal blockages, are appearing with increasing frequency, especially in California and throughout the Southwest. Arabian and Morgan horses seem to be particularly susceptible. The basic tonic dose (see "Horsing Around," at left) is a good starting point, but if you live in prime enterolith territory and/or have a high-risk breed, ask your vet to recommend the optimum dose for your steed.

Word to the Wise

Do not use vinegar in galvanized metal watering containers. The acid in the vinegar will eat away at the metal and leach dangerous chemicals into the water.

Here's to Healthy Hooves!

Help fend off thrush and other fungal infections by soaking your horse's feet several times a week in a solution of ¼ cup of vinegar per gallon of water. Either ACV or white vinegar will create an environment in which foul fungi cannot thrive.

Shine Him Up

Getting set for a horse show, or maybe riding in a parade? If so, give your mount star power by spraying his coat with a solution of ½ cup of vinegar per quart of water. As with dogs, use white vinegar on a white or light-colored horse and ACV on darker-colored equines.

Make DIY Horsefly Traps

All those pesky flies that hang around your barn and trailer will soon be goners if you make up a herd of these terrific traps. For each one, you'll need a 2-liter plastic bottle, a pair of sturdy scissors or a sharp knife, ½ cup of apple cider vinegar (the cheapest kind you can find), ½ cup of sugar, water, a long spoon or stir stick, and duct tape. Once you've got your supplies in hand, follow this routine:

STEP 1. Cut off the top quarter of the bottle, being careful to maintain a straight line all the way around.

STEP 2. Pour the vinegar and sugar into the bottom portion of the bottle. Then fill it about halfway up with water, and stir the bait thoroughly.

STEP 3. Invert the top of the bottle, and fit it inside the bottom to create a funnel. Seal the two pieces together with duct tape.

Make as many traps as you need, and set them out in all the enclosed areas where the demons like to linger. They'll zoom in to get the cocktail inside—and they won't get out alive.

FANTASTIC FORMULA

Super-Safe Horsefly Spray

Horseflies do a lot more than make life miserable for your resident equine. They can spread internal and external parasites, as well as numerous diseases, including the often deadly anthrax. But commercial fly repellents—especially those containing DEET—pack their own load of toxic trouble. Enter this all-natural formula. It sends a potent "Keep Away!" message to flies and other insects, but it's also gentle enough to use on foals.

2 cups of apple cider vinegar

1 cup of Avon® Skin So Soft bath oil

2 tsp. of eucalyptus oil*

1 cup of water

Mix the ingredients together in a spray bottle, and keep it nearby in the barn. Spritz your ponies as needed, carefully avoiding their eyes.
* Or substitute 2 teaspoons of citronella oil.

part THREE
Outside Your Home

In Part 2, we focused on vinegar's astounding powers as a household helper for work and play. Now we'll venture into the great outdoors to see how this ancient product can help you keep your home's exterior in tip-top shape, from the top of the roof to the foot of the foundation—and beyond. For example, you'll discover simple, easy-as-pie tricks for cleaning your barbecue grill, sprucing up your outdoor furniture, and making your car shine like the morning sun. First, though, I'll share a passel of Grandma Putt's (and my) favorite tips for putting the prodigious power of vinegar to work in your yard and garden.

chapter eight

LAWN & GARDEN

When vinegar took its first bow in the garden is anyone's guess. But one thing is certain: For thousands of years since then, this fabulous five-star fluid has presented one crowd-pleasing encore after another. In this chapter, I'll tell you how this legendary performer can put your yard in the spotlight.

GROWING & TENDING PLANTS

Turn Seeds into Speed Demons

Before you plant any flower, herb, or vegetable seeds—indoors or out—soak them overnight in a solution made from ½ cup of apple cider vinegar and 1 pint of warm water. Come morning, remove the seeds from their bath, rinse them with clear water, and tuck them into the soil or seed-starting mix (as the case may be). Soon, sprouts will all but jump out of their shells! **Note:** *If you're working with thick-coated seeds like morning glories, moonflowers, or gourds, either nick them slightly with a sharp knife, or rub them lightly with fine sandpaper before you drop them into the drink.*

Intensive Care for Woody Wonders

Seeds with woody coats, like those of beets and parsnips, get off to a faster start when soaked in a mixture of 1 cup of ACV and ¼ cup of mild dishwashing liquid per 2 cups of warm water before planting. Leave the seeds for 24 hours, then rinse them with clear water, and plant them according to the directions on the seed packet. **Note:** *For this task, or any other plant-care purposes, use a clear, unscented dishwashing liquid—and whatever you do, avoid any product that has antibacterial properties. It'll destroy the friendly bacteria that plants need for good health.*

{ **WHENEVER YOU'RE FEEDING PLANTS** or giving seeds a pre-planting soak, always use organic, unprocessed apple cider vinegar. The ever-lovin' mother in it will serve up nutrients that are just as essential for plants as they are for people and pets. }

Test for Alkaline Soil

You say you have no idea whether your soil is sweet or sour? Put a tablespoon of dried garden soil on a plate, and add a few drops of white vinegar to it. If the soil fizzes, that means it's extremely alkaline—most likely above 7.5 on the pH scale—though how much above is anybody's guess. In this case, a more exact, laboratory test is called for because very few garden plants will tolerate soil with a pH that's above 7.5. **Note:** *To check for the opposite problem—severe acidity—put about a tablespoon of wet soil on a plate, and add a pinch of baking soda to it. If the soil fizzes, then the pH is most likely below 5.0.*

You'll Wonder Where the Yellow Went

The sudden appearance of yellow leaves on plants that love acid soil, like azaleas, rhododendrons, and camellias, often means one of two things: Either the soil's pH has risen above their comfort level, or the plants' ability to absorb iron has been compromised. Fortunately, the same slick trick should resolve either problem. First, mix up a solution of 2 tablespoons of apple cider vinegar per quart of water. Then, once a week for three weeks, pour 1 cup of the potion onto the soil around each stricken plant. **Note:** *If this remedy doesn't put the green back in the foliage—and you can find no sign of pests or disease symptoms—dig up a soil sample and have it tested by your closest Cooperative Extension Service or a private testing lab that it might recommend.*

SUBURBAN LEGEND ALERT!

According to many self-proclaimed gardening "experts" who write online, you can substantially raise your soil's acidity by simply drenching it with a vinegar-water solution. Well, folks, I'm here to tell you it just ain't so! It takes a lot of hard work, as well as persistence and patience, to lower the pH of highly alkaline soil. And sometimes it's downright impossible to bring it within the near-neutral range that most popular garden plants need to thrive. The long and short of it is: While vinegar can perform plenty of near miracles in your yard and garden, this isn't one of them!

Some Like It Sour

Many of Grandma Putt's favorite flowering shrubs, including azaleas, gardenias, rhododendrons, hydrangeas, and camellias, had one thing in common: They craved acidic soil. And every year, without fail, those plants put on a show that was the talk of the town. Yours will too—that is, if you're as persistent as Grandma was in performing an extra bit of TLC: Every week or so, and after every rain, water the bushes with a solution of 3 tablespoons of white vinegar per gallon of water. Just be sure to discontinue this routine when the first blooms appear; otherwise, the vinegar could harm the plants or shorten the life of the flowers. **Note:** *Just bear in mind that while an occasional sour cocktail will give these flowering wonders a big performance boost, the plants still need to be grown in soil with a pH below 6.5. Otherwise, no amount of vinegar will make them happy.*

More Happy Vinegar Drinkers

Grandma Putt's beloved flowering shrubs (see "Some Like It Sour," at left) aren't the only common garden plants that appreciate a weekly drink of vinegar-rich water. So do a number of other shrubs, including mountain laurel, American holly, junipers, and viburnum, as well as nearly all ferns. All of this crowd will also respond to your kindness by putting on a grander, more glorious show (and, in some cases, a bigger harvest):

Perennials: Bleeding hearts, butterfly weed, cardinal flowers, lupines, creeping phlox,

OLD-TIME Vim and Vinegar

Few things are more frustrating than gathering armfuls of fresh flowers from your garden, arranging them in beautiful vases—and then, within days, seeing them droop and go limp. Well, if you're Johnny on the spot, you can bring those blooms back to their peak of loveliness the way Grandma Putt did: First, cut ¼ inch or so off the bottom of each flower stem. Then put the flowers into a clean vase with fresh water, and add 2 tablespoons of white vinegar and 1 tablespoon of sugar to each quart of water. Those posies'll perk up in no time at all!

Note: *Be sure to cut the stems at roughly a 45-degree angle so they can soak up the maximum amount of perk-up solution.*

and most types of daylilies.

Vegetables: Asparagus, carrots, cauliflower, celery, cucumbers, garlic, lettuce, onions, potatoes, spinach, sweet peppers, tomatoes, and winter squash (including pumpkins).

Perk Up Your Houseplants

Do your houseplants look less than chipper—even malnourished—despite the fact that you feed them regularly with a high-quality plant food? If so, and you have hard water, then it's all but guaranteed to be the root of the problem. That's because essential plant nutrients are less available in hard water, which is alkaline. Fortunately, there's an ultra-simple solution to this dilemma: Every time you water your plants, add 1 tablespoon of apple cider vinegar per gallon of H_2O. It'll shift the water's pH into the neutral range so your plants' roots can absorb more nourishment. Plus, ACV contains about 50 trace nutrients that will give your green pals even more get-up-and-grow power.

QUICK & QUIRKY

Save the Trowel—

The good news: You finally found your favorite trowel that's been missing for months. The bad news: It was lying under a bush in your yard, and now it's covered with a thick layer of rust. Don't despair! Just soak the blade overnight in full-strength white vinegar. The brown crust will dissolve like magic.

Tend Your Tool Handles

If you're like most folks I know, your plant-tending tools take quite a beating—and that can put major stress on their wooden handles. To keep mine from cracking and splintering, I use this routine that Grandma Putt taught me many moons ago:

STEP 1. In a glass jar with a tight-fitting lid, mix 1 part white vinegar, 1 part boiled linseed oil, and 1 part turpentine.

STEP 2. Pour some of the mixture on an old cotton sock or soft cotton cloth, and rub it up and down the handle until the whole thing is covered. Wait about 10 minutes for the liquid to soak in, and then repeat the treatment.

Word to the Wise

Working with lime can make your skin rough and flaky. So whenever you use that pH adjuster on your lawn or garden, wash your hands with vinegar as soon as you're done. Besides keeping your skin smooth, it'll help heal any small cuts and scratches you've picked up along the way.

STEP 3. Wait another 10 minutes, and wipe any excess off with a clean, dry cloth.

Store the leftover potion in a cool, dark place, where it will keep indefinitely. **Note:** *Perform this chore about once a month, or whenever you notice that the wood is starting to look a tad pale and dry. That way, your gardening tools—and other kinds, too—should stay in fine fettle for years to come.*

Clean Your Mower Blades

After mowing your lawn, always—and I mean *always*—wipe the blades thoroughly with a cloth dampened with white vinegar. That way, you'll remove any grass that's clinging to the blades. That's important for two reasons:

- Even sharp blades can't do their best work when they're

plastered with a lot of old hacked-off grass. Instead, they're likely to tear the grass, leaving it with frayed tips that I like to think of as revolving doors: Water goes out; sun damage and disease come in.

- Whenever you mow, there's always a good chance that some of the grass lingering on the blades will harbor insects, their eggs, or both. But when you wipe that populated greenery away, you'll take any potential troublemakers with it.

De-Spot Flowerpots

As all you container garden lovers know, both soilborne minerals and fertilizer salts can soak right through terra-cotta pots—causing those unsightly white splotches. The best way to make them vanish: Reach for good old white vinegar. Depending on the severity of the marks, use it in one of these three ways:

> **TO REMOVE A THICK, TOUGH,** crusty buildup from a terra-cotta pot, soak either the whole pot or just the affected part in full-strength vinegar overnight. If you treat the whole pot, soak it in clear water for a few hours afterward to dilute the vinegar absorbed by the clay.

- As soon as you notice the beginnings of any white spots, pour some vinegar on a rag, and wipe the stains away.

- For more stubborn mineral residue, wet the white marks with vinegar, wait about 15 minutes for it to loosen the gunk, and scrub it off with a stiff brush.

- When the whole pot has a thin white coat, soak it overnight in a solution of 1 part vinegar to 5 parts water. Then scrub the crud away.

4 Fine Ways to Slam Slugs

There are a gazillion effective methods for eliminating these slimy, voracious pests, but here's a quartet of the best:

- Shortly after dark, when the slimers slink out to feed, fill a handheld spray bottle with white vinegar, head out to the garden, and let 'em have it. Or (as Grandma Putt generally did) pour the tangy stuff into squirt guns, put a bounty on the slugs' heads, and send a posse of youngsters out to do the job for you.

- If your aim isn't so good, pour a cup or so of white vinegar into a bucket, grab the slugs with a pair of retired, long-handled tongs, and dump the varmints into the drink.

- For an easy overnighter, wait until dusk, and then set citrus rinds, cabbage leaves, or potato chunks among your plants. In the morning, scoop up the traps, slugs and all, and toss them into your bucket of doom.

- Not quite up to a hunting trip at any time of day or night? No worries! Just bury shallow containers, such as cat food

OLD-TIME
Vim and Vinegar

To keep your cabbage plants free of cantankerous caterpillars, use this no-fail trick of Grandma Putt's: Mix a table-spoon of vinegar with enough milk to measure 1 cup. Then drop a teaspoon or so of the mixture into the center of each plant. It worked like a charm for Grandma Putt—and it still does for me, too!

Wicked Wonder Salsa

This tasty-sounding salsa is only a little hotter than the stuff you might put on nachos—but it's lethal to every kind of bad bug you can name. It's even been known to kill black widow spiders!

2 lbs. of ripe tomatoes*

1 lb. of fresh chili peppers

1 large onion

2 garlic cloves

1 cup of white vinegar

½ tsp. of black pepper

Roughly chop the first four ingredients, and liquefy them in a blender or food processor. Add the vinegar and pepper, and blend briefly to mix them in. Strain the mixture through a paper coffee filter or several layers of cheesecloth, and pour the liquid into a handheld spray bottle. Then take careful aim, and blast the fiery stuff directly on the pests. Just be sure to spray on a calm day. If this salsa drifts into your eyes or mouth, it'll burn like crazy!

Bruised or cracked ones are fine— so don't waste the cream of your crop on the enemy!

cans or retired cake pans, up to their rims throughout your garden. Then pour in a mixture of 1 teaspoon of brown sugar per cup of apple cider vinegar. The malevolent mollusks will belly up to the bar, fall in, and drown!

Note: *The last three methods will also send plant-slashing snails to their just rewards.*

Curtail Codling Moths

These are the culprits responsible for the old joke that goes, "What's worse than biting into an apple and finding a worm? Finding half a worm!" Although codling moths are most famous for ruining apple harvests from coast to coast, they also target crabapple, pear, quince, and sometimes plum and walnut trees. Once the worms are inside your fruit, there's nothing you can do about it, but you can prevent the next generation (at least a sizable part of it) from seeing the light of day. Here's your moth birth-control plan: Gather up some 1-gallon plastic milk or vinegar jugs, and make a solution that's 1 part molasses to 1 part apple cider vinegar. Pour 1 to 2 inches of the mixture into each jug, tie a cord around the handle, and cover the opening with ⅛- to ¼-inch mesh screen to keep honeybees out. Then hang the traps from branches. The moths will fly in for a sip, and they won't fly out. **Note:** *This trap also deals a deadly blow to disease-carrying mosquitoes.*

Pickle Bark Beetles

These tiny pests zero in on woody plants that are diseased, dead, or under stress; but once they're in the neighborhood, they sometimes attack healthy trees and shrubs, too. The larvae chew through and just under the bark, cutting off the flow of nutrients in the process. Once they've tunneled into a plant, no insecticide can reach them. But you can catch the adults on the fly, simply by setting jars of white vinegar among your troubled woodies. The beetles will dive right in— and they won't get out alive.

ONLY WHITE VINEGAR will work for battling bark beetles because its odor mimics the scent of a tree's distress signal.

Make a Berry Good Berry Bug Trap

Are bad bugs bashing your blackberries and raspberries? If so, then this trap can save your crop. To make it, shove a banana peel into a 1-gallon plastic jug, and add 2 cups of sugar and 1 cup of vinegar. Pour in enough water to reach about 2 inches below the top. Then screw the lid on the bottle and give 'er a good shake. Remove the lid, and set the jug among your berry bushes, or hang it from a low limb on a nearby tree.

Make as many traps as you need to guard your cane fruits, and replace them as needed throughout the summer.

Foil Fruit Flies

Yuck! You piled bushels of vegetables on your porch while you got your canning gear ready. And now there are clouds of fruit flies feasting on your bounty. So try this simple trick: Mix ¼ cup of apple cider vinegar and 1 teaspoon of dishwashing liquid in 2 cups of water, and pour the solution into a jar. Then set the jar next to your plagued produce. The fruit flies will be drawn to the vinegar, dip into the water for a taste, and drown (thanks to the soap, which will coat their tiny bodies). Replace the solution every couple of days to keep the vinegar scent fresh and clear out the dead bugs.

Nix Nasty Gnats

Fungus gnats bear a close resemblance to fruit flies, but they don't munch on fresh produce. In fact, the adults don't harm plant material of any kind—and they don't bite people or pets, either.

GOOD-BYE, GOOD GUYS

Even beneficial bugs can drive you crazy when they're buzzing at your windows. Well, this spray will make the little guys go elsewhere for fun and games, but it won't hurt them one bit. To make it, mix ¼ cup of vinegar, 1 tablespoon of essential oil of bay, and 3 cups of water in a handheld spray bottle. Then use the potion to clean the outside of the glass in your usual way. If the bugs are bouncing off the screens, thoroughly spray the mesh, too. Just make sure you spray from the inside out, so you don't wind up with puddles on  the floor! **Note:** *You can find essential oil of bay in herbal-supply and craft stores.*

It's the larvae that cause the trouble. When you see the tiny bugs flitting around your houseplants, it means just one thing: The adult females are fixin' to lay eggs in the soil. And once those eggs hatch, the larvae will start sucking the life-giving juices out of the plants' roots and the base of the stem. The good news is that it's a snap to snag the mamas—but you need to move fast before the maternity ward opens. Here's your five-step action plan:

Word to the Wise

Vinegar can't kill any fungus gnat larvae that are already in the soil. But you can wipe 'em out using another of Grandma Putt's favorite down-home products—namely, hydrogen peroxide. For the lowdown on that score, see "Stop Trouble at the Roots" on page 272.

STEP 1. Pour ½ inch of apple cider vinegar into a disposable plastic cup. Add a drop or two of dishwashing liquid, and stir until it's thoroughly mixed with the vinegar.

STEP 2. Drop a small piece of ripe fruit into the container, making sure it protrudes above the surface of the liquid.

STEP 3. Cover the top of the cup with transparent tape, leaving a ⅛-inch opening in the center.

STEP 4. Set the trap close to your plagued plant(s), and check it daily. If you see gnats congregating on the taped surface, don't disturb them—they'll soon find a way to the hole in search of the tantalizing fruit and vinegar cocktail.

STEP 5. Empty and refill the trap every few days, or as often as needed, until your bait no longer has any takers.

Note: *In most cases, all the fungus gnats in your house will find their way to the trap within a few days.*

OUTSIDE YOUR HOME

STOP TROUBLE AT THE ROOTS

Fungus gnats are a nuisance, but they only live for about a week. Unfortunately, during their brief life, they lay approximately 300 eggs. And when the larvae emerge, they can severely stunt or even kill the healthiest of houseplants. Geraniums, African violets, carnations, and poinsettias are all particularly susceptible to these baby bad guys.

The good news is that if you reach the scene early, you can save the day. First, though, to find out whether the minute marauders are actually present, set a few inch-long pieces of peeled, raw potato on the soil surface. Go about your business for four hours or so, and then check back. If you spy any tiny, black-headed larvae on the tater chunks, immediately dispose of them in your outdoor garbage can—not the compost bin. Then take care of the rest of the clan as follows:

▶ Let the soil dry out to a depth of 2 inches. This is where the larvae live, but without moisture, they go into suspended development—where they're sitting ducks for the next step.

▶ Water your plants with a solution made from 1 part 3% hydrogen peroxide (with no added ingredients) to 4 parts water. It will kill the larvae on contact, but won't harm your plants. (It will fizz, but don't be alarmed—that's normal.)

▶ Continue to monitor the adult population, and reapply the peroxide drench weekly as long as gnats are appearing in your traps (see "Nix Nasty Gnats" on page 270).

▶ As extra insurance, you can water your plants with the anti-larval formula once a month to prevent further infestations.

Herbal Vinegar: It's Not Just for People Anymore

And it never has been. Grandma Putt used herbal-infused vinegar to fend off a whole lot of destructive garden thugs, and you can, too. To make the pest-repelling potion, just follow the simple instructions on page 114. But in this case, increase the herbs by a third to one-half to make a good, strong infusion. Also, instead of using high-quality culinary vinegar, go with the cheapest unprocessed ACV you can buy in bulk, either online or at your local feed-and-seed establishment. As for which herbal armament you choose to use, these were Grandma's favorite additives:

Basil protects tomato plants from just about every pest.

Mint keeps aphids away from crucifer crops, including Brussels sprouts, cabbage, and cauliflower.

FANTASTIC FORMULA

Anti-Aphid Spray

Aphids attack just about every kind of vegetation you can name, including turfgrass—spreading fatal plant viruses in the process. But the terrors are no match for this potent potion.

- **1 cup of water**
- **1 cup of white vinegar**
- **½ cup of salt**
- **¼ cup of baking soda**
- **¼ cup of powdered citric acid**
- **2 tsp. of aloe vera juice**
- **2 tsp. of sesame seed oil**
- **12 drops of sage oil**
- **10 drops of grapefruit seed extract**

Mix all of the ingredients together in a large handheld spray bottle. Shake well before each use, and spritz your plagued plants from top to bottom. Pay special attention to the undersides of leaves, where aphids love to linger.

Oregano guards against pests that attack cucumber, melon, squash, and other members of the cucurbit clan.

Sage is an all-around bug deterrent for all vegetable plants.

Note: *White vinegar will also work just fine for pest-repelling purposes, but mother-enriched apple cider vinegar will give your plants a small nutrient boost at the same time.*

Go One-on-One with Mealybugs

In northern climes, these tiny sap suckers are most famous for the damage they do in sunrooms and home greenhouses. But they also target a wide range of outdoor plants. Fortunately, if the victim is small, or you catch the invasion in its early stages, it's easy to head off a full-scale attack: Just dab each cottony-looking bug with a cotton swab dipped in white vinegar. It'll bite the dust instantly.

Vanquish Ants with Vinegar

Ants rarely damage plants of any kind. In fact, these tiny guys actually improve growing conditions for all plants. Besides breaking down organic matter into soil-building humus, they dig literally thousands of miles of little tunnels in the ground. And those openings allow free passage for water, nutrients, and even earthworms. But, hey, nobody's perfect! Around the yard and garden, ants have two

QUICK & QUIRKY

Get Tough—If ants have turned your favorite tree into an aphid ranch, boil a 50-50 solution of white vinegar and water. Then scrape the top off the mound, and quickly pour the mixture into the nest. If the potion reaches its target, the queen will be an instant goner, and any workers that survive will die off. Repeat in a week if the colony still shows signs of activity.

major flaws: They make first-class nuisances of themselves at picnics and barbecues, and (much worse) they "farm" sap-sucking insects like aphids, so they can have a steady supply of the honeydew that the little monsters produce. Depending on what kind of mischief your ants are up to, put white vinegar to work in one (or several) of these ways:

WHEN THE BLASTED ANTS ARE DRIVING YOU TO DRINK (or simply increasing your consumption), spray them with straight vinegar. Then wipe the bodies away with damp paper towels and toss 'em into the compost bin.

- Create borders around your deck or patio by thoroughly spraying the perimeter.

- Soak cotton balls in vinegar, tuck them into small jar or bottle lids, and set them out in any areas where you don't want ants to roam.

- Saturate any travel paths that you've noticed. This will disrupt the scent trails the ants follow, and they'll quickly move on to other territory.

No Ants in the Nectar!

It's enough to throw any bird lover into a hissy fit: You look out your window and see a line of ants marching down the wire hanger of your hummingbird feeder and into the sweet syrup. Well, you can put a quick end to those shenanigans. How? Just mix 1 tablespoon of ground cloves in 1 cup of white vinegar in a handheld spray bottle, and spritz it on the trail leading to the "chuck wagon." The little gluttons will take their "sweet teeth" elsewhere, and leave the sweet stuff for the hummers.

Word to the Wise

To fend off fire blight attacks, it's absolutely essential to control insects, especially aphids and psylla, which spread the disease. Laying out the welcome mat for birds can go a long way in helping you battle these and hordes of other bad bugs (see "Your Flying Pest-Control Squad" beginning on page 281). Also, don't overfeed your trees, and avoid high-nitrogen fertilizers. They encourage exactly the kind of lush, leafy growth that fire blight bacteria flock to.

Put Out Fire Blight

This bacterial disease strikes apples and pears, and it spreads like (yes) wildfire in warm, moist weather. First, reddish, water-soaked lesions appear on the bark of limbs and branches, and on warm days, an orangey-brown liquid oozes out. Infected shoots look as though they'd been scorched. Branch tips wilt and turn under at the ends, like a shepherd's crook. Your mission:

At the first sign of trouble, prune off all infected branches at least 12 inches below the wilted section. Then remove all suckers and water sprouts, where more bacteria could be lurking.

After each cut, to avoid spreading the disease, dip your shears or saw in a solution of 1 part bleach to 4 parts water.

Finally, spray the tree from top to bottom with a solution of 4 parts vinegar to 6 parts water. Then spray again two weeks later.

Fight Foul Fungi

Fungal diseases are the most common garden ailments of all. One of the most dreaded is black spot, the arch nemesis of roses and aspen trees. But there are more kinds than you can even imagine. They can strike flowers or vegetables at any time during the growing season, but they're most likely to occur during periods of wet or humid weather. And the spores multiply like crazy when the air is stagnant. So here's your simple battle plan:

Provide excellent air circulation for your plants, thinning them out if needed.

Spray them once a week during the growing season with a solution of 1½ tablespoons of baking soda, 1 tablespoon of white vinegar, and 1 teaspoon of vegetable oil per gallon of water. Use a handheld spray bottle, and make sure you spritz the stems, as well as the top and underside of each and every leaf.

Repeat the process after every rain.

Note: *When you apply your antifungal spray (or any other problem-solving potion), be sure to do the job in the morning so your plants have plenty of time to dry off before nightfall. Fungal spores love dark, damp gardens!*

Turn Off Tomcats

When male felines are leaving your garden smelling anything but flowery, relief is close at hand. Fill a handheld spray bottle with full-strength white vinegar, and spritz the places where the boys are making their mark. The scent will confuse and repel the rascals. Don't spray your plants, though—straight vinegar could kill them. Instead, take aim at your garden fence or a patch of weeds. And remember to renew the repellent after every rain!

> **THE CONTAINMENT POLICY**
> Here's an ultra-simple way to keep cats, rabbits, and other critters from ravaging your decorative container plants: Saturate small pieces of wood with white vinegar, and set them on the soil. The diners will take their appetites elsewhere, but the repellents will blend right in with the scenery.

Ward Off Wascawy Wabbits

Are Bugs and his buddies running rampant through your glorious garden? If so, here's your no-fail defense strategy: Gather up a bunch of corncobs, and soak them in full-strength white vinegar for 8 to 12 hours. Then set them in strategic locations throughout your veggie patch and any flower beds the cute culprits are targeting. Resoak and reset the cobs every 14 days or so, and they'll keep hungry hoppers away from your heavenly harvest.

A Trio of Tricks to Deter Deer and Repulse Raccoons

There's almost nothing that these ravenous rascals won't devour—but there are a few aromas that will say, loud and clear, "This diner is closed!" One of them is (you guessed it) vinegar. You can put this magic bullet to work in three ways:

- Saturate rags in vinegar, and tack them to your garden fence, or tie them onto posts that you've stuck into the soil throughout the danger zone.

- Tie vinegar-soaked rags onto your trash can lids.

- If you routinely leave your trash out in plastic garbage bags—or whenever you have more critter-tempting residue than your cans can accommodate—give each sack a big splash of vinegar.

PEOPLE PESTS

Bug Off, You Bullies!

Are you looking for a really effective insect repellent that doesn't contain toxic chemicals? Look no further! Here's a formula that bugs hate, but it's safe enough to use on kids. What's more, it's a snap to make using plants you might have right in your garden.

Here's the process:

- Put ½ cup each of fresh lavender, mint, thyme, and rose-scented geraniums in a bowl.

- Heat 1 cup of white vinegar just to the boiling point, and pour it over the herbs. Cover the bowl, and let the herbs steep until the vinegar has cooled to room temperature.

- Strain out the solids and pour the liquid into a handheld spray bottle.

Spritz all your exposed skin with the potion before you head outdoors, and reapply it every couple of hours. Annoying bugs will bug you no more! **Note:** *Store your repellent in the refrigerator, where it will keep for about two months. And put the strained-out herbs on the ground in your garden to help keep your plants safe from bad bugs.*

THE NEXT TIME YOU'RE SETTING THE STAGE FOR OUTDOOR FUN, spray lavender vinegar on the ground around your table and grill. For good measure, set a dish or two of it on top of the dining table and any food-prep surfaces. Then enjoy the festivities in peace and quiet!

Bye-Bye, Blackflies

Every time you step outdoors, does it seem as though black-flies turn your body into their own movable feast? Well, you can solve that problem in a jiffy. Just rub apple cider vinegar on your exposed skin. These little hellions are surprisingly picky eaters, and while they may still annoy you by circling your head, they won't actually zoom in for a bite.

FANTASTIC FORMULA

Life of the Party Bug Repellent

When you're planning a special out-door event, like a graduation party or a wedding reception, whip up a big batch of this extra-strength potion.* It repels mosquitoes and just about every other annoying, biting bug under the sun (or moon).

- **¼ cup of distilled water**
- **¼ cup of vinegar (either white or ACV)**
- **15 drops of lavender oil (prefer-ably *Lavandula angustifolia*)****
- **10 drops of lemon eucalyptus oil**
- **10 drops of tea tree oil**
- **6 drops of bergamot oil**
- **6 drops of lime oil**

Thoroughly mix all of the ingredients together. Spritz the air with the mixture, spray it on furniture, and set bowls of it around the space to keep beastly bugs from crashing the party. (This formula is not intended for topical use on humans or pets.)

* Multiply the ingredients as needed.
** All the essential oils are available online or in herbal-supply stores.

Tick Off Ticks

Ticks have gained nation-wide infamy for spreading Lyme disease and the potentially fatal Rocky Mountain spotted fever. And whether you're out hiking in the woods or working (or playing) in your yard, you're a tempt-ing target for these tiny disease-carrying demons. But you can keep the blood-sucking creeps away with this simple strategy: Mix ½ cup of vinegar and ¼ cup of water, and add 10 drops of either geranium, lemon-grass, or rosemary oil (take your pick—ticks loathe all of 'em!). Before heading into the great outdoors, spray your hair and any exposed skin with the mixture. **Note:** *This formula will also keep your pets tick-free. Just be sure that when you spray, you keep it far away from your pal's eyes!*

Keep Your Hummers on the Job

A hummingbird feeder is not just a source of lively entertainment. It's also a surefire way to entice these voracious insect-eating birds to your yard to lend a hand with your pest-control chores. But there is one catch: Hummers are mighty finicky about the cleanliness of their dining area. If your feeder is dirty, sticky, or crusted over with dried sugar water, they'll take their appetites elsewhere. So to keep your work crew happy and healthy, disinfect their nectar holder frequently. Here's how:

- Take the feeder apart, submerge the components in a bucket filled with 1 part hot water to 2 parts vinegar, and let them soak for three to four hours.

- Use a bottle brush or special hummingbird feeder brush to scrub the inside of the tank. Also thoroughly scrub the base and the flower-shaped dispenser holes. (Use a toothpick to unclog them if necessary.)

- Rinse well with cold water, and let it air-dry outdoors in full sunlight before you fill 'er back up with nectar.

> **A LOT OF HUMMER FANS** I know keep two nectar feeders on hand so that one can be open and serving its customers while the other is in the wash (so to speak).

Spruce Up Your Songbird Feeder

Avian dining facilities that serve up seed or suet demand slightly different treatment than nectar feeders do—and it's best to do the job outdoors. Start by rounding up your supplies. You'll need a scrub brush, an old toothbrush, rubber gloves, a garden hose, unscented dishwashing liquid, a jug of white vinegar, and a bucket or tub that's big enough to hold your feeder(s). Then proceed as follows:

Fill the container with hot water and a few squirts of dishwashing liquid. Then drop each feeder into the drink, and scrub all the parts you can reach.

Rinse the feeders with the hose, aiming the spray into any nooks and crannies that your brushes couldn't penetrate.

Empty the tub, then fill it with clean water and 4 cups of vinegar. Let the feeders soak in the solution for 60 minutes or so. Then rinse them thoroughly and let them air-dry in the sun before replenishing their supply of seed or suet.

Note: *If you operate more than a couple of feeders, you might want to set up a rotating schedule to avoid the time-consuming task of scrubbing them all at once.*

Word to  the Wise

Avian experts recommend cleaning songbird feeders once a month, year-round, and hummingbird feeders every three or four days. The reason: A dirty dining area is a prime breeding ground for all kinds of foul fungi and bad bacteria that can—and routinely do—cause fatal diseases in birds.

Bathe Your Birdbath

The birds that visit your watering hole expect to find fresh and sparkling clean water to drink and bathe in. If that liquid isn't up to their standards, they'll take their lovely feathers—and their big bad-bug appetites—elsewhere. So periodically give your birdbath a thorough cleaning following this routine:

STEP 1. After the birds have

gone to bed, empty the bowl, fill it with white vinegar, and let it sit overnight.

STEP 2. Wipe the surface with a cloth.

STEP 3. Rinse it thoroughly before filling it with fresh water.

The birds in your neighborhood will give your yard a five-star hospitality rating! **Note:** *How often you need to perform this chore depends on how much use your birdbath gets, as well as the quantity of windblown leaves, dust, and other debris flying around the vicinity.*

PLAY LORD (OR LADY) OF THE RINGS
Whenever you refill your birdbath, add a teaspoon or so of apple cider vinegar to the water. It'll accomplish three fabulous feats:

▶ Prevent white lines from forming inside the basin as the mineral-laden water evaporates

▶ Slow down the growth of algae

▶ Deliver the same healthful boost to your avian visitors as it can for pet birds and other critters (see Chapter 7 for the lowdown on that score)

Note: *For this purpose, always use pure, unprocessed ACV.*

WICKED WEEDS

Kiss Weeds Good-Bye

White vinegar, applied straight from a handheld spray bottle, is a nightmare come true for shallow-rooted weeds. For best results, pull off the plant's green tops, then point your sprayer downward, and saturate the crown. (This trick is especially helpful for those impossible-to-get-at spots like cracks in a concrete driveway, or narrow spaces between stone or brick pavers.) **Note:** *Whenever you use this or any vinegar-based potion to kill weeds, be* *extra careful not to get the solution on plants that you want to keep! If necessary, cover them with boxes, buckets, or other protective devices.*

Death and Destruction to Dandelions

How? First mix together 1 cup of salt and 1 teaspoon of dishwashing liquid per gallon of white vinegar. Pour the solution into a handheld spray bottle. Turn the nozzle to the straight-stream setting—not the fan-type spray. Then give each plant this 1, 2, 3 punch:

- Blast the center of each flower. This will prevent it from setting seed and kill any seeds that may be starting to form.

- Spray the foliage from top to bottom.

- Finally, aim at the ground, and saturate the base of the stem so the vinegar can soak down into the roots.

Note: *For best results, do this job on a hot day when the sun is at its brightest and when no rain is forecast for the next 48 to 72 hours.*

QUICK & QUIRKY

Give Charlie the Brush-Off—To wipe out creeping Charlie, plantain, and other broad-leaved weeds, duct-tape a foam paintbrush to a 2- to 3-foot branch or dowel. Then dip the brush in vinegar, and dab it onto the leaves. They'll bite the dust—and you won't even have to bend over!

Extra-Strength Weed Remover

This potent potion is tailor-made for tackling the toughest weeds in your yard—like those deep-rooted perennials that just keep on coming back …coming back…and coming back! To make it, bring 1 quart of water to a boil, then stir in 5 tablespoons of white vinegar and 2 tablespoons of salt. While the liquid is still boiling (or as close to it as possible), pour it directly on the weeds.

Wild Weed Wipeout Tonic

When you've got weeds that just won't take "no" for an answer, mix 1 tablespoon each of white vinegar, gin or vodka, and dishwashing liquid per quart of hot water. Pour the solution into a handheld spray bottle, and drench the stubborn interlopers to the point of runoff. It'll knock 'em flat!

Be the Boss of Moss

Moss can add just the right touch of old-time character to a brick or stone wall. But if there's too much of it—or if you don't like that fuzzy green stuff at all—grab a handheld spray bottle. Fill it with a pint of water, and add 2 tablespoons each of vinegar and gin. Then take careful aim (so you don't hit any other plants) and thoroughly drench the moss. **Note:** *Just be aware that if your afflicted structure is in the kind of damp, shady spot that moss loves—and you can't or don't care to alter those conditions—you will have to repeat this routine periodically.*

That's Historical

For thousands of years, folks have been using ordinary household vinegar to solve garden-variety problems of all kinds. Then about 12 years ago, somebody decided to "improve" it by upping the acid level from 5 to 20 percent. The result is: "horticultural vinegar." Don't fall for it! Not only is it expensive and stronger than you need, but it sure ain't food-safe! It's a petroleum derivative made from 99 percent glacial acetic acid (not grain). It's dangerous to breathe and can severely damage your skin and eyes. And don't be fooled by the 10 percent vinegars being sold in garden centers. Many, if not most of them, are the 20 percent stuff that's been cut with water.

chapter nine ▸ *OUTDOOR STRUCTURES*

If you're like most folks I know, you have at least one major thing in common with my Grandma Putt: You want the outside of your home sweet home to look every bit as shipshape as the inside. And you can accomplish that noble goal using the same hardworking wonder "drug" she used—namely (what else?) vinegar. It's inexpensive and readily available. But the best part is that its lightly acidic nature makes it an outstanding all-purpose solution for your outside living spaces.

HARD SURFACES

Get Burn Marks Off Brick

No matter how careful you are, accidents will happen. When you wind up with burn marks on your brick patio, fire pit, or outdoor hearth—perhaps courtesy of a toppled candle, a dropped piece of kindling, or a wayward charcoal briquette—don't panic. Just reach for white vinegar. Sponge it onto the spots and rinse with clear water. Bingo: nice clean bricks once again!

Clean Brick or Stone

Keep your patio or walkway looking its very best by mopping it regularly with a solution made from 1 cup of white vinegar in a bucket of warm water. Of course, how often you need to perform this chore depends on weather conditions, as well as how much traffic the surface gets and how clean you want it to look.

Banish Bird Droppings

Sure, it's fun to watch your fine feathered friends flutter and frolic around your yard. That is until they start using your patio or driveway for target practice. The good news is that you can make those sloppy splotches disappear in no time flat. How? Just spray them with full-strength apple cider vinegar. Or, if you prefer, pour a splash of ACV onto an old rag, and wipe the offensive droppings away.

Can the Calcium Buildup

To remove unsightly calcium deposits from brick, limestone, or concrete, spray the marks with a half-and-half mixture of white vinegar and water. Then go about your business. The acidic solution will take it from there, and the marks will soon be history!

> **FOR INDOOR OR OUTDOOR CLEANING** purposes, use the cheapest apple cider vinegar you can buy in bulk—don't waste the healthy, unprocessed kind on inanimate objects!

Demolish Mold or Mildew

Just like any other surface that's in a damp, shady site, a wall, patio, or walkway can fall victim to these foul fungi. To send 'em packing, simply scrub the stricken surface with full-strength white vinegar and a stiff nylon brush. Don't use a wire brush because metal particles could get trapped in the brick, leaving you with rust stains to clean off. **Note:** *To tell for sure whether you're dealing with potentially damaging mildew or simple dirt, dab a few drops of chlorine bleach on the area in question. If it remains dark in color, it's dirt. But if it gets lighter or changes color, it's mildew.*

Clear Concrete from Your Skin

When you're working with concrete, cement, or mortar mixes—even if you're wearing gloves—it's a good bet that some of the stuff will splash onto your skin, where it will dry almost immediately. And if it stays there too long, it can cause your skin to crack. In extreme cases, it could even lead to eczema. So don't dawdle! Use straight white vinegar to wipe any dried concrete off your skin. Then follow up by washing with warm, soapy water.

Good Riddance to Bad Rust

Got rust marks on your concrete patio—perhaps courtesy of metal furniture? No problem! Just pour full-strength white vinegar onto the spots, and give the acid about five minutes to react with the rust. Then, while the vinegar is still wet, scrub it with a stiff nylon brush. Rinse with clear water, and repeat the process as needed until you've banished the blemishes.

QUICK & QUIRKY

Wash before You Work—Before you head outdoors to work (or play) in cold weather, wash your hands with vinegar (either white or ACV), and dry them thoroughly without rinsing. The vinegar will make your fingers stay limber longer, whether you wear gloves or not.

Restore the Color to Concrete Pavers

As tinted concrete weathers, the mineral salts used in the mixture come to the surface. The result: pavers that look faded and dusty, with white powdery spots here and there. To bring back the original color, scrub the blocks with a sturdy nylon brush dipped in a half-and-half solution of vinegar and water. Wait about 15 minutes so the acid in the vinegar can dissolve the mineral buildup, and then rinse the patio or walkway with a strong blast from the garden hose. If you can still see some whitish spots, repeat the treatment, and do it again once a month or so to keep the natural buildup under control. **Note:** *To stop minerals from weathering out of the concrete altogether and to make the color of your pavers really pop, apply a penetrating sealer that's available at most hardware stores.*

Keep Plaster Pliable

Plastering over (a.k.a. rendering) an outdoor wall is a simple way to add a major touch of class to any home or garden. There's just one problem: It can be mighty tricky to keep the plaster from hardening before you're done with the job. The simple solution: Add a tablespoon or two of white vinegar to your mixture. It'll slow down the hardening process and buy you some valuable time to get your wall looking just right.

Paint Aluminum Siding Perfectly

There's nothing like a fresh coat of paint to give your house a whole new lease on life. But if those walls are covered with aluminum siding, you need to do some crucial prep work before you whip out your brush and paint bucket. Specifically, you need to etch the surface by coating it with an acid that causes a chemical reaction, which in turn produces a slight all-over engraving. Otherwise, the paint will peel right off. The ideal acid for the job is (you guessed it) white vinegar. Here's the drill:

STEP 1. Coat the siding with a half-and-half solution of vinegar and water. Keep a close eye on it, applying more solution if it begins to dry. You want to make sure the surface stays wet until the acid has done its work. You'll know the aluminum is properly etched when it turns dull and darker.

STEP 2. Wipe the siding with warm, soapy water. Rinse thoroughly with clear water, and pat it dry with a lint-free towel. Then let the surface air-dry completely.

STEP 3. Apply one or two coats of aluminum primer, following the manufacturer's directions. Using a brush is fine, but a small roller will give you a smoother, more even surface. Let it dry for the recommended amount of time.

{ **FOR ROUTINE CLEANING,** spray aluminum siding with a 50-50 solution of vinegar and water, then rinse it off with a garden hose. }

STEP 4. Paint the primed surface with exterior acrylic latex paint that has the highest percentage of acrylic resin possible. Again, follow the manufacturer's directions, and use either a brush or roller, as you prefer. (If you opt for a brush, be sure to use long, even strokes.)

Then stand back and admire your spankin' new house! **Note:** *Follow this same routine when you're painting an aluminum boat.*

The Vexatious Vinyl Pressure-Washing Myth

True or false? The only way to get vinyl siding sparkling clean is to go at it with a high-powered pressure washer.

A resounding false! In fact, some siding manufacturers strongly advise against using pressure washers at all, while others recommend keeping the pressure low. According to the Vinyl Siding Institute, the best way to clean their namesake product is to use a soft cloth or a soft-bristled brush to apply your cleaner of choice. One of the most effective—especially when you're dealing with light mold or mildew stains—is none other than vinegar and water. Here are the specific guidelines:

- Use a solution made of roughly 3 parts white vinegar to 7 parts water.

- Before you start, mix up a gritty paste made from ½ cup of baking soda per ¼ cup of water. Use it to scrub off any stubborn stains that you encounter.

- To prevent streaking, start at the bottom and work up toward the top of the house.

- Thoroughly rinse each section before moving upward.

GO EASY ON YOURSELF

Whenever you're setting out to clean your whole house, don't even think about tackling the entire thing in one fell swoop. Instead, deal with the most visible part first. Then divide the rest of the structure into small sections that you can finish one at a time as your schedule and energy allow. Follow this same easy-does-it principle if your fence encloses a large area or it's especially grubby. (Full  disclosure: I learned this piece of wisdom the hard way, folks!)

Keep Your Vinyl Fence Vibrant

Vinyl fences tend to be made of tougher stuff than house siding, but they're just as vulnerable to damage from a high-powered pressure washer. The good news is that for routine maintenance, a garden hose should do the job just fine, especially if you have a scrub-brush attachment to tackle any dirty patches. But there are a couple of stains that need the extra oomph that (you guessed right) vinegar can supply—namely these:

FANTASTIC FORMULA

Darn Good Deposit Remover

When lime and hard water leave extra-stubborn buildup on your swimming pool deck, concrete driveway, water spigots, planters, or any other hard outdoor surface, get rid of them with this foolproof formula:

½ cup of borax

1 cup of warm water

½ cup of white vinegar

Dissolve the borax in the water, and stir in the vinegar. Sponge the mixture onto the spots, let it sit for 10 minutes or so (longer for really stubborn stains), and wipe the ugly marks away. How's that for a quick and easy fix?

Mold and mildew. Here's one easy-to-use, all-natural formula that fence manufacturers recommend: Fill a bucket halfway with water. In a separate container, mix 2 cups of dishwashing liquid or liquid soap and ½ cup of white vinegar. Add ¼ cup of the mixture to the water, and swish it around. Then dip a rag, sponge, or soft-bristled brush in the soapy solution and scrub the spots away. Rinse with clear water, and you're good to go.

Rust and hard-water stains. These are especially prevalent in areas like the Pacific Northwest that get a lot of rain. To banish both types of blemishes, simply spray straight white vinegar onto the affected areas, and rub with a soft cloth, using light pressure. Repeat as necessary until the spots are gone. No need to rinse.

3 Keys to Winning at Vinyl Washing

Heeding this trio of simple reminders will help you do the best-possible job on your siding or your fence—and avoid unpleasant surprises:

Word to the Wise

Never use steel wool, abrasive pads, stiff-bristled brushes, or abrasive cleansers on vinyl or any other kind of plastic. If you do, you'll wind up with a scratched mess on your hands!

Read all about it. Before making the vinegar solutions on the previous two pages (see "The Vexatious Vinyl Pressure-Washing Myth" and "Keep Your Vinyl Fence Vibrant"), check the manufacturer's guidelines to ensure they're safe to use on your brand of siding or fencing. The same advice applies to any other cleaning potion.

Test first. Even if your owner's manual does not list vinegar as a no-no cleaner, don't take any chances. Apply a small amount of the solution to an out-of-the-way spot. Then wait 24 to 48 hours to make sure there is no adverse reaction before you proceed.

Protect your vegetation. Move all container plants away from the work site, and cover any inground plants that are within splashing range of your vinegar solution.

3 Positively Pleasing Plastic Solutions

If you have a plastic shed in your yard or a plastic storage box on your deck (perhaps doing double duty as a bench), you're not alone. More and more folks are relying on these inexpensive and relatively low-maintenance alternatives to wooden structures. Notice I said "relatively" low-maintenance. That's because, just like anything else that spends all its time in the great outdoors, these handy store-alls pick up their fair share of dirt, berry stains, and everything else Mother Nature throws their way. Well, guess what? At least one major plastic manufacturer recommends only one product to clean its line of outdoor structures and furniture. Of course, that star performer is none other than vinegar in any of these three forms:

- Straight apple cider vinegar

- 2 cups of white vinegar and 2 tablespoons of dishwashing liquid in a bucket of warm water

- 1 cup of white vinegar per 5 to 7 quarts of water

Whichever of that terrific trio you use, your action plan is the same: Wash off exterior dirt with a garden hose. Then either spray your cleaning formula onto the surface or wipe it on with a soft cloth or sponge, scrubbing any stains or stubborn dirt. Use a toothbrush or bottle brush to get into small nooks and crannies. Rinse with a garden hose, and dry the item with a towel to avoid the stubborn water marks that often appear on plastic.

TLC FOR TRAVERTINE

For as drop-dead elegant as it looks around a swimming pool, travertine is what my Grandma Putt would call a down-home easy keeper. For routine cleaning, all you need to do is brush the tiles with warm, soapy water using circular motions, and rinse with clear H_2O (making sure it doesn't drain into the pool). To remove stubborn stains, like tree sap and berry juice, as well as mold or mildew, mix up a thin paste of roughly 1 part vinegar to 2 parts baking soda, and spread it onto the marks. Let the mixture sit for 10 minutes, then grab your brush, and once more scrub in a circular motion until it's as clean as a whistle.

Get in the Swim

If, like a lot of swimming pools, yours is covered partly or entirely with ceramic tile, you know what a challenge it can be to remove the hard-water scale that builds up at the water line. No doubt you've also been told that the only way to remove the unsightly stuff is to use muriatic acid (which actually is a weakened form of hydrochloric acid). Well, forget that poison! Sure, it'll clean your tiles all right. But in the process, it can also hand you a whole heap of trouble—especially when you're spraying it on, which its proponents recommend. Instead, do the job with hot vinegar. Either use it straight from the pot you've heated it in, or pour it into a handheld spray bottle. Then wipe the deposits away with a soft cloth. Your pool will sparkle to beat the band!

Liven Up the Liner

White vinegar is also just what the pool doctor ordered for sprucing up a dingy vinyl liner. Just wipe it on generously with a sponge or rag, and wait a few minutes so the acid can penetrate any mildew, leaf stains, or other offending marks. Then grab a soft-bristled brush, and scrub in both vertical and horizontal directions until the discolorations are gone. Rinse thoroughly so the dirt you've removed doesn't wind up in the pool water.

IF YOU'RE CLEANING A VINYL LINER on a pool that's been drained, it's A-OK to do your post-cleaning rinse with a blast from the garden hose. But if you've only removed a few spots near the top of a still-filled pool, carefully wipe the treated areas with a damp cloth.

Easy Concrete Paint Prep

Getting ready to paint your concrete patio or garage floor? If so, then make sure that colorful surface hangs in there for the long haul, rather than peeling, as painted concrete tends to do pretty quickly. For protection, simply give the surface a primer coat of white vinegar. You can brush it on or wipe it on with a cloth—it's your call. Let the vinegar dry completely, then grab your brush or roller and get to paintin'. **Note:** *This trick will also help paint adhere better to galvanized metal.*

Window Washing 101: What the Pros Know

Professional window washers recommend cleaning your exterior windows at least twice a year using the right tools and this highly effective routine:

Whip up a batch of Heavy-Duty Window Cleaner (at right).

Remove loose dirt, cobwebs, or crumpled leaves with a soft-bristled brush.

Dip a natural sponge or a strip applicator (a squeegee look-alike with a soft, woolly fabric strip on the business end) into the cleaning solution, wring out the excess, and wash the glass. Use a nylon scrubbing pad to go after stubborn spots, such as bird droppings or tree pitch.

FANTASTIC FORMULA

Heavy-Duty Window Cleaner

When your windows are extra grimy or greasy, this formula will bring back the sparkle.

¼ cup of white vinegar

2 tbsp. of rubbing alcohol*

3 cups of warm water

Mix the ingredients together in a bucket—multiplying the recipe as needed—and go to town (see "Window Washing 101: What the Pros Know," at left).
* *Or substitute 2 tablespoons of pulp-free lemon juice.*

Pull a squeegee over the soapy pane in whatever direction you prefer (straight down, horizontally, or in a reverse-S pattern). Overlap passes, and at the end of each stroke, wipe the blade clean with a lint-free cloth.

Dry the panes and frames with a fresh lint-free cloth.

Note: *Whenever possible, wash your windows—indoors and out—on a cloudy or overcast day. Otherwise the sun will make the cleaning solution dry prematurely, causing unsightly streaks.*

OLD-TIME
Vim and *Vinegar*

To remove old, dried-out paint from window glass, wipe heated vinegar onto the splatters. It'll soften the paint, so it'll glide right off when you go at it with a plastic scraper, expired credit card, or (Grandma Putt's tool of choice) an old-fashioned single-edge razor blade.

OUTDOOR FURNISHINGS

That Sandbox Is Not Your Bathroom!

It's only natural that wandering neighborhood cats might mistake your kids' sandbox or sandpit for a giant litter box. But natural and acceptable are different things altogether! To send the misguided felines elsewhere for their potty breaks, just saturate the perimeter of their target with full-strength vinegar. Don't scrimp on the amount—this is one case where more is better. And remember to reapply the aromatic barrier after every rain. **Note:** *After a few applications, local cats should start giving your sandbox the cold shoulder. If future problems occur,* *that probably means that new felines have moved into the neighborhood, so relaunch your pungent defense tactic until they, too, get the message.*

Splash!

For tiny tots, and a lot of dogs, too, a backyard splash pool delivers some of the best fun summer has to offer. But to keep the happy times coming all season long, you need to make sure that pint-size pond stays crystal clear and clean. Here's how to do the job quickly and safely, with no harsh chemicals:

- After using it, empty the pool, and dry up any remaining water with thick rags or old towels.

- Use a brush to scrub the bottom and sides with a half-and-half solution of white vinegar and water.

- Rinse the little basin with the garden hose, and fill 'er up again.

Note: *Ideally, you should perform this routine after each use. But unless a child or pet has urinated in the water, simply topping the pool with a sturdy cover will do just fine. It'll keep out dirty debris and, more importantly, prevent mosquitoes and other nasty Nellies from using the standing water as a breeding ground.*

QUICK & QUIRKY

Shoo, Flies!—
Ward off annoying flies in your deck, porch, patio, or pool area with this nontoxic repellent: Mix equal parts of white vinegar and mouthwash in a spray bottle. Then spritz it around your furniture, and even yourself. The flies will keep their distance—guaranteed!

Great Grills o' Fire!

To keep your barbecue grill looking good and cookin' up a storm, give it the same care you provide for your outdoor metal furniture. That is, make sure the casing is clean, and when you spot dings or worn spots, paint them before rust has a chance to form. As for cleaning the business end—the grate that holds all that delicious food—here's the simplest way I know to do the job: Grab a tub or basin that's big enough to hold the rack, and pour in enough hot water to cover it. Mix in ¼ cup of dishwasher detergent and ¼ cup of vinegar. Let the grill soak for an hour or so, then rinse and dry it thoroughly. **Note:** *Some folks use the bathtub for this project. If you choose to do that, just remember to drain and sponge the tub with a vinegar-water solution immediately. Otherwise, you'll wind up with a nasty ring!*

FANTASTIC FORMULA

Garbage Can Cleanup Concoction

When your garbage can starts smelling like, well, garbage, take action ASAP because it'll only get worse. Start with this terrific tonic.

½ cup of white vinegar

2 tbsp. of dishwashing liquid

2 cups of hot water

Borax

Mix the first three ingredients in the empty garbage can, then swish them around and scrub the bottom and sides with a sponge or a long-handled brush. Rinse the can well and let it dry thoroughly. Then sprinkle borax across the bottom before replacing the bag. **Note:** *Eventually, you'll need to repeat the whole process. But simply renewing the borax layer every 30 days or so should keep bad odors at bay for at least a few months.*

Let There Be (More) Light

Propane lanterns will burn brighter, longer if you use this old-time trick: Soak the new wicks in full-strength white vinegar for three to four hours, and let them dry thoroughly before inserting them in the lamp. You'll be amazed at how much it'll ramp up the fuel's glow power!

Send Your Cooler to Spring Training

Your first neighborhood barbecue of the season is coming up this weekend, so you haul your gang-size cooler out of storage, open the lid—and get a big ol' whiff of stale, musty air. Well, don't fret. You can get rid of that odor long before the crowd arrives. First wash the chest with hot, soapy water, and dry it with a soft towel. Then set a small bowl of white vinegar into the container, close the lid, and let it sit overnight. Come morning, it'll be fresh-smelling and ready to hold whatever you need to keep on ice during the festivities.

An Iron-Clad Guarantee

Iron is tough stuff. Well-made iron furniture will give you years of faithful service if you guard against its biggest enemy—rust. Give your pieces a

That's Historical

When Henry J. Heinz launched his company in 1869, the product line consisted of pickles, horseradish, and a few sauces. The white vinegar used to process them was made in-house, too, and before long it was also being sold for home use. Fast forward to the early 1900s, when Heinz sales reps held samplings in grocery stores. They asked housewives to taste various types of culinary vinegars and select which ones they would buy. These informal predecessors to focus groups led to the introduction of new varieties, like wine, malt, and apple cider vinegars.

Fast forward again to 2012, when the company's marketing gurus held formal, targeted focus groups in which women fondly recalled their grandmothers' tips for cleaning with vinegar. The result: Heinz® All Natural Cleaning Vinegar. For more about that, see "The Real Skinny on Cleaning Vinegar" on page 305.

careful inspection at the beginning and end of the summer. (Do this every few months if you live where the outdoor-living season goes year-round.) When you find spots where the paint has chipped off, tend to them immediately this way:

- Wipe on a coat of white vinegar and let it dry (no need to rinse).

- Repaint the worn areas with a high-quality, rust-resistant paint. I find spray paint the easiest to work with, but some folks prefer the brush-on kind—it's your call.

- Dip a soft cloth in car wax, and rub the whole piece of furniture with it. Repeat this rubdown yearly, and your rust worries will be a thing of the past!

Clean Your Outdoor Furniture

Vinegar is just the ticket for getting mildew—as well as plain old dirt and grime—off your deck, porch, and patio furniture. The best way to put this prodigious cleaner to work depends on what the pieces are made of. Here are the choices:

Wood. Mix up a solution made from 1 cup of ammonia, ½ cup of white vinegar, and ¼ cup of baking soda per gallon of water. Apply the mixture with a sponge or brush, scrubbing to remove any stubborn stains. Then rinse with clear water, and dry the pieces with a clean towel. (This routine works just as well to keep wooden

Word to the Wise

To keep bugs from buggin' you while you're painting outdoors, mix 2 parts apple cider vinegar and 1 part honey or molasses in an old can, and set it near your work area. The flying hordes will head for the sweet stuff and leave you in peace.

OUTSIDE YOUR HOME

decks, porches, and fences free of mildew.)

Plastic (solid or mesh). Add 2 cups of white vinegar and 2 tablespoons of dishwashing liquid or liquid soap to a bucket of hot water. Wipe the mixture onto firm surfaces with a sponge or a soft cotton cloth. Use a soft brush to work the solution into any padding. Then rinse with clear water, wipe with a clean towel to avoid streaks, and set the pieces in the sun to dry thoroughly. (This formula also works like a charm on patio umbrellas.)

But I Don't Want to Wear It!

Aluminum furniture wins popularity contests from coast to coast for its light weight and reasonable price tag. Unfortunately, though, aluminum has one glaring flaw: If left untreated, the surface oxidizes and develops a powdery, white residue. This ugly stuff, in turn, leaves equally ugly gray marks on clothes, tablecloths, and seat cushions. To ensure that your aluminum furniture keeps itself to itself, wipe it down with a solution of equal parts of vinegar and water. Let it dry, then spray on a coat or two of either clear lacquer or exterior paint to finish up.

Stain Outdoor Furniture...

Or anything else that's made of wood. How? Simply mix white vinegar with water-based ink in the color of your choice. The finished surface will be the color of the ink with a silvery sheen supplied by the vinegar. Apply the mixture to the wood surface with a rag or a paintbrush. Then wipe off any excess with a soft, clean cloth and let it dry.

{ **AS YOU MIGHT SURMISE,** the more ink you use to stain your wood furniture, the darker the stain will be, so the amount is your call. }

De-Gunk Your Fountain

There's nothing like the gentle splash of a fountain to add a touch of relaxation and elegance to your yard. That is, until algae or hard-water buildup—or both—get out of hand and intrude on your moment of Zen. Fortunately, you can probably solve both problems at once. First, check your owner's manual to make sure the magic ingredient—white vinegar—won't harm the fountain or void your warranty. If you get the green light from the manufacturer, then follow these six simple steps to make your wonderful water feature sparkling clean—and calming—again:

STEP 1. Drain the water by either pulling the plug or using a wet/dry vacuum to empty the basin.

STEP 2. Remove any stones from the bottom, drop them into a bucket of water with 1½ cups of chlorine bleach added to it, and let them soak while you proceed with Step 3.

STEP 3. Tackle the mineral buildup by covering the afflicted areas with rags saturated with white vinegar. Leave them in place for 30 minutes or so.

STEP 4. While you're waiting for the vinegar to work on the mineral buildup, fish the stones out of the bucket they've been soaking in, and scrub each one with a stiff brush. (Don't forget to wear gloves and clothes that can bear up to bleach splashes!) Then rinse them extra thoroughly with a strong blast from your garden hose, and set them aside for now.

STEP 5. Dip a stiff scrub brush into full-strength white vinegar, and go to town on the mineral deposits and algae in the basin. Use a retired toothbrush or bottle brush to get into the cracks and crevices.

STEP 6. Rinse the basin thoroughly with the garden hose, and refill it. Replace the clean stones, and plug the pump back in. Then sit back, relax, and enjoy!

OLD-TIME *Vim and Vinegar*

When a skunk comes a-callin' and leaves some fragrant evidence behind, reach for this easy remedy of Grandma Putt's: In a bucket, mix 1 cup of white vinegar and 1 tablespoon of dishwashing liquid in 2 ½ gallons of warm water, and thoroughly saturate walls, stairs, or other objects your local skunk has left his mark on. Everybody will breathe easier! **Note:** *Use this tonic only on nonliving things—not on pets, people, or plants. If your poor pooch was the target of the skunk's stink, see page 242 for the anti-aromatic answer.*

THE REAL SKINNY ON CLEANING VINEGAR

Since Heinz introduced its extra-strength cleaning vinegar in 2012 (see "That's Historical" on page 300), a number of other brands have come on the market. While upping the normal 5 percent acidity of distilled white vinegar to 6 percent does sound like a small difference, the actual acid concentration is 20 percent greater than that of "regular" vinegar. That added oomph can come in mighty handy when you're dealing with extra-grimy messes. But if you choose to clean with vinegar because of its food-safe nature and the convenience of having a double-duty product on hand, there are a few things you need to keep in mind. For instance:

▶ While the Heinz product is made from edible grain and technically is, as the website proclaims, "safe for cooking," you have to make some major recipe adjustments to effectively deal with the much higher acidity.

▶ Some of the copycat cleaning products are made from the same kinds of petroleum distillates used in the new high-powered horticultural vinegars. In fact, they are actually labeled "Not for Food Consumption."

▶ Edibility aside, an acidic substance that is 20 percent more potent than regular vinegar is not something you want to keep within reach of a child or pet—and certainly it should not be used as an internal or topical remedy for anyone.

The bottom line: If you want to use one of these superpowered vinegars, go for it. But handle it as you would any other commercial cleaning product—with care, and by keeping it out of reach of curious little hands (or paws)!

chapter ten ▶ BY LAND OR BY SEA

Vinegar's cleanup prowess doesn't stop at the edge of your property line. It's also a world champ when it comes to maintaining the good looks—and resale value—of boats and every kind of motor vehicle, from a spankin' new luxury car to a vintage Harley-Davidson bike.

CARS & OTHER MOTOR VEHICLES

Longer Life for Your Lifesavers

When you're driving through heavy, blowing rain or thickly falling snow, your vehicle's windshield wipers can literally spell the difference between life and death. To keep those hard workers on the job longer and functioning better, wipe the blades every week or so with a rag soaked in white vinegar. It'll clean and soften the rubber, so it can continue to perform flawlessly. **Note:** *When you use your wipers during a rainstorm, and your windshield just gets blurrier, it's all but certain that the blades are overdue for a good cleaning.*

Deal with Deposits

Hard water can leave unsightly mineral deposits on just about anything it touches—including your car's windows. One of the primary depositors is the spray from your windshield sprinklers, but giving Old Betsy a bath, or taking her to the local car wash, can also make a streaky mess of your windows. To make all your auto glass clear and clean again, simply spray the surface with straight white vinegar and let it sit for five minutes. Then scrub the streaks and splotches with a damp sponge, and finish by wiping away all the residue with a clean, damp cloth.

Save Your Road Trip

Getting ready to hit the road with a carsick-prone passenger? If so, then make sure you pack two essential pieces of travel gear: a bottle of white vinegar and a shallow, unbreakable bowl. This way, you'll be all set to eliminate the odor left behind by any tossed "cookies." Once you've cleaned up the mess, just fill the bowl with vinegar and let it sit in the vehicle overnight. By morning, your car will be fresh-smelling and ready to roll again. **Note:** *Of course, this anti-aroma trick works just as well for queasy stomachs that act up right in your own neighborhood (maybe on the way to the vet's office).*

De-Diesel Your Duds

If your vehicle runs on diesel fuel, then you know that even a tiny spill leaves your clothes with a horrible odor that refuses to go away—

Word to the Wise

A bowlful of vinegar will rid your car of any unwanted aroma, no matter what the source, including French fries, soccer gear, and spilled coffee. Just remember to take the dish out before you start driving away, or your car will smell like salad dressing— and you'll have a pool of vinegar to sop up besides!

unless, of course, you launder the afflicted garments with a cup or so of white vinegar added to the wash cycle. If an aroma still lingers after the cleaning, repeat the process, and any remaining smell should be so faint that only a dog could detect it.

Unstick Bumper Stickers

When you're out on the road, you see bumper stickers touting everything from political candidates to car owners' favorite vacation destinations or their prowess as marathon runners. But those self-branding labels come with a daunting challenge: getting them off your car when the election's over or when it's simply time for a change of bumper decor. Enter the star of our book: vinegar! Just coat the sticker generously with the fabulous fluid, wait 10 to 15 minutes until it's thoroughly penetrated the paper, and then scrape the sticker off. If any gooey residue remains, sponge on more vinegar, and scrape the bumper again—no need to wait this time. A retired credit card is the perfect tool for this job. One word of caution: Never use a metal scraper or a razor blade because it could—and most likely will—scratch the bumper. **Note:** *This trick works just as well for removing car window decals that have outlived their original purposes, such as an expired inspection sticker or a parking permit for a place where you no longer work.*

That's Historical

What do you do when a reckless driver cuts you off in traffic or insists on "riding" your bumper? Well, you could express your road rage the way a Roman charioteer might have done: by looking the so-and-so square in the eyes (or, in this case, glancing in your rearview mirror), and saying three times, "Mayest thou have neither salt nor vinegar in thy house."

According to folklore, targets of this curse were destined to be poor for the rest of their lives. I can't guarantee that'll happen to your adversary, but reciting the curse might give you a chuckle or two to help lower your stress level!

Wipe Off Winter Woes

Road salt and chemical deicers make for easier and safer going in the winter, all right. But they do have a couple of downsides: When they splash up on your car, they look as ugly as sin—and, worse, if the dried stuff stays there for any length of time, it can damage the finish and eat away at the metal. So as soon as you reach your destination, wipe away any fresh spots and thin coatings with a soft cloth dipped in a half-and-half solution of vinegar and water. Use straight vinegar to tackle thicker, dried-on crud. Either way, your vehicle will look better—and last longer, too!

An Inside Job

You can buy specialized products to clean just about everything under the sun, and your car's interior is no exception. But good old vinegar can perform as well as anything you'll find at your local auto-supply shop—and for a fraction of the price. Here's all you need to do:

Plastic, vinyl, or wood. Mix equal parts of white vinegar and water in a spray bottle, and spritz the surfaces that need clean-

OLD-TIME *Vim and Vinegar*

When I bought my first little car, Grandma Putt gave me my first automotive emergency kit: a roll of paper towels and a spray bottle filled with a half-and-half solution of vinegar and water. She told me I should keep them in my trunk so I'd always be prepared to clean my windows, mirrors, and headlights or wipe up spills. To this day, I still follow that advice, and you should, too. But in the winter, be sure to leave an inch or so of empty space at the top of the bottle. So if the solution freezes, it'll have room to expand without bursting the bottle and making a mess.

ing. Let the solution soak in for a minute or so (longer if you're dealing with major dirt). Then wipe with a soft, clean cloth.

Fabric upholstery and carpet. A once-over with a vacuum cleaner is fine for routine cleaning, but when more intensive action is called for, get tough with one of these two tactics:

FANTASTIC FORMULA

Automotive Anti-Frost Formula

There are few more annoying cold-weather predicaments than waking up to find your car windows covered in frost or a thick coat of ice. This simple elixir can end your ice-scraping days for good (provided you remember to use it every time you have to park your car outdoors on a frosty night).

6 cups of white vinegar

2 cups of water

Mix the vinegar and water together in a bucket or pan, drench a cloth with the solution, and give all your windows and mirrors a good once-over. Or pour the potion into a spray bottle and spritz the solution all over the glass. The next morning, you'll wake up to ice- and frost-free windows!

- To remove light stains or snow-salt residue, sponge a half-and-half mixture of vinegar and water onto the material, and blot it up.

- Tackle deeper stains with a paste made from equal parts of white vinegar and baking soda. Spread the paste onto the spots, and work it in using a small, stiff-bristled brush. Let the paste dry, then vacuum it up. Repeat the process as necessary (but it probably won't be).

Work Wheel Wonders

Metal car wheels pick up road dirt, grit, and brake dust like nobody's business. Fortunately, it's an easy business to send the crud packin'. Simply spray the wheels with a 50-50 solution of white vinegar and water, and use a sponge, rag, or (if necessary) cotton swab to work the solution into all the nooks and crannies. Give it a few minutes to penetrate the grime, then rinse it off with a garden hose. If any dirt remains, repeat the process until your wheels look wonderfully radiant.

Home, Home on the Go

When you vacation or (as some folks do) actually live in an RV or on a boat, you have a trio of special reasons to take vinegar along, namely these:

- The active ingredients in most commercial cleaning products are toxic chemicals, and to cover up their odors, the manufacturers use artificial fragrances that are made from other noxious substances. In a small, enclosed space, it's difficult to get the kind of ventilation required to use those products comfortably and safely. And if you have just the slightest chemical sensitivity, even a short trip could be a nightmare.

- No matter how tightly you lock down the contents of your

ADJUST THE AROMA

Lots of folks enjoy the smell of vinegar because it reminds them of favorite food treats like pickles or fish-and-chips. But if you don't care for the scent, it could pose a problem for you in an enclosed space such as a car, RV, or travel trailer. So here's a simple solution: Put lemon or orange peels in a jug of white vinegar, and let it sit for a week or so. (The more rinds you use and the longer the vinegar sits, the more citrusy it will smell.) When it's reached the desired aroma, pour equal parts of the infused vinegar and water into a spray bottle, and you'll have the perfect mixture to clean with.

cabinets, you'll have a lot more spills and splashes than you have in a stationary home—and therefore more chances for children or pets to dabble in the resulting puddles. When your cleaning agent of choice is vinegar, you can rest easy, knowing that no harm will be done.

- In a tight space, the more jobs an item can perform, the more valuable it is to keep around. That makes vinegar worth its weight in gold!

A Vintage Vehicle Deserves a Vintage Cleaner

You rarely see chrome on new cars or trucks, but if you have an old-timer, keep that trim gleaming with the same shiner-upper Grandma Putt used: full-strength white vinegar. Just wipe it on with a soft, clean cloth—no need to rinse. (Of course, this same timely TLC works just as well to shine up the bright work on a motorcycle, bicycle, or boat.)

IF YOUR CHROME still looks cruddy after polishing it with vinegar, sprinkle a little baking soda on the cloth for extra cleaning power.

Rejuvenate a Rusty Bike

It's exciting, all right: You snagged a classic mid-century Schwinn® for peanuts at a tag sale. On the downside, it's sporting more rusty patches than Howdy Doody had freckles. Well, don't despair. Here's how to get that baby back in shape fast:

- Find a container that's big enough to hold the bike frame—a plastic under-the-bed storage box should do the trick nicely—and fill it with white vinegar.

- Remove the seat, tires, and chain (more about that coming up) and immerse the frame. Put the lid on the box, and let the bike soak for two to three hours.

- Take the frame out of the drink and wipe it off with a rag. Then very gently brush the rusted areas using a soft, copper-wire brush or a nonabrasive plastic scrubber. The brown patches should fall right off. If any stubborn spots remain, repeat the process, soaking only the affected sections if that's possible given their locations.

- After all the rust has gone bye-bye, rinse the frame with clear water, and wipe it very lightly with WD-40® or a similar lubricant to prevent further rusting.

Then reassemble your bike, and go for an old-fashioned joyride! **Note:** *If the wheel rims are also rusty, chances are you'll need a separate container for them, but the procedure is the same.*

Don't Soak the Chain!

Some bicycle experts warn against soaking a bike's chain in vinegar because (they say) the acid could loosen the links and make them come apart. So, rather than risk trouble, while your frame is soaking, scrub the rust from your two-wheeler's chain using a toothbrush or scouring pad dipped in vinegar. Then apply a light coat of lubricant to fend off future rust attacks.

HIKE HAPPY TRAILS!
Whenever you set out on a long hike or overnight backpacking trip, make sure you bring along plenty of water. And be sure to add several drops of apple cider vinegar to the H_2O in your canteen or thermos bottle. It'll keep your drinking supply fresh longer and also increase its thirst-quenching power.

Be a Happy Camper

When you open up an RV or camping trailer that's been stored for the winter, you can be slammed with a blast of stale, stagnant air that smells unpleasant to say the least. Well, don't panic. Just fill a spray bottle with white vinegar and thoroughly spritz the walls, countertops, floors, and storage spaces. Lightly spray any pillows, mattresses, and seat cushions, and set them out in the sun to dry.

Pop! Goes the Camper

When your traveling vacation home is a pop-up camper, rather than a standard RV or trailer, it's not always easy to keep it properly ventilated. And that puts you at constant risk for a mildew invasion. Fortunately, it's easy to send the spores on their unmerry way. Do the job on a bright, sunny day, and proceed as follows:

Mix ¼ cup of soap flakes in a gallon of water, adding more soap if necessary until you've got nice suds. Then dip an abrasive sponge in the solution, and scrub away any dirt and debris from the surface.

Soak a terry-cloth towel or similar cloth in white vinegar, and scrub using an up-and-down motion. Get the canvas as wet as you can without having the vinegar run off. Let the wet camper sit for 5 to 15 minutes (depending on the severity of the mildew).

Aggressively scrub the vinegar-soaked canvas with a brush or abrasive sponge to remove deeply embedded spores. If any remain, reapply the vinegar and scrub again.

Word to the Wise

To keep future mildew attacks to a minimum, always give your pop-up camper the best ventilation you possibly can, and try not to fold it up when it's even the least bit damp. (Yes, I know that's mission all-but-impossible, so just do your best, and keep plenty of vinegar and soap flakes on hand!)

Saturate a clean cloth with water, and wring it out onto the canvas to rinse away the vinegar and the sinister spores.

Position the camper in direct sunlight, and let the rays dry the canvas before you "un-pop" your sleeping quarters.

Timely Treatment for Troubled Tents

It happens every summer: Folks haul their tents out of their winter napping spots, unfold the fabric, and see mildew. That should come as no surprise, given the fact that garages and basements rank among the most common off-season storage areas for tents and other camping gear. Don't waste time berating yourself for your poor choice of a hibernation spot. Just bundle that tent up and haul it outside quickly before mildew spores start spreading. Brush the material thoroughly. Then mix up a half-and-half mixture of vinegar and water, wipe the mildew away, and spread the tent out on the lawn to let the sun finish the job.

To prevent future trouble, make sure your tent—and all your camping gear—is thoroughly dry before stowing it away between uses. And at the end of the season, stash it in a dry, well-ventilated area. **Note:** *This mildew-removal method may also work for other types of outdoor gear, including backpacks, sleeping bags, and waders. Then again, depending on the brand and the fabric, it may not—at least not without damaging the goods that probably cost you*

OLD-TIME

Vim and Vinegar

In addition to its other camping uses, vinegar makes a fine stand-in for two important items you might forget to pack: deodorant and insect repellent. That's because its acidity creates a hostile environment for bacteria that cause body odor and bugs that want to bite you!

*a pretty penny. So don't take any chances. Before using vinegar or any
other anti-mildew formula, consult your owner's manual or the manufacturer's website for specific guidelines.*

Deodorize Your Sleeping Bag

It's no secret that a sleeping bag picks up odors galore. The easiest
way to get rid of them—without harming the fabric or stuffing—is
the spray and hang method. Simply spray the affected area(s) with
a half-and-half solution of white vinegar and water, and hang the
bag outside to dry. The triple-threat combo of vinegar, sunshine, and
fresh air will take it from there.

BOATS

Head Off Head Pain

Today's marine toilets need minimal maintenance, but if you ignore
yours completely, you'll wind up with a whopper of a headache
(pun intended). That's because a head that's flushed with salt water accumulates calcium deposits in its discharge channels, hoses,
and valves. If that scale is allowed to build up, it will lead to total
blockage—and if Mr. Murphy's law is operating as usual, it's all but
guaranteed to happen when you're miles from the closest shore.
Fortunately, you can avoid this nightmare by performing the following simple process once a month:

- Pour a pint of white vinegar into the head, then give it a
  single pump every four to five minutes.

- Once the vinegar has passed all the way through the system,
  pump a gallon of fresh water through the lines to flush them out.

That's all there is to it!

More Helpful Head Hints

Bathroom problems that are annoying on dry land can be absolute nightmares on a boat. Here's how to fend off a couple of the worst:

Odors. Once a week or so—without fail—pour ½ to 1 cup of vinegar into the toilet bowl. Use a scrubber to remove any built-up mineral deposits in the bowl, and then dry flush once or twice (no more). This way, the acidic fluid will remain in the hoses long enough to kill unpleasant odors and also keep bronze fittings clean and smooth by cutting through accumulated calcium. The result: an amazingly sweet-smelling head.

Hose woes. This ploy is a must when you're about to leave your vessel unattended, either in the water or in dry storage, for a period of time. First, pour a half-and-half mixture of vinegar and oil into the toilet bowl and dry flush. Then cover the bowl with plastic wrap to prevent evaporation. The vinegar-oil combo will keep all the working parts clean and lubricated and will dissolve any crystallized salt in the hoses. When you return to your boat, your plumbing will function (and smell) just fine.

DON'T SWEAT THE SMALL SPACE

Small refrigerator space, that is. When chilling capacity is at a premium, or even nonexistent, vinegar can help keep you well fed. Here are just two prime examples of what it can do:

Preserve cheese. It'll stay fresh and fine to eat for weeks with this trick: Saturate cheesecloth in vinegar, wrap it around blocks of cheese, and store them in airtight plastic containers.

Pickle fish. When you catch one that's too big to eat at a single

sitting, don't toss out the extra. It'll keep for a couple of weeks if you preserve it in vinegar with your choice of herbs and/or spices. For some taste-tempting recipes, see Chapter 4.

Banish Boat-Seat Mildew

Anything that spends as much time in a damp environment as a boat seat does is bound to pick up its fair share of mildew. Fortunately, it's easy to clean the yucky stuff off. Just grab a bucket, a garden hose, a jug of white vinegar, a box of baking soda, and a scrub brush. Then proceed as follows, working on one cushion or one small section of upholstery at a time:

Remove the cushions if you can. If you've got upholstered seats that are not removable, dock or anchor the boat in a sunny spot. Take off any cover or lower any canopy that may be over the seats.

Fill the bucket with a half-and-half solution of vinegar and water.

Rinse the seat with clear water. Then sprinkle the surface with a generous layer of baking soda, and scrub-a-dub-dub, paying special attention to the mildewed areas.

Pour or sponge on the vinegar-water solution. (As usual, when you mix vinegar and baking soda, there will be bubbling action.) Don't rinse! Just leave the seat in bright sunlight until it's thoroughly dry. This way, the vinegar will kill any lingering mildew spores and prevent them from hatching into future trouble.

TO RETARD THE GROWTH OF MOLD AND MILDEW on your boat's interior woodwork, wipe it down after every cruise with a 50-50 mix of vinegar and water.

Repeat the process with every vinyl-covered seating surface on your vessel. **Note:** *Ignore any advice you may hear to use bleach for cleaning mold or mildew from your boat's seats. It'll kill the spores, all right, but it may also damage the vinyl and will definitely cause the stitching to deteriorate.*

Stop Vinyl Vexations Before They Start

Developing these three boat-healthy habits can go a long way toward keeping your vessel's vinyl seats free of mold and mildew:

- Whenever swimming and sunbathing, cover the seats with thick, dry towels. Otherwise, the combination of sunscreen residue, moisture from wet bathing suits, and sweat from bodies will issue an invitation to mold and mildew spores.

- When the seats have gotten wet, let them dry completely, in bright sunlight if possible, before you cover them or your whole boat.

- The minute you spot any new mildew stains beginning to form, wipe them with full-strength vinegar and let the the seats dry in the sun.

FANTASTIC FORMULA

Crackerjack Canvas Cover Cleaner

As every boat owner knows, both mooring and travel covers take a beating and gather mountains of dirt. But tossing any cover in a washing machine or using harsh cleaners can shrink the canvas and damage its water repellency. Whenever your cover needs more than a simple hosing off, reach for this strong but gentle formula.

1 cup of borax powder

1 cup of white vinegar

2 cups of warm water

Mix the ingredients together in a bucket. Sponge the mixture generously onto the soiled area(s), and let it sit for about 10 minutes. Scrub any stubborn spots, then rinse thoroughly. Be sure to let the canvas dry completely before you fold it up. **Note:** *Multiply the ingredients to accommodate the size of the cover.*

Darn Good Dacron Sail Cleaner

In order to look and perform their best, Dacron® sails demand a good bath every year. To do the job, first spread each sail out on a soft, grassy lawn—not on a hard surface like gravel or concrete! Then, using a soft-bristled brush, gently wash it with a solution made from 1 cup of white vinegar and 2 tablespoons of Woolite® per gallon of water. Rinse thoroughly with clear water to remove all of the soap residue. Hang the sails up in a spot that has good air circulation until they're completely dry. Then fold them—avoiding any windows in the material—and store them in a space that's well ventilated and well removed from any source of heat. **Note:** *Never use anything but plain old H_2O on nylon sails like spinnakers or drifters.*

Keep Your Bass Boat Beautiful

If you own a bass boat or similar fishing craft, you know that keeping that baby spanking clean is far more than a cosmetic nicety. It's also a crucial factor in maintaining the resale or trade-in value of your sizable investment. You also know that if you use a sport boat regularly, no matter how careful you are, all kinds of dirt and grime get tracked onto the nonremovable carpet and work their way into the fibers. For that reason, in addition to Johnny-on-the-spot vacuuming, experts (such as the folks who put out *Bass Fishing* magazine) recommend a thorough, no-holds-barred scrubbing at least two or three times a year. Here's how to do the job right:

STEP 1. Gather your supplies. You'll need a heavy-duty wet/dry vacuum cleaner, a garden hose, a 2-gallon hand-pump sprayer, two clean scrub brushes (one soft- and one medium-bristled), and—yep, you guessed it—a jug of white vinegar.

STEP 2. Park your boat on a slight slope, attached to a tow vehicle if possible, with the transom facing downhill. Make sure the boat is level from side to side so that water will drain out through the floor. Then pull the drain plug.

STEP 3. Pour 2 to 3 pints of white vinegar into your pump sprayer, and fill the balance of the container with water.

STEP 4. Vacuum up any loose dirt. Then, starting at the front of the boat, thoroughly saturate the carpet using a garden hose with the spray nozzle removed.

STEP 5. Working on one section of carpet at a time (again starting at the front of the boat), use your soft brush to loosen any stuck-on dirt, then drench the area again with water from the hose.

STEP 6. Spray the vinegar-water mixture onto the area, once again to the saturation point. Let the

> **THE SAME CARPET-CLEANING ROUTINE THAT KEEPS BASS BOATS SHIPSHAPE** works just as well on pontoon boats, which generally have the same kind of nonremovable, polypropylene floor covering.

solution set in for four to five minutes, and then scrub again to loosen up any stains or stubborn dirt.

STEP 7. Turn the hose back on, and rinse the area thoroughly as you continue to scrub.

STEP 8. Repeat steps 5 through 7 on the remainder of the carpeting. When you're finished, use the wet/dry vacuum to remove all excess moisture, and then let the boat sit in the sun for a few hours until it's dry.

STEP 9. Brush the dried carpet against the grain using your medium-bristled brush. This will lift the fibers, making your boat's carpet look fluffy and new again.

PAINT, PAINT, PAINT YOUR BOAT

Painting the hull of your boat can be a time-consuming mess. But it's an essential chore if you want your vessel to keep performing at its peak. So gather up your supplies and get started. But first—if it's made of aluminum—wash the whole thing down with white vinegar, which will etch the surface so the paint will hold. Once it's dried, apply a coat of metal primer, followed  by the waterproof paint of your choice. That's all there is to it!

One Gel of a Cleaner

Every so-called fiberglass boat is actually composed of a thick layer of fiberglass resin covered by a very thin plastic cover called gelcoat. If you use an abrasive cleaner on the hull, it'll wear right through that fragile coating and either reveal the base color or leave a glaring dull spot. So don't take any chances. Whenever you wash your boat, use a mixture of ½ cup of household ammonia, ½ cup of white vinegar, and 2 tablespoons of cornstarch dissolved in 1 gallon of warm water.

Water Spots, Begone!

If you're the proud owner of a fiberglass boat, especially one that's black or another dark color, you know that water spots can make an unsightly mess of the hull. Fortunately, adopting one simple habit can make those splotches a thing of the past. What is it? Every time you take your beloved craft out of the water, spray it with a 50-50 solution of white vinegar and water, and wipe with a soft, clean cloth. The spots will vanish before your very eyes!

Help for Spotty Windows

Just like fiberglass hulls, soft vinyl (a.k.a. isinglass) windows can collect more than their fair share of water spots. To remove them without damaging the delicate surface, spray the vinyl with a solution made from 1 part white vinegar to 9 parts water. Then wipe very gently with a clean, soft, all-cotton cloth. Old diapers or pieces cut from retired flannel sheets, flannel shirts, or T-shirts are perfect. Never, ever use paper towels on vinyl windows, or you'll scratch them. And steer clear of commercial household window cleaners, which could destroy your windows in a matter of months.

Word to the Wise

Over time, acrylic portholes can become too hazy to see through. So keep a clear view of the watery world outside your cabin. Mix equal parts of white vinegar and water and wipe away the haze using a chamois cloth or other soft cotton towel.

Remedies & Recipes

Throughout this book, you've found dozens of vinegar-based concoctions designed to improve your health, enhance your good looks, or help ease your workload around the old homestead—indoors and out. The roots of some of these potions date back literally thousands of years. Others I learned at my Grandma Putt's knee. Still others are the brainchildren of 21st-century health, beauty, and household gurus. But regardless of their origin or purpose, they all have one thing in common: They're almost miraculous at performing the job at hand.

To make it easy to put your finger on the specific tonic you need, when you need it, I've rounded up all of the recipes in this special bonus section. So, for example, whether you want to alleviate arthritis aches, clean a grimy oven, de-flea your pet, or shave years off your appearance, you'll find the solution right here!

▶ **Arthritis Ache Reliever**

> 1 part apple cider vinegar   1 tsp. of Knox® orange-flavored
> 1 part raw honey   gelatin powder (not
> 6 oz. of water   sweetened Jello-0®)

Combine the vinegar and honey, and store the mixture in a tightly lidded glass jar at room temperature. Once a day, stir 1 teaspoon of the combo and 1 teaspoon of the gelatin powder into a 6-ounce glass of water, and drink it down. Before you know it, your joints should be jumpin' again! *For related text, see page 5.*

▶ **Bursitis Pain Banisher**

> ½ cup of apple cider vinegar   1 tsp. of cayenne pepper
> 2 tbsp. of honey   12 oz. of water

Ease your discomfort with a simple routine that works from the inside out. One hour before breakfast each morning, mix all of the ingredients together in a glass and drink up. Repeat the process until your joints are back in business. *For related text, see page 6.*

▶ **Cure for Nighttime Muscle Miseries**

> 1 tbsp. of calcium lactate   1 tsp. of raw honey
> 1 tsp. of apple cider vinegar   Warm water

Muscle cramps seem a thousand times worse when they strike at night. So mix all of the ingredients together in a glass. Drink it down, and the pain should back off within 20 minutes or so, allowing you to get some sleep. *For related text, see page 8.*

▶ Leapin' Liniment!

½ cup of apple cider vinegar   2 egg whites
¼ cup of olive oil

Mix all of the ingredients together in a bowl. Then massage the lotion into the painful areas, and wipe off the excess with a soft cotton cloth. *For related text, see page 7.*

▶ Toothache Tamer

2 tbsp. of apple cider vinegar   4 oz. of warm water
1 tbsp. of salt

Mix all of the ingredients together in a glass, and rinse your mouth with the mixture. It should ease your misery until you can get to the dentist's office for a permanent fix. *For related text, see page 3.*

▶ Toothache Tamer, Take 2

1 piece of brown paper   Black pepper
   the size of your cheek   Adhesive bandage
Vinegar (any kind)

Soak the paper in the vinegar, and then sprinkle one side of it with black pepper. Lay the peppered side of the paper against your face where the toothache is. Hold it in place with a bandage, and keep it there for at least 60 minutes. *For related text, see page 3.*

INTERNAL AILMENTS

▶ Beefed-Up Chicken Soup

1 cup of soup or broth   1 crushed garlic clove
1 tbsp. of apple cider vinegar Dash of hot-pepper sauce

Heat up the soup or broth, and stir in the remaining ingredients. Pour it into a bowl or mug, and sip your cold symptoms away. *For related text, see page 14.*

▶ Breathe-Easy Asthma Reliever

3 garlic bulbs, peeled and separated into cloves

2 cups of water

1 cup of apple cider vinegar

¼ cup of raw, organic honey

Put the garlic in a nonreactive pan with the water, and simmer until the garlic cloves are soft and there is about 1 cup of water left in the pan. Using a slotted spoon, transfer the garlic to a jar with a tight-fitting lid. Add the vinegar and honey to the water in the pan, and boil the mixture until it's syrupy. Pour the syrup over the garlic in the jar, put the lid on, and let it sit overnight, or for at least eight hours. Every morning on an empty stomach, swallow one or two garlic cloves along with 1 teaspoon of the syrup. *For related text, see page 13.*

▶ Cholesterol-Clobbering Punch

2 cups of 100 percent apple juice

2 cups of 100 percent cranberry juice

2 cups of 100 percent white grape juice

⅓ cup of apple cider vinegar

Mix all of the ingredients together in a jug or pitcher, and keep it in the refrigerator. Drink one 8-ounce glass each morning and evening—and watch your cholesterol numbers plummet! *For related text, see page 45.*

▶ Cure for Coughs, Colds & Sore Throats

1 part apple cider vinegar

1 part honey

1 part warm water

¼ tsp. of grated fresh ginger per cup of the mixture

Mix all of the ingredients together in a glass jar with a tight-fitting cover, and store it at room temperature. Take 1 teaspoon three times a day. *For related text, see page 16.*

▶ External Bronchitis Reliever

Extra virgin olive oil	2 clean, soft, chest-size cloths
1 cup of chopped onions	Plastic wrap
1 tsp. of apple cider vinegar	Heating pad
Pinch of cornstarch	

Coat a cast-iron skillet with the oil, and add the onions, vinegar, and cornstarch. Cook over low heat to make a paste. Let it cool to a comfortable temperature, and then spread it on one of the cloths. Lay it, paste side down, on your bare chest. Cover it with plastic wrap, add the other cloth, and top everything with a heating pad set on low. Relax for an hour or so. The onion will be absorbed into your body and open up your bronchial tubes. You'll know the paste has penetrated into your system because you'll have the onion breath to prove it! *For related text, see page 15.*

▶ Four Thieves Vinegar

2 tbsp. of dried food-grade lavender	2 tbsp. of dried thyme
2 tbsp. of dried mint	4–8 cloves of minced fresh garlic
2 tbsp. of dried rosemary	1 32-oz. bottle of apple cider vinegar
2 tbsp. of dried sage	

Put the first six ingredients in a glass jar, and pour the vinegar over them. Cover the jar tightly, and leave it in a cool, dark place for six to eight weeks, shaking it daily if possible. When time's up, strain the tonic into smaller containers for easier use. Store them away from heat and light. Use it, as folks have been doing since the 17th century, to cure and fend off flu and cold viruses. If your jar has a metal lid, cover the opening with plastic wrap before you screw on the cap; otherwise, the vinegar will react with the metal. *For related text, see "Good Things from Bad Guys" on page 22.*

▶ Raspberry Sore-Throat Solution

2 cups of ripe red raspberries 1 cup of sugar
2 ½ cups of white-wine vinegar

Put the berries in a bowl, and add the vinegar. Cover, and refrigerate for three days. Then pour the mixture into a saucepan, stir in the sugar, and bring to a low boil. Simmer for 15 minutes, and remove from the heat. When the mixture has cooled, strain it through a cheesecloth. Pour the potion into a glass bottle, refrigerate it, and gargle with it as needed. *For related text, see page 16.*

EXTERNAL WOES

▶ Corn-Conquering Formula

1 slice of raw onion 1 cup of vinegar (any kind)
1 slice of white bread

Put the ingredients in a bowl, and let it sit for 24 hours. The next night, put the bread on top of the corn, lay the onion on top of the bread, cover it with a bandage, and go to bed. There's a good chance the corn will fall off overnight. If it doesn't, repeat the procedure until the painful bump is history. *For related text, see page 38.*

▶ Itch-Eradicating Tub Soak

½ cup of apple cider vinegar ½ cup of wheat germ
½ cup of olive or sesame oil

Add the ingredients to your bathwater, and settle in for 20 minutes or so. Then follow up with your favorite moisturizer. This is the perfect antidote when your skin is parched and itchy, whether the cause is an arid climate or moisture-robbing furnace heat. *For related text, see page 63.*

▶ Nail-Fungus Fighter Tonic

1 part antiseptic mouthwash	1 part warm water
1 part vinegar (either white or apple cider)	1 tbsp. of ground cinnamon

Mix all of the ingredients together in a bowl or basin. Then soak your afflicted hand or foot for 20 minutes every day. Granted, it will take longer to work than a doctor's prescription, but it will kill the foul fungi with no side effects. *For related text, see page 31.*

▶ Scalp Psoriasis Treatment

1 cup of olive oil	Apple cider vinegar
2 drops of calendula oil	Water
1 drop of oregano oil	

Combine the oils in a bowl. Then step into the shower, massage the mixture into your scalp, and shampoo as usual. Rinse with a half-and-half solution of apple cider vinegar and water. Repeat daily or as needed until you've doused the flare-up. *For related text, see page 32.*

PROBLEM-PREVENTION POTIONS

▶ All-Purpose Cure-All

1 cup of apple cider vinegar	8 peeled garlic cloves
1 cup of raw honey	Water or fruit juice

Combine all of the ingredients in a blender on high speed for 60 seconds. Pour the blend into a glass jar that has a tight-fitting lid, and let it sit in the refrigerator for five days. Then every day (ideally before breakfast) take 2 teaspoons of the mixture stirred into a glass of water or fruit juice. This fabulous formula can help cure or prevent almost every ailment under the sun, including Alzheimer's disease, arthritis, asthma, high blood pressure, obesity, ulcers, and cancer, as well as muscle aches and colds. *For related text, see page 43.*

▶ Fire Cider

½ cup of chopped onion	1 tsp. of ground cayenne
½ cup of freshly grated ginger	pepper
½ cup of freshly grated	1 qt. of apple cider
horseradish	vinegar
10 garlic cloves, chopped	Raw honey to taste
or crushed	(optional)

Put the first five ingredients in a glass jar with a tight-fitting lid, and fill the balance of the jar with the vinegar. Store the jar in a cool, dark place for 30 days, shaking it daily. When the time's up, strain the potion into a clean jar, pressing hard to squeeze as much liquid as possible out of the pulp. Set the pulp aside. If desired, pour the honey into the vinegar, and stir well. Take 1 tablespoon every day to maintain good health, or 3 tablespoons a day if you feel cold symptoms coming on or your stress level is elevated. *For related text, see "5 Fine Ways to Put Fire Cider to Work" on page 42.*

▶ Fire Water

½ cup of apple cider vinegar	1 tsp. of honey (optional)
½ cup of hot water	1 tsp. of sea salt
1 tsp. of ground cayenne	½ tsp. of freshly squeezed
pepper	lemon juice

Stir all of the ingredients together in a mug or heat-proof glass. Then sip it while the potion is still hot. (It's surprisingly tasty!) Repeat as needed throughout the day. It can help cure a sore throat, fend off cold and flu viruses, unstuff your sinuses, rev up your energy, and give a great big boost to your immune system. Besides adding a sweet, healthy kick of its own, the honey will tone down the pepper's power. *For related text, see page 19.*

REMEDIES & RECIPES

▶ Perfect Produce Cleaner

2 tbsp. of vinegar (any kind)　　1 cup of water
1 tbsp. of lemon juice

Mix all of the ingredients together in a spray bottle, and keep it by the kitchen sink. Then spray all your fresh fruits and vegetables thoroughly and rinse with clear water. It will rid them of any toxic chemicals and other residue. *For related text, see page 45.*

▶ Sam Houston's Health Tonic

5 parts grape juice　　　　1 part apple cider vinegar
3 parts apple juice

Mix all of the ingredients together in a jug or jar, and drink ½ cup of the tasty beverage each day. It kept Sam healthy well into old age—and it just might do the same for you. *For related text, see page 6.*

▶ Toxin-Tossin' Bath Blend

¼ cup of baking soda　　　¹⁄₃ cup of apple cider vinegar
¼ cup of Epsom salts　　　10 drops of peppermint or
¼ cup of sea salt　　　　　　or lavender oil (optional)
1 qt. of boiling water

Dissolve the first three ingredients in the boiling water, and set the mixture aside. Fill your bathtub with warm water, and pour in the vinegar. Add the other ingredients, and swish the water around with your hand to disperse them. Then step into the tub, relax, and soak for 30 minutes or so. In addition to removing toxins from your system, it'll boost your magnesium levels, soothe skin irritations of all kinds, and relax you all over. For best results, use it just before bedtime. Caution: You may feel a little light-headed, so be careful getting out of the tub! This recipe makes enough for one bath. *For related text, see page 9.*

▶ **Amazing Anti-Aging Mask**

¼ cup of dried lentils   ½ tsp. of white-wine vinegar

¼ cup of tomato puree   About ½ inch of turmeric paste

Grind the lentils in a food processor or coffee grinder. Mix the powder with the remaining ingredients. Spread the mixture onto your freshly washed face, leave it on for about 15 minutes, and rinse with warm water. *For related text, see page 56.*

▶ **Anti-Wrinkle Scrub**

¼ cup of uncooked   1 tsp. of apple cider vinegar
   oatmeal (not instant)   ½ tsp. of warm water

2 ½ tsp. of raw honey

Combine all of the ingredients in a bowl. Smooth the mixture onto your face, and let it sit for 10 minutes. Then, with a soft washcloth dipped in warm water, gently scrub your skin using circular motions. Rinse with warm water, and follow up with your favorite moisturizer. In addition to removing surface debris, this scrub encourages the growth of new cells, and decreases the depth of wrinkles. *For related text, see page 58.*

▶ **Avocado Mask**

½ avocado, mashed   1 tbsp. of apple
¼ cup of uncooked oatmeal   cider vinegar
2 tbsp. of honey   1 tsp. of lemon juice

Mix all of the ingredients together in a small bowl. Smooth the concoction onto your face, being careful not to get it in your eyes. Wait 20 minutes or so, then rinse with warm water. *For related text, see page 56.*

REMEDIES & RECIPES

▶ Beautifying Body Cleanser

½ cucumber, not peeled
½ lemon, peeled and seeded
¼ russet potato, not peeled
¼ cup of baking soda

2 tbsp. of chopped strawberries
2 tbsp. of skim milk
2 tsp. of apple cider vinegar

Mix all of the ingredients together in a blender on medium-high speed until smooth. Moisten your skin and massage the mixture all over your body. Rinse with warm water, then with cool water. Leftovers will keep for two days in the fridge. *For related text, see page 62.*

▶ Coconut-Orange Deodorant

2 tbsp. of chopped iceberg
lettuce
2 tbsp. of chopped parsley
2 tbsp. of chopped
watercress

1 tsp. of apple cider vinegar
2 tsp. of coconut extract
3 drops of orange extract
¼ cup of baking soda
¼ cup of cornstarch

Liquefy the first three ingredients in a blender. Strain the mixture through a paper towel into a bowl, then stir in the vinegar and extracts. Sift the baking soda and cornstarch into another bowl. Dab the liquid onto your underarm skin with a cotton ball. When the solution has dried, apply the powder to the area to absorb wetness. Refrigerate the leftovers in a covered container, and use them within two days. *For related text, see page 66.*

▶ Cracked-Heel Softener

1 tbsp. of coarse sea salt
1 tbsp. of raw honey

1 tbsp. of rice vinegar

Mix all of the ingredients together, and scrub the dead skin away. Then slather on a rich hand or foot cream, put on a pair of cotton socks, and leave them on overnight. The next morning, your heels will be noticeably softer. *For related text, see page 64.*

▶ Cuticle-Softening Treatment

¼ cup of pineapple flesh (fresh or canned)

2 tsp. of honey

2 tsp. of olive oil

¼ tsp. of apple cider vinegar

1 egg yolk

Mix the ingredients in a blender on medium speed for 15 seconds. Then quickly rub the mixture onto your hands, concentrating on your cuticles and the skin around your nails. Put on plastic gloves and leave them on for 15 minutes, then rinse your hands with warm water. Apply the treatment at least once a week—or as often as every day, depending on the dryness of the weather and your skin. Cover and refrigerate any leftovers, and use them within three days, shaking thoroughly before each use to re-blend the oil. *For related text, see page 65.*

▶ Exfoliating Foot Soak

10 cups of hot water

1 cup of apple cider vinegar

½ cup of sea salt

Juice of 2 lemons

Mix all of the ingredients together in a pan or foot basin. Soak your feet for about 15 minutes, pat dry, and use a pumice stone to slough off any flaky skin. Then shower to rinse off the salad-dressing aroma. *For related text, see page 65.*

▶ Facial Mask for Very Dry Skin

2 tbsp. of raw honey

¼ tsp. of vinegar

½ tsp. of sweet almond oil

Heat the honey in a microwave-safe container until it's soft and pliable but not hot (20 to 30 seconds). Stir in the vinegar and oil, and immediately spread the blend onto your face. Leave it on for 15 minutes, then rinse with warm water. The honey and oil in this simple blend soften and moisturize, while the vinegar tones and helps balance your skin. *For related text, see page 56.*

▶ 5-Star Facial Mask

1 cup of uncooked oatmeal	1½ tbsp. white-wine vinegar
1 tbsp. of wheat bran	1 tbsp. of plain yogurt
2 tbsp. of buttermilk	1 tsp. of fresh mint leaves
2 tbsp. of whipping cream	½ medium cucumber, unpeeled

Grind the oatmeal and bran to a fine powder in a blender. Mix in the remaining ingredients. Spread the mask onto your face, leave it on for 15 minutes, then rinse. *For related text, see page 56.*

▶ Germ-Fighting Facial Toner

2 cups of boiling water	½ tsp. of unfiltered apple
1 handful of fresh parsley,	cider vinegar
chopped	20 drops of tea tree oil

Pour the water over the parsley, and let it steep, covered, for 10 minutes or so. Then strain out the solids, and mix the liquid with the vinegar and tea tree oil. Pour the mixture into a jar with a tight-fitting lid, and put it in the refrigerator, where it will keep for up to three weeks. Use it as you would any other facial toner to fight off blemish-causing fungi and bacteria. *For related text, see page 52.*

▶ Homemade Beauty Mayonnaise

1 egg	1¼ cups of extra virgin olive oil
1 tsp. of salt	½ cup of apple cider vinegar

In a blender, mix the egg, salt, and ¼ cup of the oil. With the machine still running, slowly pour in another ¼ cup of oil followed by ¼ cup of the vinegar. Follow up with another ¼ cup of the oil and the rest of the vinegar. Continue blending as you slowly add the remaining oil until you have thick, white, creamy mayonnaise. Pour your creation into a clean container with a tight-fitting lid, store it in the refrigerator, and use it in any beauty treatment that calls for mayonnaise. *For related text, see page 82.*

► Hot-Weather Toner for Oily Skin

1 tbsp. of fresh lemon juice   1 tsp. of pineapple juice
1 tbsp. of fresh lime juice   ¼ cup of water
1 tsp. of apple cider vinegar

Mix all of the ingredients together in a container with a tight-fitting lid. After cleansing, apply the formula to your face with a cotton ball, concentrating on the area that extends across your forehead, down your nose, and down to your chin (a.k.a. the t-zone). Use the toner every day if your skin is extremely oily. For moderately oily skin, every other day should be fine. Keep the covered container in the refrigerator, and use the contents within five days. *For related text, see page 54.*

► Non-Drying Facial Toner

1 tbsp. of raw honey   ½ cup of peppermint infusion
¼ cup of hot water   ¼ cup of apple cider vinegar

Mix the honey in the hot water. Then stir in the peppermint infusion and vinegar and mix thoroughly. Pour the blend into a bottle with a tight-fitting stopper. Store it at room temperature, and use it as you would any toner. *For related text, see page 55.*

► Post-Sun Skin Softener

3 tbsp. of rose water   ¼ tbsp. of glycerin
2 tbsp. of aloe vera gel   5 drops of peppermint oil
½ tbsp. of apple cider vinegar   Distilled water

Mix the first five ingredients in a 4-ounce spray bottle, and shake hard until the aloe is thoroughly blended in. Fill the balance of the bottle with distilled water, and store the potion in the refrigerator. Immediately after your time in the sun, spray the mixture on all exposed areas, and let it dry before covering your skin. *For related text, see page 60.*

▶ Rosy Vinegar Splash

1 cup of rose petals	1 cup of rose water
4 cups of white-wine vinegar, heated to near boiling	

Put the flowers in a sterilized glass jar, pour in the vinegar, cover the jar, and set it in a dark place at room temperature for 10 days, shaking it occasionally. Then strain the liquid into a fresh jar, and add the rose water. To use the potion, pour 1 tablespoon of it into a bowl, add 1 cup of warm water, splash it onto your face, and pat dry. It will help hydrate your skin, keeping it firm and supple. *For related text, see page 52.*

▶ Smoothing & Firming Facial Mask

3 tbsp. of alcohol-free witch hazel	1 egg white
1 tsp. of apple cider vinegar	

Mix the witch hazel and vinegar in a bowl, then lightly beat in the egg white. Whip the mixture until it's foamy, and pop it into the refrigerator for five minutes or so. Apply the frothy stuff to your warm, moist skin with a cotton pad. Leave it on for at least 30 minutes (the longer the better). For best results, repeat the procedure at least once a week. *For related text, see page 55.*

▶ Summertime Clarifying Mask

4 tbsp. of canned pumpkin puree	½ tbsp. of rose water
3 tbsp. of apple cider vinegar	

Mix the ingredients in a bowl, then spread the mixture onto your face, and leave it on for 15 to 20 minutes. Rinse with warm water, and follow up with your usual cleansing and moisturizing routine. The mask will clear out pore-clogging crud caused by heat, sweat, dirt, and melting makeup—and fend off blemish breakouts, leaving your skin soft and radiant. *For related text, see page 56.*

▶ Vinegar-Flaxseed Skin Lotion

4 tbsp. of cracked flaxseed	6 tbsp. of glycerin
2 cups of warm water	3–4 drops of your favorite
2 cups of apple cider vinegar	essential oil (optional)

Put the flaxseed and water in a pan, and let it sit, covered, for 24 hours. Then bring the water to a boil, reduce the heat, and simmer for 15 minutes. Strain off the flaxseed, add the vinegar and glycerin, and bring the mixture just to the boiling point. Remove the pan from the heat, add the oil if desired, and beat thoroughly. Pour the potion into bottles, store them at room temperature, and use the lotion as you would any other moisturizer. *For related text, see page 59.*

HAIR CARE

▶ All-Natural Shampoo

2 tbsp. of extra virgin olive oil	1 tsp. of vinegar
1 tbsp. of lemon juice	1 egg

Mix all of the ingredients thoroughly in a blender. Pour the mixture into a plastic bottle, take it to the sink, tub, or shower, and use it as you would any other shampoo. *For related text, see page 71.*

▶ Brunette Color Reviver

½ cup of cocoa powder	1 tsp. of apple cider vinegar
½ cup of plain yogurt	1 tsp. of honey

Mix all of the ingredients together to form a smooth paste. Apply the mixture to your freshly shampooed hair, and leave it on for two to three minutes. Then rinse and style as usual. *For related text, see page 79.*

▶ Conditioner for Oily Hair

½ avocado, mashed
2 tbsp. of freshly squeezed
  lemon juice
2 tbsp. of apple cider vinegar
1 tbsp. of mayonnaise
  (full-fat—not "lite")

Mix the ingredients together in a bowl. Apply the combo to your hair shafts, avoiding your scalp. Wait 20 minutes, then massage the mixture onto your scalp and leave it on for 5 more minutes. Rinse thoroughly with very warm water. Then shampoo twice with a deep-cleansing shampoo. Refrigerate any leftovers in a lidded glass jar and use them within seven days. *For related text, see page 71.*

▶ Frizz-Fighting Conditioner

1 cup of beer (full-strength—
  not "lite")
¼ cup of vinegar
20 drops of lemon oil
20 drops of rosemary oil
20 drops of sage oil

Mix all of the ingredients together in a measuring cup. After shampooing as usual, pour the rinse over your wet hair. Massage it into your scalp, and let it sit for three to four minutes, then rinse with clear water. *For related text, see page 70.*

▶ Herbal Conditioning Rinse

1 ½ cups of water
1 cup of fresh or dried
  rosemary leaves
½ cup of apple cider vinegar
10 drops of peppermint oil
10 drops of rosemary oil

Bring the water to a boil and add the rosemary. Reduce the heat to low and steep, covered, for 45 minutes. Strain, let the tea cool to room temperature, and stir in the vinegar and oils. Pour the solution into spray bottles. After shampooing and rinsing, spray the potion onto your hair and massage it into your scalp. Store the rinse at room temperature. Do not use this treatment on color-treated or processed hair. *For related text, see page 72.*

▶ Herbal Dandruff Treatment

2 tsp. of dried rosemary	⅔ cup of boiling water
2 tsp. of dried thyme	⅔ cup of vinegar

Put the herbs in a teapot or a heat-proof glass or ceramic bowl. Pour in the boiling water. Cover the container and steep for 15 to 20 minutes. Strain the solution into a clean 10-ounce bottle with a tight-fitting lid. Add the vinegar and shake thoroughly. Between uses, store the potion in a cool, dark place, such as a kitchen cabinet that's well removed from the stove.

To use the formula, shampoo your hair as usual and rinse thoroughly. Then massage a dime- to nickel-size amount of the treatment into your scalp. For added healing power, massage an equal amount into your scalp just before you go to bed. *For related text, see page 76.*

▶ High-Intensity Hair Cleaner

4 tbsp. of aloe vera gel	5 oz. of water
2 tbsp. of rice vinegar	

Mix all of the ingredients together in a spray bottle, shaking vigorously until the ingredients are thoroughly blended. Separate your hair into six sections, and working with one section at a time, spray the mixture generously onto your scalp and along the length of the hair shafts. Work the formula into your hair with your fingertips. Then squeeze out the cleanser—and the dirt with it. Repeat the process, only this time, leave the cleanser on your hair for five minutes, and then rinse with warm water. Repeat this step if necessary. Follow up with your usual shampoo and conditioner. It'll remove whatever crud is making your hair dull and lifeless, whether it's styling-product residue or plain old dirt from city streets or a long, shampoo-less camping trip. *For related text, see page 74.*

▶ Nettle Hair-Growth Formula

1 tbsp. of fresh nettles, chopped   2 cups of warm water
1 cup of vinegar

Simmer the nettles in the vinegar for 15 minutes. Strain the vinegar into a jar with a tight-fitting lid, and store it in a cool, dark place. At shampoo time, mix ¼ of the infused vinegar in the warm water, and use it as a final rinse. It'll help maintain a healthy scalp and encourage hair growth. Be sure to wear gloves when handling nettles. The hairs sting like the dickens! *For related text, see page 81.*

▶ Quick and Easy Dandruff Treatment

5 aspirin tablets, mashed   ⅓ cup of witch hazel
⅓ cup of vinegar

Put all of the ingredients in a plastic bottle, cap it, and shake it thoroughly. After you shampoo as usual, comb the solution through your hair. Wait 10 minutes, rinse it out with warm water, and say farewell to the flakes. *For related text, see page 75.*

▶ Scalp-Moisturizing Dandruff Scrub

½ cup of olive oil   1 tbsp. of apple cider vinegar
2 tbsp. of cornmeal   Shower cap or plastic wrap

Put all of the ingredients in a small bowl, and stir to make a thick paste. Wet your hair with warm water, scoop up a handful of the mixture, and warm it up by rubbing your hands together. Massage it into your scalp. Put on a shower cap, or cover your hair with plastic wrap, and go about your business for 30 minutes or so. Remove the topper, and shampoo as usual. It will add moisture to your scalp, combating the dry skin that (according to the folks at the Mayo Clinic) is the most common cause of dandruff. This formula does not keep well, so discard any leftovers. *For related text, see page 76.*

▶ Scentsational De-Gunking Treatment

¼ cup of vodka

2 tbsp. of apple cider vinegar

2 tbsp. of apple juice

1 tsp. of lemon extract

1 tsp. of orange extract

Put all of the ingredients in a blender and mix on high for 20 seconds, or just long enough to disperse the extracts (be aware that the potion will not be completely homogenized). Pour the mixture into a spray bottle, shake vigorously, and spray your hair thoroughly before shampooing and conditioning. The elixir will penetrate deep into your hair, removing product buildup, clarifying the shafts, and letting their natural highlights shine through. Refrigerate the final product immediately and use it (and any leftovers) within five days. *For related text, see page 74.*

▶ Thickening, Softening Hair Rinse

4 cups of water

3 tbsp. of vinegar

1 tsp. of borax

½ cup of dried lavender flowers

½ cup of dried rosemary

Bring the water to a rolling boil in a large pot. Remove the pot from the stove, and stir in the vinegar and borax. Add the lavender and rosemary, and mix until they're thoroughly wet. Cover the pot, and let it sit for at least two to four hours (longer if possible; the longer the potion steeps, the stronger it will be). When the mixture has reached a caramel-brown color, strain out the herbs, pour the liquid into a jar with a tight-fitting lid, and tuck it into the fridge, where it will keep for up to two weeks.

To use the potion, shampoo as usual, then pour the rinse over your hair so that it's completely saturated. Rinse with clear water, and follow up with your normal drying and styling procedure. *For related text, see page 80.*

▶ Two-Step Daily Dandruff Treatment

1 tbsp. of apple cider vinegar	½ cup of warm water
1 tbsp. of lemon extract	1 tbsp. of apple cider vinegar
3 egg yolks	1 cup of warm water

To make the shampoo, put the first four ingredients in a blender, and mix on low for 20 seconds. Make the rinse by whisking the vinegar into the water. Massage the shampoo into your scalp, and leave it on for 10 minutes. Then pour the rinse over your hair. Rinse, then follow up with conditioner. Depending on the severity of your dandruff, you may not need to use this gentle formula every day—but it won't cause problems if you do. *For related text, see page 78.*

KITCHEN & BATHROOM CLEANERS

▶ All-Around Antibacterial Cleaner

½ cup of baking soda	¼ cup of witch hazel
½ cup of water	1 tsp. of tea tree oil
½ cup of white vinegar	

Mix all of the ingredients together in a spray bottle, and use the mixture to clean your bathroom fixtures and kitchen appliances (inside and out), as well as countertops and ceramic-tile surfaces throughout your house. *For related text, see page 176.*

▶ Amazing Aluminum Cleaner

½ cup of baking soda	½ cup of white vinegar
½ cup of cream of tartar	¼ cup of soap flakes

Combine the baking soda and cream of tartar in a bowl. Add the vinegar, and mix to form a paste. Stir in the soap flakes, and transfer the mixture to a glass jar with a tight-fitting lid and label it. Apply the paste with a plain steel wool pad, and rinse with clear water. *For related text, see page 171.*

▶ DIY Do-It-All Cleaner

1 cup of clear ammonia	¼ cup of baking soda
½ cup of white vinegar	1 gal. of hot water

Mix all of the ingredients together in a bucket. Then pour the solution into a spray bottle and go to town. Or, if you'd prefer, mop or sponge it on straight from the pail. This old-time recipe cleans floors, greasy countertops, kitchen and bathroom fixtures, as well as appliances—both large and small. It even kills mildew. What's more, there's no need to rinse! *For related text, see page 161.*

▶ Fragrant Floor Cleaner

1 cup of white vinegar	1 tsp. of lavender or eucalyptus oil
1–2 tbsp. of liquid castile	1 tsp. of rosemary oil
soap (optional)	1 gal. of hot water (at least 130°F)

Mix all of the ingredients together in a bucket, and mop your floor as usual. If you've used the castile soap, rinse with clear water. Otherwise, you can skip this step. This delightfully aromatic (and thoroughly nontoxic) potion works equally well on ceramic tile, rubber, vinyl, cork, and linoleum floors. *For related text, see page 184.*

▶ Glass Shower Door Cleaner

⅓ cup of vinegar	5 drops of eucalyptus oil
3 cups of distilled water	5 drops of sage oil

Mix all of the ingredients together in a spray bottle. Spritz the solution onto the glass, and polish with a clean, dry cloth, and kiss streaks and smears good-bye! Any leftover mixture will last for six months. This fabulous formula works wonders on frequently fogged bathroom windows. *For related text, see page 179.*

▶ Old-Time Extra-Grubby Floor Cleaner

2 cups of white vinegar	2 tbsp. of liquid castile soap
¼ cup of washing soda	2 gal. of very hot water

Mix all of the ingredients together in a bucket. Mop the solution onto the floor, and let it air-dry. It leaves even the dirtiest floor as clean as a whistle and as shiny as a new penny—without waxing. *For related text, see page 183.*

▶ Oven Cleaner, Over Easy

5 tbsp. of baking soda	A few drops of grease-cutting
4 tbsp. of white vinegar	dishwashing liquid

Mix all of the ingredients together to make a thick paste. Heat the oven to 350°F and leave it on for 5 minutes. When the time is up, turn the oven off, and carefully spread the paste across the floor and walls of the oven, concentrating on any especially grimy spots. Wait 60 minutes or so, and then scrub with a sponge or plastic scouring pad. Wipe the crud away, and rinse thoroughly with clear water. Dampen a clean sponge with full-strength vinegar, and wipe down the whole oven to prevent future greasy buildup. *For related text, see page 155.*

▶ Potent Porcelain Stove Cleaner

2 tsp. of white vinegar	1 squirt of grease-cutting
1 tsp. of borax	dishwashing liquid
½ tsp. of baking soda	2 cups of water

Mix all of the ingredients thoroughly in a spray bottle. Spray and wipe your porcelain stove top, drip pans, gas burner grates, oven, and even the glass windows in your oven door. For dried-on spills, soak the spots with the potion, and wait about 15 minutes before wiping it off. Shake the bottle frequently as you work, and store it in a cool cabinet between uses. Do not use this formula on stainless steel appliances or smooth-surface cooktops. *For related text, see page 152.*

▶ Wood Cabinet Polish

½ cup of linseed oil 1 ½ tsp. of lemon juice
½ cup of malt vinegar

Mix the oil and vinegar together in a small jar or bowl, and then stir in the lemon juice. Apply the polish with a soft, clean cloth, adding a little elbow grease, and your kitchen cabinets will be the talk of the town. *For related text, see page 164.*

GENERAL HOUSEHOLD CLEANERS

▶ All-Around Stain Zapper

¼ cup of ammonia 1 tbsp. of dishwashing liquid
¼ cup of white vinegar 1 qt. of water
2 tbsp. of baking soda

Pour all of the ingredients into a spray bottle, put the lid on, and shake the bottle to mix well. When a stain appears, spray the pretreater onto the spot, and work it into the fibers with an old clean toothbrush. Wait a minute or two, and if the mark is still visible, repeat the process. Once the item is stain-free, drop it into the washer with the rest of the load, and run the machine as usual. *For related text, see page 221.*

▶ Baseboard Bonanza

1 tbsp. of cornstarch ⅓ cup of white vinegar
2 cups of boiling water

Measure the cornstarch into a spray bottle, then carefully add the water through a funnel, and stir until the cornstarch has dissolved. Add the vinegar, and stir again. After vacuuming with a soft brush attachment, spray the potion on your baseboards, and wipe them clean. *For related text, see page 186.*

▶ Bravo Brass Cleaner

½ cup of all-purpose flour

½ cup of dry laundry detergent
 (without bleach)

½ cup of salt

¾ cup of white vinegar

¼ cup of lemon juice
 (fresh or bottled)

½ cup of hot tap water

Mix the flour, detergent, and salt together in a bowl. Add the remaining ingredients, and blend thoroughly. Dip a soft, clean cotton cloth into the mixture, and rub it onto the brass, taking care to get into all the nooks and crannies. Buff with a second cloth. Store any leftover cleaner in a jar with a tight-fitting lid. This formula works just as well on copper cookware as it does on brass accessories and hardware. *For related text, see page 207.*

▶ Carpet Scorch Lifter

1 cup of white vinegar

½ cup of unscented talcum powder

2 onions, coarsely chopped

Add the ingredients to a pot, and bring the mixture to a boil, stirring constantly. Let it cool to room temperature, then use a sponge to spread it over the mark. When the spot is dry, brush or vacuum away the residue. Your carpet should look as good as new! This formula works like a charm on light scorch marks, but deeper burns require a "cut and paste" repair job. *For related text, see page 190.*

▶ Lemon-Scented Furniture Polish

1 cup of olive oil

2 tbsp. of white vinegar

½ cup of water

1 tsp. of lemon oil

Mix all of the ingredients together in a dark glass jar and store it, tightly closed, at room temperature. Shake well before using. Pour a small amount onto a soft cotton cloth, and wipe it onto your wooden furniture. Buff with another clean, dry cloth. Then stand back and admire yourself in the shiny surface! *For related text, see page 196.*

▶ Simple Saddle Soap

¼ cup of white vinegar

2 tbsp. of beeswax
(available in craft stores)

⅛ cup of linseed oil
(not boiled)

⅛ cup of vegetable-based
dishwashing liquid (like
Seventh Generation™
Free & Clear Natural
Dish Liquid)

Put the vinegar and beeswax in a small pan and heat on low until the wax has melted. In a small bowl, mix the linseed oil with the dishwashing liquid. Add the solution to the wax mixture, stirring until all of the ingredients are thoroughly blended. Pour the mixture into a shallow, heat-resistant container with a lid (like a candy tin or a glass jar that once held shoe cream). Use the soap to clean anything that's made of leather, including car and furniture upholstery, home accessories, handbags, briefcases, footwear, and even leather-bound books. *For related text, see page 198.*

▶ Wonderful Wood-Paneled Wall Cleaner

1 cup of white vinegar

¼ cup of lemon juice

2 cups of water

Old panty hose
or nylon stockings

Mix all of the ingredients together in a bucket. Then bunch up a handful of old panty hose, dip the wad into the solution, and wipe the paneling clean. For best results, work from the bottom of the wall upward to avoid messy runs, drips, or errors. The texture of panty hose or other nylon stockings provides the perfect abrasive, yet gentle, scrubbing action for this job. Multiply the formula as needed to suit the size of your room. *For related text, see page 192.*

▶ After-Bath Comfort Rinse

½ cup of brewed green
tea, cooled

1 cup of distilled water
½ cup of vinegar

Pour the ingredients into a glass bottle or jar, fasten the cap securely, and shake well. After bathing Fido, soothe his skin by applying
the rinse to his coat and massaging it into his skin. Then, either rinse
with clear water and let your pup air-dry. Store any leftovers in the
refrigerator in a tightly capped glass container up to two weeks, but
pitch it if you detect any sign of mold. *For related text, see page 250.*

▶ Fabulous Flea Shampoo

1 8-oz. bottle of pet shampoo
1 tbsp. of aloe vera juice or gel
10 drops of tea tree oil

Vinegar
Water

Add the aloe vera and tea tree oil to the shampoo and shake well.
Wash and rinse your pet as you would normally, but don't dry him.
Wait for 6 to 10 minutes (doing whatever it takes to keep him from
rolling on the ground!). While you're waiting, mix 1 tablespoon of
vinegar per pint of lukewarm water. Either spray or sponge it on as
a final rinse, and let it air-dry. *For related text, see page 246.*

▶ Horsefly Spray

2 cups of apple cider vinegar
1 cup of Avon® Skin So Soft bath oil

2 tsp. of eucalyptus oil
1 cup of water

Mix all of the ingredients together in a spray bottle and keep it close at
hand in the barn. Then spritz your ponies as needed, being careful to
avoid their eyes. This formula sends a potent "Keep Away!" message to
flies and other insects that spread potentially lethal diseases, but it's
gentle enough to use even on young foals. *For related text, see page 258.*

▶ Panacea for Itchy Pets

1 part vinegar   Lavender oil

1 part water

Mix the vinegar, water, and a few drops of the oil in a covered container, and apply the mixture generously to the affected areas two or three times a day. You can either spray it or gently dab it on—whichever is less stressful for your pet. The vinegar will deliver potent antibacterial and antifungal properties and will also help restore the proper pH to your pal's skin. The lavender oil offers additional analgesic, anti-histamine, and anti-inflammatory properties. It also helps repel fleas. Use white vinegar on a white or light-colored dog or cat. For a black or dark-toned animal, use apple cider vinegar. *For related text, see page 245.*

LAWN & GARDEN CARE

▶ All-Natural Fungicide

1½ tbsp. of baking soda   1 tsp. of vegetable oil

1 tbsp. of white vinegar   1 gal. of water

Mix all of the ingredients together in a bucket, and pour the mixture into a handheld spray bottle. Spray all your plants once a week during the growing season, making sure to cover the stems, as well as the top and underside of each and every leaf. Be especially diligent during periods of wet or humid weather. And be sure to repeat the process after every rain. When you apply your antifungal spray (or any other problem-solving potion), be sure to do the job in the morning so that your plants have plenty of time to dry off before nightfall. Fungal spores love dark, damp gardens! *For related text, see page 276.*

▶ Anti-Aphid Spray

1 cup of water	2 tsp. of aloe vera juice
1 cup of white vinegar	2 tsp. of sesame seed oil
½ cup of salt	12 drops of sage oil
¼ cup of baking soda	10 drops of grapefruit seed extract
¼ cup of powdered citric acid	

Mix all of the ingredients together in a large handheld spray bottle. Shake well before each use, and spritz your plagued plants from top to bottom. Pay special attention to the undersides of leaves, where aphids love to linger. *For related text, see page 273.*

▶ Dandelion Destruction Formula

1 gal. of white vinegar	1 tsp. of dishwashing liquid
1 cup of salt	

Combine all of the ingredients, and pour the mixture into a handheld spray bottle. Turn the nozzle to the straight-stream setting and blast the center of each flower. This will prevent it from setting seed and kill any seeds that may be starting to form. Then spray the foliage from top to bottom. Finally, aim at the ground, and saturate the base of the stem so that the vinegar can soak down into the roots. For best results, do this job on a hot day when the sun is at its brightest and when no rain is in the forecast. *For related text, see page 284.*

▶ Good-Bye, Good Guy Spray

¼ cup of vinegar	3 cups of water
1 tbsp. of essential oil of bay	

Mix all of the ingredients together in a handheld spray bottle. Then, to fend off the beneficial bugs that keep flying at your closed windows, use the potion to clean the outside of the glass. *For related text, see page 270.*

▶ Life of the Party Bug Repellent

¼ cup of distilled water	10 drops of lemon eucalyptus oil
¼ cup of vinegar (either white or apple cider)	10 drops of tea tree oil
	6 drops of bergamot oil
15 drops of lavender oil	6 drops of lime oil

Thoroughly mix all of the ingredients together, multiplying the quantities as needed. Spritz the air with the mixture, spray it on furniture, and set bowls of it around the space to keep beastly bugs from crashing the party. *For related text, see page 280.*

▶ Moss-Removal Remedy

16 oz. of water	2 tbsp. of vinegar
2 tbsp. of gin	

Mix all of the ingredients together in a handheld spray bottle. Then take careful aim and thoroughly drench the moss. Just be aware that if your unwanted moss is growing in the kind of damp, shady spot that it craves, you will have to repeat this routine periodically. *For related text, see page 285.*

▶ Super-Safe Insect Repellent

½ cup of fresh lavender	½ cup of fresh thyme
½ cup of fresh mint	1 cup of white vinegar
½ cup of fresh rose-scented geraniums	

Put the first four ingredients in a heat-proof bowl. Heat the vinegar just to the boiling point, and pour it over the herbs. Cover the bowl, and let the herbs steep until the vinegar has cooled to room temperature. Strain out the solids and pour the liquid into a handheld spray bottle. Store your repellent in the refrigerator for up to two months. Then, before you head outdoors, spritz yourself with the potion. *For related text, see page 278.*

▶ Tick Off Ticks Spray

½ cup of vinegar
¼ cup of water

10 drops of lemongrass,
geranium, or rosemary oil

Mix the vinegar and water together in a spray bottle, and add the essential oil of your choice (ticks loathe all of the ones listed above!). Before heading into the great outdoors, spray your hair and any exposed skin with the mixture. **Note:** *This formula will also keep your pets tick-free. For related text, see page 280.*

▶ Tool Handle TLC Formula

1 part boiled linseed oil
1 part turpentine

1 part white vinegar

Mix all of the ingredients together in a glass jar with a tight-fitting lid. To keep wooden handles from cracking and splintering, pour some of it on an old cotton sock, and rub it up and down the handle until the whole thing is covered. Wait about 10 minutes for the liquid to soak in, and then repeat the treatment. Wait another 10 minutes, and wipe any excess off with a clean, dry cloth. Store the leftover potion indefinitely in a cool, dark place. *For related text, see page 264.*

▶ Wicked Wonder Salsa

2 lbs. of ripe tomatoes
1 lb. of fresh chili peppers
1 large onion

2 garlic cloves
1 cup of white vinegar
½ tsp. of black pepper

Roughly chop the first four ingredients, then liquefy them in a blender or food processor. Add the vinegar and pepper, and blend briefly to mix them in. Strain the mixture through a paper coffee filter, and pour the liquid into a handheld spray bottle. Then take careful aim, and blast the fiery stuff directly on garden pests. Just be sure to spray on a calm day. If this salsa drifts into your eyes or mouth, it'll burn like crazy! *For related text, see page 268.*

▶ Crackerjack Canvas Cover Cleaner

1 cup of borax powder   2 cups of warm water
1 cup of white vinegar

Mix the ingredients together in a bucket. Sponge the mixture generously onto the soiled area(s), and let it sit for 10 minutes or so. Scrub any stubborn spots, then rinse thoroughly. Be sure to let the canvas dry completely before you fold it up. *For related text, see page 319.*

▶ Darn Good Deposit Remover

½ cup of borax   ½ cup of white vinegar
1 cup of warm water

Dissolve the borax in the water, and stir in the vinegar. Sponge the mixture onto any lime or hard-water buildup on your swimming pool deck, concrete driveway, water spigots, planters, or any other hard outdoor surface. Let it sit for 10 minutes or so, and wipe the ugly marks away. *For related text, see page 292.*

▶ Fiberglass Boat Cleaner

½ cup of household ammonia   2 tbsp. of cornstarch
½ cup of white vinegar   1 gal. of warm water

Mix the ingredients in a bucket. Dip a sponge or soft cloth into the mixture, and wash your vessel from stem to stern. Then rinse with clear water, and dry the hull thoroughly with a soft cloth to avoid water spots. Every so-called fiberglass boat is actually composed of a thick layer of fiberglass resin covered by a very thin plastic gelcoat cover. If you use an abrasive cleaner, it'll wear right through that fragile coating and either reveal the base color or leave a glaring dull spot. *For related text, see page 322.*

REMEDIES & RECIPES

▶ Garbage Can Cleanup Concoction

½ cup of white vinegar 2 cups of hot water
2 tbsp. of dishwashing liquid Borax

Mix the first three ingredients in the empty garbage can, then swish them around and scrub the bottom and sides with a sponge or a long-handled brush. Rinse the can well and let it dry thoroughly. Then sprinkle borax across the bottom before replacing the bag. *For related text, see page 299.*

▶ Heavy-Duty Window Cleaner

¼ cup of white vinegar 3 cups of warm water
2 tbsp. of rubbing alcohol

Mix all of the ingredients together in a bucket—multiplying the recipe as needed—and go to town. It'll bring back the sparkle to even the grimiest windows. *For related text, see page 296.*

▶ Outdoor Wooden Furniture Cleaner

1 cup of ammonia ¼ cup of baking soda
½ cup of white vinegar 1 gal. of water

Mix all of the ingredients together, and apply the mixture with a sponge or brush, scrubbing to remove any stubborn stains. Then rinse with clear water, and dry the pieces with a clean towel. *For related text, see page 301.*

▶ Plastic Furniture Cleaner

2 cups of white vinegar 1 gal. of hot water
2 tbsp. of dishwashing liquid

Mix the ingredients in a bucket. Wipe the mixture onto firm surfaces with a sponge or a soft cotton cloth. Use a soft brush to work the solution into any padding. After rinsing, wipe with a towel to avoid streaks, and set the pieces in the sun to dry. *For related text, see page 302.*

Index

A

Acid reflux, 25
Adhesive removal, 177–178, 209–210, 308
After-Bath Comfort Rinse, 250, 350
Aftershave, 67
Age spots, 61–62
Aging, premature, 40
Air conditioners
  algae eviction, 203–204
  filter cleaning, 202, 204–205
  grille cleaning, 200
Air fresheners. *See* Deodorizing techniques
Algae, in air conditioners, 203–204
Alkalinity
  good health and, 39
  of soil, 261
All-Around Antibacterial Cleaner, 176, 344
All-Around Stain Zapper, 221, 347
Allergies
  in humans, 13–14
  in pets, 250
All-Natural Fungicide, 351
All-Natural Shampoo, 71, 339
All-Purpose Cure-All, 330
Almond oil, 57, 335
Aloe vera
  hair-care use, 74–75, 341
  pest-control use, 273, 352
  pet-care use, 246, 350
  skin-care use, 60
Aluminum foil, as scrubber, 166

Aluminum items
  Amazing Aluminum Cleaner, 171, 344
  cookware, 169–170
  furniture, 302
  siding, 289–290
Alzheimer's disease, 43
Amazing Aluminum Cleaner, 171, 344
Amazing Anti-Aging Mask, 57, 333
Ammonia
  kitchen use, 164
  laundry use, 221, 347
  in multipurpose cleaner, 161, 345
  outdoor-cleaning uses, 301, 322, 355, 356
Antacid tablets, 162
Anti-Aging Mask, Amazing, 57, 333
Anti-aging remedy, 44–45
Anti-Aphid Spray, 273, 352
Antibacterial Cleaner, All-Around, 176, 344
Antioxidants, 10, 85
Antiques, 195, 208
Anti-Wrinkle Scrub, 333
Ants, 107, 274–275
Aphids, 273, 276, 352
Apple cider vinegar
  buying in bulk, 255
  culinary uses, 84–85
  homemade, 20–21
  substitution for, 106
  type to use, 3
  use cautions, 15
Apple juice
  hair-care use, 74, 343

medicinal uses, 6, 45, 327, 332
Apples
  in fruit salad, 145
  hair-care use, 81
  Spinach-Apple Salad, 122–123
Apple seed magic trick, 232
Appliances. *See specific appliances*
Apricot Dipping Sauce, 140
Arthritis
  Arthritis Ache Reliever, 325
  in humans, 4, 5, 43
  in pets, 251
Ashtrays (collectibles), 210
Aspirin, for hair care, 76, 342
Asthma, 13–14, 43, 327
Atherosclerosis, 40
Athlete's foot, 34
Automotive Anti-Frost Formula, 310
Avocados
  Avocado-Cucumber Salsa, 138
  Avocado Mask, 57, 333
  hair-care use, 71–72, 340
Avon® Skin So Soft bath oil, 258

B

Baby and child care
  baby bottles, 227
  crayon marks, 231
  diapers and diaper pails, 228–229
  fun and games, 232–235
  high chairs, 229–230
  Homemade Baby Wipes, 230

T

Tableware, 170–171, 172–174

Taffy, Old-Time Vinegar & Molasses, 144–145

Talcum powder, 190, 348

Tamago-su (egg vinegar), 44

Tarragon
  Mustard-Tarragon Marinade, 120
  preserving, 97

Teakettles, 171–172

Teapots, 171

Tea stains, 170–171, 218

Tea tree oil
  cleaning use, 176
  in insect repellent, 280, 353
  pet-care use, 246, 350
  skin-care use, 52, 336

Tents, mildewed, 315–316

Texas Caviar, 139

Thermos bottles, 174

Thickening, Softening Hair Rinse, 343

Thrush, 18–19

Thyme
  hair-care use, 76, 341
  in insect repellent, 279, 353
  lemon-thyme vinegar, 115
  medicinal use, 23, 328
  properties of, 11, 51
  thyme vinegar, 146
  using in recipes, 43

Ticks
  Tick Off Ticks Spray, 280, 354
  Timely Tick Repellent, 48
  vinegar use and, 250

Tinctures, herbal, 9–10

Toilets, 180–181. *See also* Marine toilets

Tomatoes
  pest-control use, 268, 354
  skin-care use, 57, 333
  Tomato-Potato Basil Soup, 127

Tomato juice, 104

Tool care, 264–265, 354

Tool Handle TLC Formula, 354

Toothaches, 3

Toothache Tamer, 326

Toothache Tamer, Take 2, 326

Tooth enamel caution, 39

Toothpaste, for cleaning floors, 182

Towels, washing, 215

Toxin-Tossin' Bath Blend, 9, 332

Toys, 228, 229

Travertine, 294

Triglycerides, 41

Turkey
  safe handling of, 99
  Turkey Soup, 127

Turmeric
  skin-care use, 57, 333
  using in recipes, 43

Turpentine, 264–265

Two-Step Daily Dandruff Treatment, 344

U

Ulcers, 43

Upholstery care, 199, 310

Urinary tract infections, in pets, 250

Urine, on carpet, 240–241

V

Vaginal yeast infections, 18

Vaporizers and steam treatments, 12, 15

Varicose veins, 33

Vases, 208–209

Vegetable dyes, 239–240

Vegetable oil, 185, 187

Vegetables. *See also specific vegetables*
  cooking, 88
  Creamy Zucchini, 116
  gas from, 91
  growing, 264
  limp, 87
  preparing, 88

Vegetable vinegar, 118

Very Fine Vinegar Fruitcake, 145

Vinaigrette dressing, 109, 121

Vinegar. *See also specific types*
  cookware and, 98
  drinking, 18
  factoids, 54, 112
  hair-care cautions, 69, 74, 80
  hair-care power, 73
  health cautions, 12, 21, 39, 242
  history of, 113, 158
  pet-care cautions, 248
  safety of, 231
  shelf life, 26, 114
  stain cautions, 211, 244
  storing, 63
  substitutions for, 106
  type for cleaning use, 287